The Healing Power of Education

Afrocentric Pedagogy as a Tool for Restoration and Liberation

Marcia J. Watson-Vandiver
Greg Wiggan

Foreword by Joyce E. King

TEACHERS COLLEGE PRESS

TEACHERS COLLEGE | COLUMBIA UNIVERSITY
NEW YORK AND LONDON

Published by Teachers College Press,® 1234 Amsterdam Avenue, New York, NY 10027

Library of Congress Cataloging-in-Publication Data

Names: Watson-Vandiver, Marcia J., author. | Wiggan, Greg A., 1976- author.
Title: The healing power of education : Afrocentric pedagogy as a tool for
    restoration and liberation / Marcia J. Watson-Vandiver, Greg Wiggan.
Description: New York, NY : Teachers College Press, [2021] | Includes
    bibliographical references and index.
Identifiers: LCCN 2020056485 (print) | LCCN 2020056486 (ebook) | ISBN
    9780807765364 (paperback) | ISBN 9780807765371 (hardcover) | ISBN
    9780807779576 (ebook)
Subjects: LCSH: African Americans—Education. | Holistic education—United
    States. | Curriculum change—United States. | Afrocentrism.
Classification: LCC LC2717 .W38 2021 (print) | LCC LC2717 (ebook) | DDC
    371.829/96073—dc23
LC record available at https://lccn.loc.gov/2020056485
LC ebook record available at https://lccn.loc.gov/2020056486

ISBN 978-0-8077-6536-4 (paper)
ISBN 978-0-8077-6537-1 (hardcover)
ISBN 978-0-8077-7957-6 (ebook)

Printed on acid-free paper
Manufactured in the United States of America

Contents

Foreword

If one looks at healing as an act of making healthy, we can argue that nothing heals a person better than knowing who s/he is, (descendancy) what s/he is about (purpose) and where s/he is going.

—Edwards et al., "The Role of Ancestors in Healing"

A culturally centered curriculum . . . allows students to explore themselves, explore who they are, and truth. Teach kids the truth.

—Mr. Griffin, this volume, p. 117

Recently, I was invited to review a manuscript on the topic of Afrocentric education that was submitted to a multicultural education–focused journal. The author maintained that the submission reported the results of the only survey of student perceptions of "Afrocentric praxis"—using a survey instrument that was supposedly adapted from my book with Ellen E. Swartz, *The Afrocentric Praxis of Teaching for Freedom*. So, I mused, "That's why I am being invited to review this submission." To my surprise, however, what I had thought would be a routine academic task felt more like stepping in front of and trying to stop a moving train that had already left the station heading in the wrong direction! The manuscript's numerous factual errors and unsubstantiated false assertions about Afrocentric education were absolutely astounding. The more I read, the more I struggled to make sense of the (perhaps well-intentioned but) dated allegations about Afrocentric education—as misogynistic, patriarchal, essentialist, divisive— none of which referenced any scholarship of Afrocentric theorists.' I remain quite perplexed that such a flawed discussion of Afrocentric education could get so near to publication in a reputable academic journal with no attention to the extant theory and scholarship, such as the extensive body of research that Marcia Watson-Vandiver and Greg Wiggan review so thoroughly in *The Healing Power of Education: Afrocentric Pedagogy as a Tool for Liberation*.

Breaking new ground, this volume fills a significant gap in the literature by offering new and original insights with regard to our understanding of the Afrocentric paradigm in education. First, Watson-Vandiver and Wiggan have assembled and comprehensively discuss an impressive array of empirical studies conducted on curriculum and pedagogy in African-centered and Afrocentric schools. Second, the clarity of curriculum concepts and powerful pedagogical examples they present, as well as the historical and contemporary linkages in their analysis, make this volume an indispensable handbook on Afrocentric theory, practice, and research. How refreshingly accurate and profoundly informative that this book begins not with slavery tropes, but with an overview starting with the classical foundations in ancient Kemet (Egypt) and precolonial indigenous African educational history, and proceeds to consider Pan-African and Black Nationalist precursors of Afrocentric education. Third, by introducing the concept of and using an "introspective lens," their unique case study of the perspectives and lived experiences of the students and the teachers in an all-Black high-achieving 21st-century Afrocentric school reveals how teaching "right knowledge" and "corrective history" restores Black students' identity, promotes their success, and heals students from the trauma of miseducation and the falsifications of curriculum violence.

Finally, it is the meaning of the self-healing power of education, that is to say, the power of "Afrocentric pedagogy as a tool for liberation," that Watson-Vandiver and Wiggan introduce that also makes this book exceptionally noteworthy. Demonstrating that "self-healing is both an individual and a collective approach to restoration and uplift," this book affirms that Black identity is *inherently communal*. Thus, the inherent connection between self and community and self-healing "eventually leads to collective and communal healing." To say that this understanding of Afrocentricity as a paradigm of communal healing is profound is an understatement. Rather, regarding Afrocentric pedagogy as a tool for "making us healthy" indicates that this educational model is indispensable not only to heal Black students, but also for the health and wellness of everyone in this society—a society that is traumatized by the emotional and spiritual damage of dehumanizing racial domination. Marcia Watson-Vandiver and Greg Wiggan have given us a book that is liberating for us all.

—Joyce E. King, Ph.D.,
Benjamin E. Mays Endowed Chair for
Urban Teaching, Learning & Leadership,
Georgia State University,
March 8, 2021

Preface

Student achievement and school reform are some of the most pervasive topics in public school discourse. However, the curriculum is one area that remains virtually unchanged across U.S. schools. The efflorescence of federal legislative policies such as *No Child Left Behind* (NCLB), *Common Core State Standards* (CCSS), and *Race to the Top* (RTTT) have attempted to modify national assessment measures without preemptively seeking true curriculum and pedagogical reform. As a result, today's non-White students seldom have the opportunity to learn and identify with multicultural perspectives in schools. One alternative approach is to expose students to an Afrocentric education (Allen, 2009, 2010; Dei, 1994, 1996; Hilliard, 1998; Hilliard & Amankwatia, 1998; King et al., 2014; Murrell, 2002). This book examines the benefits of Afrocentric schools and the role of *education as self-healing power*. In this regard, *education as self-healing power* refers to the realignment of curriculum and pedagogy to be inclusive, factual, and counterhegemonic against falsification and dehumanization, and responds to the resultant social, psychological, and emotional damage and trauma. *The Healing Power of Education* is also introspective work, as it promotes and nurtures healing from negative self- and group concepts. It disrupts misappropriations in regard to cultural, social, and psychological domination of oppressed groups, and fosters their healing and wholeness. *The Healing Power of Education* promotes wellness against the enduring legacies of miseducation and domination. In this sense, it is an ongoing work to cleanse from falsification and internalized domination. Since Europeans colonized or enslaved more than 80% of the entire world for centuries, there is necessary and purposeful work that must be done to promote healing from this negative and enduring force. In the context of this book, *enslavement* is not just physical bondage but also psychological, social, cultural, and spiritual oppression.

Oppressed people have a great deal of trauma—social, emotional, and intellectual—that results principally from their historical enslavement as well as their present domination. We see the symptoms of this in self-hatred, dehumanization, and private and public adoration for their oppressor. They must heal from this. Education can play a vital role in helping to correct miseducation. In other words, "right knowledge" can help to correct misinformation and misconceptions both in the oppressed and the oppressor. The recent killings of Walter Wallace Jr. (Philadelphia), George Floyd (Minneapolis), Breonna Taylor (Louisville), Ahmaud Arbery (Brunswick, Georgia), and Tony McDade (Tallahassee, Florida), among so many others, along with the xenophobia and racism witnessed in the Covid-19 (severe acute respiratory syndrome coronavirus 2) pandemic, show that even today the complicated milieu of American racism persists (Costello & Duvall, 2020; Deliso, 2020; Huerta, 2020; Human Rights Watch, 2020; McLaughlin, 2020; Murphy, 2020). Additionally, the 2020 presidential election and victory of President Joe Biden and Vice President Kamala Harris has increased racial tensions and unrest between those who want to cling to old traditions of racism and White supremacist thinking and those who want progress and inclusion, all of which points to a need for national healing. Recent federal attacks on critical race theory (Lang, 2020) and the *1619 Project* (Perez & Guadiano, 2020), for example, along with the insurrection of domestic terrorists at the U.S. Capitol Building on January 6, 2021 (Leatherby et al., 2021; Simon & Sidner, 2021), showcase increased divisions in relation to our nation's fundamental understandings of race. Whereas schools would seem like optimal spaces for critical inquiry, most classrooms have been standardized generally to avoid critical race discussions (Dei, 2003, 2012; George & Puente, 2015; Moulthorp, 2015). There is thus a need to explore the transformative power of education in addressing critical issues facing our society (Baker, 2020), which can help each of us become a source of healing.

If we do not heal, we transmit that pain and poison onto others. In this sense, schools have been instrumental in transmitting curriculum violence and miseducation. However, they can also become places of healing and restoration through proper care and support, and the delivery of "right knowledge" from a master teacher. When schooling lacks right knowledge, education is not taking place; to be most effective, schooling must be critical and introspective, while challenging systems and institutions of oppression (Freire, 2000). Thus, many people, especially the oppressed, are schooled, but not educated; are credentialed in miseducation, but are not educated (Woodson, 1933/1977).

In some respect, all human beings experience difficulty and traumatic moments over the course of their lives. And where there is trauma, healing is required. In the United States, minority groups experience various forms of systemic oppression, ranging from facing daily microaggressions to deliberate forms of institutional racism. However, this is exponentially worse for African-descent groups, who phenotypically cannot assimilate, and are oppressed and who have lived and continue to live in societies and cultural systems, and operate within institutions that deny or undermine their very existence as human beings. In the book, *Christopher Columbus and the Afrikan Holocaust* John Henrik Clarke describes the destructive forces of slavery, colonialism, and imperialism, both physical and psychological, and their enduring institutional and interpersonal legacies on Africans and African descent people (Clarke, 1993). Africans and African descendants collectively endured more than 400 years of slavery and over 200 years of colonialism, as well as the precipitations of their modern and contemporary legacies. A process of healing thus remains compulsory. Enslavement and oppression have erased cultural artifacts, collective memory, and heritage. As Joyce King argues, reclaiming "heritage knowledge" is key to the healing process. To heal, decolonization of the mind must take place (Ngũgĩ, 1986). To this point, South African freedom fighter Stephen (Steve) Biko noted that the most powerful tool in the hand of the oppressor is the mind of the oppressed. As such, this mind must be healed from miseducation, falsification, and even, at times, self-hate. Similarly, Ani argues that the *Asili*—the central seed of a culture, and in the case of African-descent people—of European cultural domination has been destructive to positive African identity development constructs (Ani, 1994). In this way, *education as self-healing power*, in both its institutional and noninstitutional forms, must play a central role in the healing and restoration of all people, but particularly the oppressed. By *healing*, we are referring to the restorative process or act of becoming whole again—whole in thinking, living, and being. In the same way that a child is not born a criminal or a deviant, but is whole and complete and may learn how to become a deviant, oppressed groups have learned and been conditioned into destructive ways of thinking and being, which they must heal from.

OBJECTIVES OF THIS BOOK

This book examines Afrocentric schools, which are educational institutions that take an unapologetic stance against hegemonic curriculum development and pedagogical practices. The purpose of this book is to explore the experiences and perceptions of students and teachers at an Afrocentric school. The following objectives help to guide the book's overall contributions. Specifically, this book seeks to:

- Situate the need for Afrocentric education within the context of history
- Qualitatively explore the perceptions of students and teachers at Afrocentric schools
- Examine Afrocentric educational experiences within 21st-century contexts
- Introduce and enhance the current understanding of Afrocentric education as a tool for nurturing healing and restoration

ORGANIZATION OF CHAPTERS

Chapter 1 introduces the book and develops the theme of *education as healing power*, primarily for African American students but also for all students. This chapter explains the role that education plays in personal healing and restoration. It includes a theoretical explanation of Afrocentricity, and also provides an overview of student achievement in the 21st century, which shows modest performance across all demographic types.

Chapter 2 provides a brief overview of precolonial African history. In doing so, the chapter highlights critical omissions within U.S. school curricula and raises key multicultural and diversity issues in education. This background helps to contextualize the subsequent chapters of the book and provides foundational history on the early formations of Black historical movements.

Chapter 3 synthesizes previous research on Afrocentric schools in the 20th and 21st centuries and provides an overview of Afrocentricity and its utility within 21st-century contexts. This chapter includes an in-depth analysis of curriculum and pedagogy in these schools and outlines the historical formation of Afrocentric education. The chapter concludes with a synthesis of the current status of Afrocentric education in the United States.

Chapter 4 provides an exposition of the study's site: Asa G. Hilliard Academy (AGHA, a pseudonym), a high-performing school with 100% African American students and teachers. This chapter provides descriptive information on the school, as well as snapshots of participants.

Chapters 5 and 6 outline the major findings and themes that emerged from the case study. Chapter 5 details the experiences of students and teachers at AGHA, the high-performing Afrocentric school noted in this study. The themes that emerge in this chapter include Unique Learning Environment, Support System, and Devotion, which from the perspective of students and teachers are integral aspects of AGHA. Similarly, Chapter 6 details the role of "right knowledge" in mediating trauma and promoting healing with oppressed groups. The themes that emerge in this chapter include Black Education, Reframing Afrocentricity, and Restorative Education and Black Identity.

Chapter 7 presents a synthesized discussion on each theme as it relates to the overall premise and theoretical framework of the book. The chapter also presents national, state, and local policy recommendations. The chapter concludes with implications for further research on Afrocentric schools, curriculum design, and inclusion. Appendix M outlines the research method used in the book's case study. Since this research seeks to explain, in depth, the role of Afrocentricity in helping oppressed groups to heal from social, cultural, and psychological trauma, this appendix examines an Afrocentric school model in its entirety. We attempt here to reveal how Afrocentricity can be used as an alternative curriculum model through classroom observation, interviews, and student discourse analysis.

CHAPTER 1

Introduction

Education as Healing

Only yesterday Zeus went off to the Ocean River to feast with the Aethiopians [Ethiopians], loyal, lordly men, and all of the gods went with him.

—Homer, *The Iliad* 1.423–424, 762 BCE

Do not be proud and arrogant with your knowledge.

—Ptahhotep, 2388 BCE

African American student achievement has received substantial attention in academic research (Delpit, 2006a; Irvine, 1990; King, 2005; Kozol, 2005; Kunjufu, 2002; Ladson-Billings, 1994; Perry et al., 2003). The *National Assessment of Educational Progress* (NAEP) reports that 20% of 4th-grade and 18% of 8th-grade Black students are at or above proficiency in reading (NAEP, 2017a), while 19% of 4th-grade and 13% of 8th-grade Black students are at or above proficiency in mathematics (NAEP, 2017b). This report also suggests that 47% of 4th-grade and 45% of 8th-grade White students are at or above proficiency in reading (NAEP, 2017a), while 51% of 5th-grade and 44% of 8th-grade White students are at or above proficiency in mathematics (NAEP, 2017b). These figures are undoubtedly disturbing across both racial groups. Clearly, both groups are underachieving. Recent reform initiatives such as *Common Core* and *Race to the Top* have aimed to "fix" the problem of African American student underachievement, yet many of these efforts have focused on *treating* Black children without preemptively seeking to address the systematic root causes of today's educational problems, such as lack of teacher preparation and urban school inequality. These efforts are in vain, good intentions notwithstanding.

Today's African American students face educational disparities that are systemic, pervasive, and long-lasting (Irvine, 1990; Kozol, 2005; Kunjufu, 2002; Mickelson, 2001). It is important to better understand these educational conditions in order to explain and address African American student achievement. Due to the U.S. contextualization of this book, the terms

"Black" and "African American" are used interchangeably. It is important to note that this book problematizes the oversimplification and over-promotion of quantitative achievement scores. Achievement is not just standardized academic measures, but personal growth and development as well. While high-performing schools and exemplary student achievement are laudable, the focus on scores is myopic without a holistic approach that promotes both academic growth and social and personal growth (King, 2005; Wiggan & Watson-Vandiver, 2018). Additionally, the awareness of cultural knowledge and corrective history is equally important for students today. Thus, we instead promote the importance of holistic education that leads to healing and restoration. It is important to note, however, that since the site for this book's case study is 100% African American and high-performing, we use this as leverage to better understand both the academic and social practices that promote educational excellence among Black students.

One compounding problem that most public schools encounter is the lack of multiculturalism, diversity, and nonhegemonic perspectives in school curricula. Schools have promoted for decades the same inaccurate and erroneous views of history, views that are more or less White-washed. Today's public school curriculum systemically perpetuates cultural hegemony and White, Eurocentric ethos (Delpit, 2006a; King, 2005; Perry et al., 2003; Sizemore, 1990). In this context, hegemony is the cultural dominance of one group over all other groups. It is, in essence, normalizing the cultural ethos of one culture over all others (Gramsci, 1999). Curricular hegemony is not a new phenomenon, as described over 80 years ago in Carter G. Woodson's seminal work, *The Mis-Education of the Negro* (1933/1977), but its dangerous effects have intensified through current modes of instruction. Today's curriculum content has been simplified for the sake of state assessments, which has de-emphasized critical thinking. The lack of multiculturalism in the curriculum now teaches students cultural tidbits, menial information without contextualization or inquiry, and purges out diverse perspectives (Ladson-Billings, 1994; Nieto, 1992). For students who are not of European descent, there is little room to probe or explore information or history that reflects their own cultural identity. Additionally, much of the cultural misinformation found in schools promotes myopic stereotypes and discrimination. This was recently seen in the 2020 Covid-19 pandemic, where Asian and Pacific Islanders were often targets of discrimination, xenophobia, and intolerance (Huerta, 2020; Human Rights Watch, 2020). Thus, a more comprehensive understanding of multicultural education is much needed in schools and society. In this regard, *education as self-healing power* posits the importance of holistically addressing cultural misinformation and falsification.

Education as self-healing power is an introspective ontological process that promotes restoration from negative self- and group concepts. It realigns misappropriations in regard to cultural, social, and psychological domination of oppressed groups, and fosters healing and wholeness. It is important to note that self-healing is both an individual and collective group framework. We believe in the relationship between the individual and the community, and assert that self-healing leads to communal healing. In this regard, successful educational outcomes are denoted by a positive self-identity that affirms decolonial understandings of Blackness and Black people (Hilliard, 1998; King & Swartz, 2016, 2018; Murrell, 2002). In relation to the synergy between school and society, it is important to examine ways in which contemporary education can better promote culturally holistic education.

Traditional schools pejoratively ignore non-White cultures, and solely teach Eurocentric perspectives. Many traditional schools expose students to multiculturalism only via cultural history months or diversity events. As a response to both inadequate and failing public schools, the emergence of nontraditional school models has surfaced. One alternative approach to schools is Afrocentric (also known as Africentric or African-centered) education. Afrocentric schools embed into the school culture the tenets of Afrocentricity, which is the theoretical framework that places African people at the *center* of analysis (Asante, 1991, 2003). According to Asante (1991), Dei (1996), and Dragnea and Erling (2008), Afrocentric education focuses on cultural, academic, and social goals. Within Afrocentric schools, "teachers teach Black students about their culture, about life, and about their role in society and the world while maintaining high expectations and demanding excellence" (Dragnea & Erling, 2008, p. 3). Thus, Afrocentric education is a response to the unaddressed problems within traditional schooling.

It is important to conceptualize the differences between Afrocentricity, which guides Afrocentric schools, versus the Eurocentric framework found in traditional education. Afrocentricity is defined as "a mode of thought and action in which the centrality of African interest, values and perspectives predominate" (Asante, 2003, p. 2). Asante (2003) continues:

> In regards to theory, it is the placing of African people in the center of any analysis of African phenomena. Thus it is possible for anyone to master the discipline of seeking the location of Africans in a given phenomena [*sic*]. In terms of action and behavior, it is a devotion to the idea that what is in the best interest of African consciousness is at the heart of ethical behavior. Finally, Afrocentricity seeks to enshrine the idea that blackness itself is a trope of ethics. Thus to be [Black] is to be against all forms of oppression, racism, classism, homophobia, patriarchy, child abuse, pedophilia and white racial domination. (p. 2)

Afrocentricity, as described above, is the bedrock of Afrocentric education. A comparison of Eurocentric and Afrocentric education is provided in Table 1.1.

Table 1.1. Contrasting Values of Teaching

Eurocentric Style of Teaching	Afrocentric Style of Teaching
Rules	Freedom
Standardization	Variation
Conformity	Creativity
Memory of Specific Facts	Memory of Essence
Regularity	Novelty
Rigid Order	Flexibility
Normality	Uniqueness
Differences Equal Defects	Sameness Equals Oppression
Precision	Approximate
Control	Experience
Mechanical	Humanistic
"Thing" Focused	"People" Focused
Constant	Evolving
Sign-Oriented	Meaning-Oriented
Duty	Loyalty

Source: Austin (2006); Kenyatta (1998).

The uniqueness of Afrocentric education is found in the teaching style, curriculum, and learning environment of students. Table 1.1 demonstrates the uniqueness of Afrocentric education. It is the Afrocentrists' aim to cultivate the best qualities in each student. Competition, individualism, and materialism are not part of the traditional precolonial African ethos, nor is it used within the Afrocentric school model (Akbar, 1998; Dei, 2012; Murrell, 2002; Rodney, 2011). Having a learning environment that validates the importance of collective unity, as demonstrated in the African tradition, is a distinguishing feature of Afrocentric education (Brown, 1996; Dillard & Neal, 2020; Lee, 1992).

Figures 1.1 and 1.2 provide illustrations of Afrocentricity in comparison to Eurocentrism. Whereas Eurocentrism informs Africa using hegemony, Afrocentricity confronts hegemony through a search of truth. Figure 1.1 displays that hegemony is centralized within Eurocentrism and Africa is marginalized. This is attributed to Eurocentrism's antithetical claims against African heritage. This proves true throughout history and is evidenced today in the systematic removal of African contributions from the traditional curriculum. In Eurocentrism, which is used in traditional public schools, all non-European cultural contributions are marginalized. As described in Figure 1.1, Eurocentrism promotes rigid binaries and creates an impenetrable understanding of knowledge. This further advances *hegemony*, meaning one monopolized perspective that dominates ideology or the universalization of the interest and perspectives of one group over all other groups (Gramsci, 1999; Lemert, 2010). People who have been the subjects of these oppressive processes for decades, and most often centuries, must have deliberate and targeted work to promote their healing and wholeness. *Education as self-healing power* provides a framework for nurturing this healing. Within the Afrocentric perspective (see Figure 1.2), the perniciousness of hegemony is addressed. It is important to note that within the Afrocentric framework, no culture is marginalized. This is because, by design, Afrocentricity acknowledges Africa as the origin of the human family tree rather than a race. Africa, also called Alkebulan, constitutes the first family of humanity. It is creation force. Afrocentricity validates the contributions of all groups, which are viewed as part of the original African Diaspora. This includes all people and cultures (Akbar, 1998; Asante, 1991). Africa's connection to all cultural groups is represented using a circle, denoting the inclusiveness of varying perspectives and the continuum of learning (see Figure 1.2). This theoretical paradigm is beneficial for students in academic settings.

As demonstrated in Figure 1.2, the tenets of Afrocentric education do not exclude or marginalize students based on race (Brown, 1996; Dei, 1994). Instead it continuously responds to hegemony, as demonstrated by the circle's fluid continuum (King et al., 2014). This is why Afrocentric schools are considered *inclusive* of all racial groups, whereas traditional education is not because it promotes a perpetual state of learning and relearning. Today, Afrocentric education reinforces anti-racism education and discourse, and

Figure 1.1. Eurocentrism Illustrated

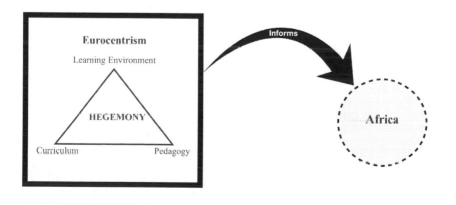

Figure 1.2. Afrocentric Theory Illustrated

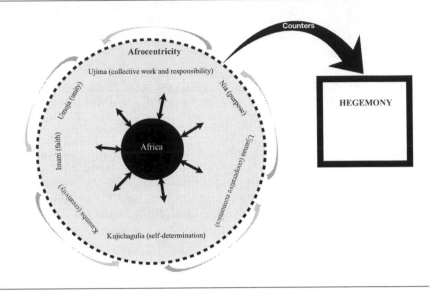

provides positive learning environments for students (Agyepong, 2010; Allen, 2009, 2010; Dei, 1994, 1996, 2003; King & Swartz, 2018; Murrell, 2002). These positive learning environments bring healing and historical realignment—known as "sankofa." The concept of sankofa is an Akan term that literally means, "go back and fetch" (King et al., 2014). Afrocentric education promotes positive self-concepts for students and retrieves "lost" historical knowledge. King and Swartz (2018) have described this as "heritage pedagogy," which is the promotion and retrieval of lost historical knowledge. Thus, it must be acknowledged that Afrocentricity is a *human* approach to education, not a racial approach (see Figure 1.2). It is important to recognize its agency across all cultural groups.

Afrocentricity's inclusion of all racial and cultural groups is a clear distinction from the Eurocentric framework found in traditional schools. Still, many incorrectly confuse the aforementioned with simply being an African version of European ethnic domination and postulations. Such propagandist perspectives seek to undermine Afrocentricity's positioning of continental Africa as the birthplace of humanity and the beginning of the human family tree, civilization, earliest writings, manuscripts, books, and spiritual and educational systems. Today, many traditional public schools attempt to implement menial multicultural education initiatives, yet fail to fundamentally address or change the curriculum. This leaves students of racial and ethnic minority groups *excluded* from the curriculum or on the margins as afterthoughts. As mentioned, students in traditional public schools are rarely taught African American history beyond slavery and the Civil Rights Movement. Latino/Latina, Caribbean, Native American, and Asian histories are often ignored as well. In traditional educational settings, students are taught the superiority of European contributions without an accurate assessment of the whole—or *inclusive*—picture. Afrocentric education, by design, offers a more inclusive approach because the curriculum starts at a different, more historically accurate place of origin, that being Africa. This recentered starting place involves the intersection of *all* students' racial and ethnic heritage—Black, White, Latino/Latina, Asian, Native American, and so on (due to topics like world history, globalization, modernization, international relations, current events, etc.). As such, Afrocentricity is not just for Blacks or African-descent students; in fact, it is useful for all learners. By deconstructing and restructuring the curricula to include a more historically accurate starting place, Afrocentric schools are considered to be more racially *inclusive* than Eurocentric (traditional) schools.

CONSISTENTLY UNDERSERVED STUDENTS

African American students are largely underserved in traditional public schools. The compounding factors of culturally irrelevant teaching, miseducation, unqualified teachers, inequitable funding, and discipline disproportionality negatively impact African American students (Chenoweth, 2007; Delpit, 2006a; Irvine, 1990; King, 2005; Kozol, 2005; Kunjufu, 2002; Ladson-Billings, 1994; Milner & Hoy, 2003; Perry et al., 2003). Yet little research has placed a concerted effort on exploring options that can reverse problems with student achievement. As noted, curriculum development is an area that remains wildly unchanged. Outside of stale state and federal assessment initiatives, there is little evidence of *true* curriculum reform. As a result, students are blatantly underserved in traditional schools. This is evidenced by the limited amount of multiculturalism found in school curricula.

Despite national curriculum reform initiatives such as *No Child Left Behind* and *Common Core State Standards*, public school curricula overwhelmingly favor Eurocentric norms and ideas. In 2012, then-President Barack Obama's administration launched *Race to the Top* (RTT), the largest-ever federal competitive grant-based school reform, which focused on the school district level, and provided funding for states that improved student achievement. The federal government attempted to reward states that were able to create policies and programs that increased achievement. However, this reform had very little impact on the national curriculum and the moderate student achievement level in the United States (Darling-Hammond, 2010, 2017).

Current school curriculum is lensed through Eurocentric hegemony, which elevates European ethos above all other cultures (Asante, 1991).

This approach limits curricular relevancy for African American students (Dei, 1996; King et al., 2014; Ladson-Billings, 1994; Murrell, 2002). Without diversity in school curricula, African American students learn from a European perspective and nothing else (Dei, 1996; Jackson, 1994). Asante (2009b) and Dei (2012) assert that African American students generally learn about their history through the lenses of slavery and colonization. In this sense, there is no proper contextualization of cultural history that spans before slavery and beyond the Civil Rights Movement (Loewen, 1995). Important Black accomplishments extend far beyond those oversimplified time periods, such as precolonial African history, the Harlem Renaissance, and Tulsa's Black Wall Street of the 1920s (Akbar, 1998; Diop, 1987; Karenga, 2002). It is important that all students, not just African Americans, learn and understand the contributions of Africans across the Diaspora. Positive images in African American history should be accessible to all students in schools (Akbar, 1998). Also, it is important to note that Afrocentric schools teach all subjects (social studies, arts, mathematics, language arts, etc.), not just history, and generally adhere to state standards. Using state standards as a guide, Afrocentric schools attempt to supplement curriculum and instruction with antiracist and counterhegemonic sources. Such supplementation is widely encouraged among critical multicultural educators (Awad, 2011; Nieto & Bode, 2008). By removing the lens of European hegemony, Afrocentric schools teach students based on historical accuracy.

PURPOSE

This book explores U.S. public schools (K–12) in the context of the curriculum, school achievement, and outcomes of African American students. It presents Afrocentricity and *self-healing power* as an alternative framework and educational model that helps promote student success and healing from miseducation and falsifications of the curriculum. As an example of such practice, the book also explores the experiences of students and teachers at an Afrocentric school in order to examine the role of education in helping oppressed groups. Afrocentric schools utilize Afrocentricity as the guiding framework for instruction and curriculum design, and disrupt hegemonic propaganda with truth.

The book examines the benefits of Afrocentric schools and the role of education as self-healing power. As mentioned in the Preface, *The Healing Power of Education* promotes a realignment of curricula and pedagogy to be inclusive, factual, and counterhegemonic against falsification and dehumanization, and their resultant social, psychological and emotional damage and trauma. Racism creates institutional oppression, which can lead to emotional and psychological injuries. Thus, education as self-healing is also introspective work, as it promotes and nurtures healing from negative self and group concepts. As mentioned, self-healing is both an individual and collective approach to restoration and uplift. Since Black identity is inherently communal, the connection between self and community works together. In this regard, self-healing eventually leads to collective and communal healing.

Collective trauma across racially oppressed groups can lead to negative realities such as self-hate, internalized racism, and deficit ideologies. All people experience a degree of trauma as part of being human, but traumatic experience is far more common for groups who have been systematically oppressed for centuries. Within the context of the United States, the recent 2020 killings of Walter Wallace Jr., George Floyd, Breonna Taylor, Ahmaud Arbery, and Tony McDade, for example, have reflected the importance of the #BlackLivesMatter movement. The evidence of racial trauma has led researchers such as DeGury (2017) to posit the notion of *Post-Traumatic Slave Syndrome* (PTSS). DeGury's research asserts that U.S. slavery has an observable and traumatic effect on the human body. In this regard, PTSS describes the etiology of the adaptive survival behaviors in African American communities that are conduits of colonialism and slavery. This typically manifests in two ways. First, multigenerational trauma is often coupled with continued oppression. Second, the lack of opportunity to adequately heal or access useful benefits is another compounding factor. To that end, there are several signs of PTSS in the human body, including but not limited to feelings of hopelessness, a self-destructive outlook, violence against self or others, learned helplessness, literacy deprivation, distorted self-concept, and aversion to one's own identified cultural/ethnic group (DeGury, 2017).

This book thus has relevance for the entire United States, as the wounds of the country's racialized past are re-emerging. As we just recently ushered in the 400th year since Africans involuntarily entered North America as slaves in Virginia in 1619, there is much to explore in the context of anti-racism and racial reconciliation (Wiggan, 2018). Considering that the perils of American slavery and racism are still evident in the United States over 400 years later, the relevance of this book is especially timely considering the recent resurgence of racial injustice and protest in the United States and around the world. Notwithstanding, since collective healing and restoration is a human project not bounded by race, the principles in this book are helpful for all groups. In fact, healing and restoration are important for all people, even for the dominant group.

In this regard, *education as self-healing* disrupts misappropriations in regard to cultural, social, and psychological domination of oppressed groups and fosters their healing and wholeness. It promotes wellness against the enduring legacies of miseducation and domination, and works to cleanse our schools of distorted history and internalized domination. Because Europeans colonized or enslaved more than 80% of the world for more than a century, purposeful work must be done to promote healing from this negative and enduring force. Enslavement is much more than just physical bondage—it includes psychological, social, cultural, and spiritual subjugation as well. As a mediating and healing process, the Afrocentric school this book investigates is high-performing, boasting higher performance than the state in mathematics and reading, respectively. The findings reveal that the students and teachers described their school as having: (a) a unique learning environment, (b) support systems, (c) devotion—or spiritual affirmations, (d) evidences of Black education, (e) a reframing of Afrocentricity, and (f) restorative education that promotes positive and transformative Black identity. The results of this research are especially important when considering the lack of multiculturalism found in traditional public schools and the state of U.S. student achievement.

Education as self-healing seeks to correct neglect, distortion, and falsehood in school curricula with respect to the experiences of oppressed groups. We hope to center the Black educational experience and learners' possibilities within the prism of collective liberation and resistance against oppression. It is suggested that corrective history and "right knowledge" are part of the healing process from the emotional damage of miseducation and curriculum violence. The term "curriculum violence" describes the pervasive psychological damages caused by cultural misinformation and European standardization (Ighodaro & Wiggan, 2011). It is "the deliberate manipulation of academic programming in a manner that ignores or compromises the intellectual and psychological well-being of learners" (Ighodaro & Wiggan, 2011, p. 2). Consequently, healing is needed. This healing is psychological and perhaps spiritual as well, for as Fu-Kiau notes (1980/2001), in an African worldview one does not necessarily separate educational from spiritual, where spirituality is higher than religion.

African spirituality, in this sense, operates with, but beyond the realms of, formalized religion and instead promotes the importance of personal and community uplift, ancestral remembrance, and a connection to spirit-self. According to indigenous religions scholar Jacob Olupona, "African spirituality simply acknowledges that beliefs and practices touch on and inform every facet of human life, and therefore African religion cannot be separated from the everyday or mundane" (Chiorazzi, 2015, para. 9). It is important to note that there are several formalized African spirituality practices, such as *Ifa* or the worship of *Amma*, but this project focuses on the nonreligious regenerating power of education to uplift marginalized groups.

Ani argues that in the Dogon tradition of Mali, West Africa, the deity Amma, the Creator, proposed that all created beings should live under the universal principle of complementarity (Ani, 1998). From an Afrocentric worldview, the Creator or creative force is far too big and expansive for a single tradition. As such, spirituality is not oppositional to various forms of manifestations of human spiritual expressions in the way that religion is often oppositional against other traditions, systems, and religions. In an

Afrocentric sense, while religion can help provide a structure or system to help bring individuals into a cosmic awareness and support spiritual development, it may or may not emit spirituality. At its core, spirituality implies staying in tune with the great Spirit or Creator force. Thus, from an African worldview, spiritual traditions do not set people apart; instead, they connect us. Exemplifying this, using an African cosmological perspective, Fu-Kiau (1980/2001) notes: "I am going-and-coming-back-being around the center of vital forces. I am because I was and re-was before, and that I will be and re-be again" (p. 5). Thus, from an African worldview, the individual is a collective of past, present, and future experiences, along with ancestral expressions and awareness. This is not to suggest that all African cultures are the same, for they are surely diverse, but as Cheikh Anta Diop (1974, 1981, 1987) explains, there are cultural continuities that span across the African, and diasporic African, parlance. Again, these interconnections are not oppositional but complementary. This is based on the fact that human behavior is a reflection of human consciousness. Thus, *education as self-healing power* positions the classroom as a safe and sacred space to promote healing. In this regard, right knowledge helps to correct miseducation and raises human consciousness, especially among racially marginalized groups.

While in the Western sense science and religion may be incongruent, in the Afrocentric parlance spirituality and science are not oppositional. There is, however, opposition to pseudoscience. For students, a realignment of right knowledge can correct misinformation and miseducation. Here, miseducation refers to the systemic falsification and degradation of historical fact within curricula, which eventually leads to the "enslavement of the mind" (Woodson, 1933/1977, p. 134). This work applies an Afrocentric theoretical framework in order to investigate Afrocentricity as a method of self-healing. More specifically, this research examines how right knowledge and corrective history can potentially help reverse the effects of social, cultural, emotional, and psychological trauma that oppressed people face in a system of domination. The trauma necessitates a paradigm of healing as a mediating force. This is a new contribution to the field, as it is primarily an introspective framework and approach to education. Additionally, there is limited research that explores Afrocentric schools within 21st century contexts.

The case study presented in this book examines teacher, administrator, and student experiences. It is important to mention that while parents are important in students' educational experiences, they are beyond the scope of this book.

CENTRAL QUESTIONS

The central questions that guide this work are: What are the experiences of students and teachers at a high-performing Afrocentric school? What role does education or "right knowledge" play in helping oppressed groups to heal from trauma or social, cultural, and psychological domination? Later chapters include learning that emerged from interviewing students, teachers, and the school's administrator at Asa G. Hilliard Academy (AGHA)—the pseudonym for the school site—a high-achieving Afrocentric school in the southeastern United States. It is important to note that while this study's site is located in the Southeast, the relevance of this topic has implications for the entire United States as it speaks to racial healing. Next, as a means of understanding the school culture and climate, classroom observations capture the enriched learning experiences of Afrocentric classrooms. Last, student written narratives describe their experiences at an Afrocentric school. The interviews, classroom observations, and student written responses ultimately connect Afrocentricity's theoretical teachings to a school model that adopts the same principles. Thus, the book's central questions also focus on understanding Afrocentricity's role in shaping educational experiences for African American students. The research questions and data collection methods capture the overall focus of this case study, which is to investigate the experiences of students attending a high-achieving Afrocentric school.

As Black researchers who support African-centered philosophy and education, we understand the importance of corrective history and decolonial frameworks for learning. We collectively share a theoretical understanding of Afrocentric education, but hope to glean insight into the daily operations and overall experiences within a high-performing African-centered school. Considering the limitations in the literature, we aim to explore ways in which education can promote academic, social, and cultural success. We believe that an expansion of educational discourse to include a more introspective lens on healing from trauma is needed in the discourse on Black education. As such, we immersed ourselves into a school [Asa G. Hilliard Academy (AGHA)] with 100% African American students, teachers, and administrators. Additionally, we selected a high-performing school as evidence of an academically successful learning environment for students.

DEFINITIONS

The following terms are important to the book and have varying definitions in preexisting research. As a result, they each require a thorough understanding.

African American: The term "African American" refers to the Diasporic African in the United States. In terms of the book, as it pertains to African American education, Black and African American are used interchangeably in order to encompass those who are either Diasporic Africans or continental Africans. It is important to note that within an Afrocentric perspective, Diasporic Blacks are considered Africans.

African-centered pedagogy: Murrell (2002) defines African-centered (which is used synonymously with Afrocentric) pedagogy as education that

> brings to light those principles of good practice that already exist and links them to contemporary ideas and innovations that apply to effective practice in African American communities. The theory of teaching and learning is called "African-centered pedagogy" and has been shaped by more than twenty-five years of teaching, community organizing, and research in and around urban schools and communities. (p. ix)

Afrocentric: As mentioned, the term "Afrocentric" literally means the centering of Africa, or the placing of Africa in the middle. It is a conceptual term that moves Africa away from the margins toward the center, and allows Africans to be *participants* rather than *objects* of interpretation (Asante, 2010). As we have noted, the Afrocentric perspective correctly places Africa at the origin of humanity and civilization, and includes, rather than excludes, all human contributions across the original human diaspora from Africa. It positions the beginning of later civilizations and contributions, and acknowledges the interconnections among the human family tree, which would later span across what would come to be called the seven continents. The entire human population is of African descent. Afrocentricity acknowledges that the original people were all Africans, who evolved based on climatic and geographical changes to later create other social, cultural, and linguistic groups, but in effect, all are descendants of Africans. In this sense, the Afrocentric perspective is not just for Black or direct African descendants; it is for the human family and is a useful framework for today's classrooms and its diverse learners. It seeks to unite and create harmony by disrupting miseducation with right knowledge. Afrocentricity thus promotes self-healing power, unity, and human and group solidarity. Some contemporary nuances are associated with the term "Afrocentric." In this book, Afrocentric is used synonymously to represent Afrocentricity, Africentric, African-centered, Afrikan-centered, and Afrocentrism.

Afrocentricity: Asante (2003) defines Afrocentricity this way:

> a mode of thought and action in which the centrality of African interest, values and perspectives predominate. In regards to theory, it is the placing of African people in the center of any analysis of African phenomena. Thus it is possible for any one to master the discipline of seeking the location of Africans in a given phenomena [sic]. In terms of action and behavior, it is a devotion to the idea that what is in the best interest of African consciousness is at the heart of ethical behavior. Finally, Afrocentricity seeks to enshrine the idea that Blackness itself is a trope of ethics. Thus to be [Black] is to be against all forms of oppression, racism, classism, homophobia, patriarchy, child abuse, pedophilia and White racial domination. (p. 2)

Alkebulan: This book acknowledges that one of the original names for the continent of Africa was Alkebulan, which means mother of humanity (ben-Jochannan, 2016).

Diaspora: The literal meaning of *diaspora* is to disperse throughout. In this context, Diaspora describes the historical moment when Africans were uprooted from the continent through the transatlantic slave trade. There is a noted difference between the terms "Diaspora" and "international" in that the former is forced and the latter is by choice. Throughout this book, the term "Diaspora" (or "Diasporic") is used to describe the African American experience.

Eurocentric: Eurocentric is the narrowed perspective of assessing values, beliefs, history, and philosophy based on Western European culture. This perspective ignores the historical contributions of Africans, and other racial groups, prior to the Greek and Roman invasions. Most traditional schools today operate under this paradigm. Afrocentric schools were formed in response to this ethnocentric perspective, and should not be confused as trying to emulate this same oppression. Rather, the latter seeks to be inclusive of all by underscoring the origins of humanity and its many later civilizations and cultural systems around the world, and their interconnections.

Hegemony: Antonio Gramsci (1999) coined the term "hegemony" to denote the propagation of one set of mainstream ideals that negate the complexities and experiences of others (Lemert, 2010).

Inclusion: The term "inclusion" is used throughout the book to signify the including or encompassing of all social, cultural, and ethnic groups. This term extends beyond race and includes socioeconomics, gender, sexuality, ability, and more. This word is central to the research and combats the notions that Afrocentric schools or Afrocentricity is separatist. Inclusion is a means to explore diversity and belonging.

Kemet: In the context of this book, the name Kemet has been recognized as the precolonial name for the country the Greeks renamed Egypt. African words have meaning, and Kemet means "land of the Black people." Kemet or Kmt and Egypt are used interchangeably in this book.

MAAFA: The term "MAAFA" was coined by Marimba Ani (1994, 1998), who suggests that the systemic oppression against African Americans in the United States is a direct result of the traumatic persecution from transatlantic slavery. Ani posits that using the term MAAFA, versus "slavery," helps to codify and conceptualize the vast genocide committed toward Black Africans in North America and throughout the Diaspora. Similarly, Hilliard and Amankwatia (2002) describe MAAFA as "the unique terror of African oppression" (p. 1). This word is Kiswahili and is used to explain the social and emotional turmoil experienced in the Black experience.

MA'AT: The MA'AT (or MAAT) is the personification of world order established in precolonial Africa (Hilliard et al., 1987). Today's Afrocentric schools are based on the principles of MA'AT, which are truth, justice, harmony, balance, order, reciprocity, and propriety (Hilliard & Amankwatia, 2002; Murrell, 2002). These principles were later contemporized into the Nguzo Saba (Karenga, 1966).

Nguzo Saba: Maulana Karenga (1966) coined the seven principles of Nguzo Saba, which are known more popularly today through the holiday Kwanzaa. The seven principles include umoja (unity), kujichagulia (self-determination), ujima (collective work and responsibility), ujamaa (cooperative economics), nia (purpose), kuumba (creativity), and imani (faith). Many Afrocentric schools embed these principles into the school culture.

90/90/90 schools: 90/90/90 represents schools with student populations of 90% or more racial minority, 90% or more free and/or reduced lunch, and 90% or more at or above state-mandated achievement levels (Kearney et al., 2012). These schools represent models of success, as they are high-achieving minority schools. From a policy perspective, it is important to examine the effective educational practices found in 90/90/90 schools in order to more widely implement these strategies.

Pan-African: Pan-African describes a historical and political movement aimed to unite people across the African Diaspora toward cultural congruence and unity. Aside from being a term to describe a political movement, Pan-African can also describe a person interested in the unification of Africa across the Diaspora. Pan-Africanism is essential to this present work because it served as a precursor to Afrocentricity and Afrocentric schools in the 19th and 20th centuries.

Right knowledge: "Right knowledge" is knowledge that is factual and free of misinformation or miseducation, as Dr. Carter G. Woodson notes. It is knowledge that is critical and transformative, both personally and socially. It is reflective and can be questioned, investigated, and revisited to determine its validity. It agitates against falsification and pseudoscience in order to reveal truth. Right knowledge helps to mitigate against regimes of domination.

Sankofa: The term "sankofa" is meant to promote the self-healing power of education. The concept of sankofa is an Akan proverb, which means literally "go back and fetch" (King et al., 2014). Afrocentric education requires students to "go back" and revisit historical propaganda, and then realign falsehoods with truth. Thus, the self-healing concepts of education are beneficial for all students.

Self-healing: Self-healing is an introspective ontological process that
promotes and nurtures restoration from negative self and group
concepts. It realigns misappropriations in regards to cultural, social,
and psychological domination of oppressed groups, and fosters healing
and wholeness.

SIGNIFICANCE OF THE WORK

Today's public education system leaves little room for curricular flexibility.
Current school curriculum is streamlined, diluted, and culturally irrelevant
for many students. This is due to the compounding effects of high-stakes
testing policies and neoliberal economics, meaning market-based policies
that increase privatization in favor of free-market capitalism, which have
irreversibly changed the U.S. educational landscape (Anyon, 2005; Darling-
Hammond, 2010; Spring, 2005; Stein, 2004). The implementation of rote
learning, drills, and memorization in order to prepare for looming state
assessments has supplanted educational rigor and critical thinking (Stein,
2004). This form of education is known as the "banking" model, in which
the teacher authoritatively "deposits" information into students, without
critical discussion and inquiry (Freire, 2000). The educational banking
model is quite popular today, and overwhelmingly describes many traditional school settings. These pedagogical styles have diluted public education into factory-style models that produce unskilled laborers rather than
problem-solving critical thinkers (Darling-Hammond, 2010; Spring, 2005).
Darling-Hammond (2010) asserts that as a result the public education system is leaving today's students virtually uncompetitive in the 21st-century
global job market.

Aside from being globally uncompetitive, there is a more pervasive and
long-lasting problem in the U.S. educational system. To start, over 80%
of the U.S. teaching workforce is White (NCES, 2017a, 2017b). Table 1.2
shows the national distribution of teachers by racial demographic groups.
Racial grouping is not significant in determining teacher quality, but it is
critical to understanding teacher perceptions of students (Jackson, 1994;
Milner & Hoy, 2003). Figure 1.3 illustrates the changing student demographics of U.S. public schools.

The lack of diversity and training in the teacher workforce creates many
classroom challenges. Classroom dissonance between students and teachers
often stems from cultural misunderstandings, stereotypes, intolerance, and
ignorance (Emdin, 2016; Kunjufu 2002; Ladson-Billings, 1994; Milner &
Hoy, 2003). Since race has been found to be one of the primary identifying factors for stereotyping and creating assumptions (Ito & Urland, 2003;
Rattan & Ambady, 2013), it is safe to conclude that African American students are viewed collectively, and categorized as a cultural "group." These

Table 1.2. Percentage Distribution of Public School Teachers by Race/Ethnicity and Selected School Characteristics: 2015–2016

	Hispanic	White	Black	Asian	Native Hawaiian/ Pacific Islander	Native American/ Alaskan Native	Two or more races
All	8.8%	80.1%	6.7%	2.3%	0.2%	0.4%	1.4%
Community type							
City	13.2%	69.5%	11%	3.8%	0.3%	0.2%	2.0%
Suburban	8.5%	81.9%	5.6%	2.2%	0.2%	0.3%	1.3%
Town	5.7%	87.9%	3.3%	0.8%	0.3%	0.8%	1.2%
Rural	4.1%	89.4%	3.9%	0.6%	0.1%	1.0%	0.9%

Figure 1.3. Percentage Distribution of Public School Students Enrolled in Pre-Kindergarten Through 12th Grade, by Race/Ethnicity: Fall 2003, Fall 2013, and Fall 2025* (Projected)

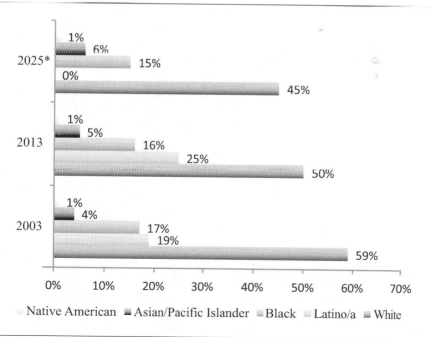

Source: National Center for Education Statistics (2017c).

identifying factors are usually based on propagated media images, rather than on factual information indicative of student behavior and character. Under these assumptions, teachers expect students to conform to certain classroom behaviors that reflect their own personal cultural ethos (Delpit, 2006a). This environment stirs indignation in both students and teachers. Chenoweth (2009) notes that many teachers possess, "unapologetic racism coupled with the sense that it [is] inefficient to waste educational resources on anyone who didn't have the ability to benefit from them" (p. 15). As Joyce King noted, White teachers exercise dysconscious racism (uncritical habits of mind or unexamined beliefs, assumptions, and actions that negatively impact Blacks or African descent people) on Black students every day in schools (King, 2005; King & Swartz, 2018). For many teachers who have not been properly trained to educate African American or urban students, their attempts at instruction are counterintuitive.

In addition to academics, teacher perceptions also influence school discipline and discipline policies (Bireda, 2002). Over the past 15 years, trend data show that African American male students are three times more likely to receive a suspension or expulsion than their White counterparts (Hilberth & Slate, 2014; Kunjufu, 2002; Skiba et al., 2002; Townsend, 2000). Even for the same discipline infractions, African American male students are more likely to receive harsher punishments than their White peers (Hilberth & Slate, 2014; Losen & Gillespie, 2012). These suspensions cause students to miss critical instructional time, which is linked to course failure, dropping out, and incarceration (Kim et al., 2010). The disparity in African American student discipline, though well researched, remains a widespread problem. This once again speaks to the disparity in the treatment of students without addressing the systemic problem.

Teacher quality is another important factor for student success (Delpit, 2006b). Urban schools, many of which serve high populations of African American students, are most likely to have uncertified teachers with outdated and inadequate classroom resources (Kozol, 2005). Table 1.3 shows the percentage of uncertified teachers teaching in public schools by school type.

Table 1.3. Percentage of Uncertified Teachers, by School Type : 2013–2014

Location	< 5%	5% to < 10%	10% to < 15%	15% to < 25%	25% or more
Urban	11.0%	11.3%	9.0%	12.0%	56.6%
Suburban	22.7%	22.4%	14.4%	15.2%	25.2%
Town	23.6%	26.2%	16.0%	11.1%	23.0%
Rural	23.1%	24.9%	15.2%	12.6%	24.3%

Source: U.S. Department of Education (2016).

Table 1.4. Adjusted Public High School Graduation Rates by Race and Gender: 2017–2018

Race/ethnicity	Graduation rate
Total	85%
White	89%
Black	79%
Hispanic	81%
Asian/Pacific Islander	92%
Native American/ Native Alaskan	74%

Source: National Center for Education Statistics (2020).

Many teachers in urban schools are unqualified to teach the subjects they are assigned. This is especially dangerous for students. In fact, the strongest predictors of student failure are the proportion of teachers without training or certification, and the proportion of vacancies open for more than 9 weeks (Darling-Hammond, 2010).

The disparities in the graduation rates may connect more deeply to the low numbers of certified teachers in urban classrooms across U.S. K–12 public schools. Table 1.4 illustrates this phenomenon. This suggests that Black and minority students in public schools are more likely to have uncertified teachers, and perhaps lower-quality instruction, across their entire educational careers. Research shows that once students reach high school, schools serving large numbers of African American students often fail to offer the necessary courses needed to graduate and matriculate into public colleges or universities (Toldson & Lewis, 2012). In fact, 90% of state flagship universities require advanced mathematics and laboratory science courses for college matriculation, yet only 29% and 40% of high schools serving low-income and African American students offer calculus and physics classes, respectively (U.S. Department of Education Office of Civil Rights, 2012). These are necessary classes for admission at the majority of universities across the nation. Therefore, student success is attributed more to teachers' instructional effectiveness, school quality, and course content than to student intelligence. African American students, portrayed as "less intelligent" on state standardized assessments, are actually "less served" instructionally. Further, school equity and quality vary across states and district lines, where low-income and minority students are subject to lower-quality instruction, fewer resources, and less access. Table 1.5 illustrates the disparities in per-student expenditure across states, with numbers adjusted for regional cost differences. Due to the geographic contextualization of this

Table 1.5. Per-Pupil Spending, Arranged by the States With the Highest Per-Student Expenditures and the Lowest Per-Student Expenditures: 2019

State	Per-pupil spending*
National average	$12,756
States with highest per-pupil spending	
1. Vermont	$20,540
2. New York	$19,697
3. Wyoming	$18,090
4. Alaska	$17,872
5. Connecticut	$17,798
6. New Jersey	$16,543
7. New Hampshire	$16,347
States with lowest per-pupil spending	
1. Utah	$7,635
2. Arizona	$8,335
3. Texas	$8,619
4. Idaho	$8,677
5. Nevada	$9,185
6. Oklahoma	$9,250
7. North Carolina	$9,367

*Figures adjusted for regional cost difference; *Source: Education Week* (2019).

book, Table 1.6 presents per-student expenditures across southern states, as determined by the U.S. Census Bureau (2018).

Table 1.5 presents the vast differences in state per-student expenditures. In fact, the United States has some of the greatest funding inequities of any industrialized nation (Learning Policy Institute, 2018). These differences can have a significant impact on school quality, student achievement, and racial inequalities (Baker, 2018; Beese & Liang, 2012). Within the United States, some of the largest economic disparities are found in the South. Table 1.7 on page 25 depicts per-student expenditures in the Southeast and displays school-funding inequity in greater detail.

Table 1.6 displays per-student expenditures in 16 southern states as designated and defined by the U.S. Census Bureau (2018). As indicated in the table, 13 of the 16 states are in the bottom 50% of per-student expenditures. These are also some of the lowest-performing states in terms of education.

Table 1.6. Per-Pupil Spending, Selected Southern States: 2018

State	Per-pupil spending	National Rank
Delaware	$15,009	12th
Maryland	$13,146	20th
West Virginia	$12,915	24th
Louisiana	$12,362	26th
Arkansas	$11,951	27th
South Carolina	$11,564	32nd
Kentucky	$11,210	34th
Virginia	$10,530	37th
Alabama	$10,386	38th
Mississippi	$10,240	40th
Georgia	$10,114	41st
Florida	$9,764	43rd
Tennessee	$9,694	44th
North Carolina	$9,367	45th
Oklahoma	$9,250	46th
Texas	$8,619	49th

*Figures adjusted for regional cost difference; *Source: Education Week* (2019).

Census data consistently indicate that the majority of African Americans live in the southern region of the United States (U.S. Census, 2011). Yet, these states report some of the lowest per-student expenditures even after regional cost difference adjustments. In relation to African American student achievement, these populations also report some of the lowest achievement ratings (NAEP, 2017a, 2017b). Thus, it is important to examine Black student achievement with a focus on fiscal equity, resources, and teacher quality.

African American school achievement has received substantial attention in academic research. Yet, with all of the aforementioned issues negatively interfering with African American achievement, there is dangerous misinformation still circulating in research that suggests that these students are somehow "inferior," lazy, or incapable (Kunjufu, 2002; Perry et al., 2003). As mentioned, most of the research erroneously focuses on the "achievement gap," which is more properly titled "opportunity," "resource," or "equity" gap. "Achievement gap" studies suggest that there is a measurable difference between Black and White student intelligence. As noted in Guthrie's (2004) seminal work, *Even the Rat Was White*, the history of these claims dates back to 19th-century research propaganda submersed in racism (Wiggan, 2007). The results from these studies are irreversibly damaging and specious. Despite the undeniable structural differences in student treatment across schools, educational research overwhelmingly continues to embrace these notions and to perpetuate false research (Perry et al., 2003).

After over a century of racist research, it is more appropriate to advocate to close the *opportunity*, *resource*, or *equity* gaps, because there are observable practices that work to reverse Black and White student underachievement, as illustrated earlier in the NAEP data (Bloom & Owens, 2013; Chenoweth, 2007, 2009). This demonstrates that instructional methods, not race, determine a child's achievement outcomes. Some examples of high African American student achievement models are exemplified in "90/90/90" schools (Kearney et al., 2012). This term represents schools with student populations of 90% or more racial minority, 90% or more free and/or reduced lunch, and 90% at or above state-mandated achievement levels. It is important to examine the effective educational practices found in 90/90/90 schools in order to more accurately address student achievement for the broader U.S. student population. Chenoweth (2007, 2009) and Bell (2001) examined how these high-performing urban schools across the United States differ from other schools. They found that administrative commitment, teacher expectations, community involvement, and adult/student mentoring are essential components in high-performing urban schools (Bell, 2001; Bloom & Owens, 2013; Chenoweth, 2007, 2009). Sadly, 90/90/90 schools are anomalies. On a larger scale, traditional public schools are failing African American students.

As mentioned, race-based research leads audiences to believe that there is something culturally, cognitively, or intellectually inadequate in African American students (Perry et al., 2003; Sizemore, 1990). This is a dangerous and deplorable claim. These claims disregard the fact that only 44% of White students in 8th grade are at or above proficiency in mathematics (NAEP, 2017b), and only 45% of 8th-grade White students are at or above proficiency in reading (NAEP, 2017a). These moderate school performance levels might suggest a need for effective national school reform for the entire country. As mentioned earlier, research on "the achievement gap" ignores the institutional and environmental factors that undermine student achievement, such as learning conditions, teacher quality, and classroom resources. Chenoweth (2009) explains, "this is one of the great failings of most schools—that students who need the best teachers often get the weakest teachers" (p. 91). There thus exists an opportunity and resource gap, not a gap in student achievement, as national data indicate that both Black and White students are underachieving (King, 2005; Kunjufu, 2002; Perry et al., 2003). As illustrative of the racism embedded in the "achievement gap" discourse, when Asians or immigrant Blacks outperform Whites, that is not called an "achievement gap;" the narrative is employed only when Whites score higher than racial minorities, particularly Black and Brown students. More importantly, traditional "achievement gap" research ignores the fact that "excellence," not a racialized achievement score, should be the primary aim for U.S. students (Perry et al., 2003). Currently, the United States is far from attaining that goal (Darling-Hammond, 2010).

A CLOSER EXAMINATION OF STUDENT ACHIEVEMENT

Most 21st-century research substantiates the fact that standardized assessments are problematic and largely skewed toward White, Eurocentric ethos (Ighodaro & Wiggan, 2011). However, they are consistently used to comparatively assess achievement, often at a detriment to African American students. As we have noted, there are overwhelming misconceptions regarding Black student achievement in educational institutions in the United States. To support the purpose of this book, it is important to reposition a more comprehensive examination of student achievement, at different analytic levels.

To start, the overall status of U.S. education, on a macro level, is misunderstood. Thus, it is important to examine U.S. student achievement comparatively and internationally. The 2015 Program for Student Assessment (PISA) compared U.S. student achievement to other Organisation for Economic Co-operation and Development (OECD) nations, and measured proficiency levels of 15-year-old students in critical subjects such as mathematics, science, and reading literacies. In mathematics literacy, the United States ranked 40th of 70 nations and scored below the OECD average (PISA, 2015a). Meanwhile, the United States ranked 25th in science literacy and 24th in reading literacy (PISA, 2015b, 2015c). We acknowledge that science and reading literacy scores were above the OECD average, but overall rankings consistently placed U.S. students in the bottom two-thirds (66%) of comparable nations.

The 2016 Progress in International Reading Literacy Study (PIRLS) also yields some imperative findings. In 4th-grade reading, U.S. students ranked 15th of 61 participating international districts (PIRLS, 2016). Similarly, the 2015 Trends in International Mathematics and Science Study (TIMSS) notes that the United States ranked 14th in 4th-grade and 10th in 8th-grade mathematics (TIMSS, 2015a). In science, the TIMSS show that U.S. students ranked 10th and 11th in 4th- and 8th-grade science, respectively (TIMSS, 2015b). In 8th-grade disciplines, the United States ranked 11th of 40 comparable nations in both mathematics and science (TIMSS, 2015a, 2015b). These results are in comparison to other participating nations and international districts. Findings from these international assessments are helpful when putting U.S. student achievement, and excellence, into a global perspective.

It is important to mention that international assessments have received some criticism in educational discourse (Torney-Purta & Amadeo, 2013). Researchers note the unavoidable inconsistencies when comparing unique and distinctive educational systems (Torney-Purta & Amadeo, 2013). Additionally, researchers also problematize student selection processes and caste hierarchies in countries where educational access is not available to all citizens (Singer & Braun, 2018). Thus, it is also important to examine student achievement on a national level. The National Assessment of Educational Progress (NAEP) presented 4th- and 8th-grade student achievement data. This report measured the percentage of students at or above proficiency in mathematics and reading (NAEP, 2017a, 2017b). Nationally, in reading, only 37% of U.S. 4th-grade students and 36% of 8th-grade students were at or above proficiency (NAEP, 2017a). In mathematics, only 40% of U.S. 4th-graders and 34% of 8th-graders were at or above proficiency (NAEP, 2017b). Note that these numbers reflect *all* racial and socioeconomic groups within U.S. public schools. Data from Tables 1.7 to 1.9 show underperformance across every student demographic and school type. These numbers are concerning, indicating systemic underperformance of U.S. students and schools in general.

As demonstrated in Table 1.7, the differences in school geographic locale are also important when considering student achievement. The aforementioned 2017 NAEP scores further disaggregate student achievement data based on school location, including city, suburb, town, and rural. For 8th-grade reading, 32% of city students, 42% of suburban students, 30% of town students, and 34% of rural students were at or above proficiency in 2017. For 8th-grade mathematics, 31% of city students, 39% of suburban students, 29% of town students, and 33% of rural students were at or above proficiency in 2017. Note that *all* geographic locations, not just urban areas, are below 50% proficient in both reading and mathematics (NAEP, 2017b). Additionally, NAEP disaggregated student proficiency data based on school type, including public and private/parochial schools (see Table 1.8). The results from the 2017 study demonstrate that 35% of U.S. public school students and 55% of private school students were proficient in 8th-grade reading (NAEP, 2017a, 2017b). Similarly, 33% of 8th-grade public school students were proficient in mathematics, while only 44% of private school students demonstrated proficiency (NAEP, 2017a, 2017b). Once again, it is important to mention that this is an averaged composite score across all racial and socioeconomic groups.

The 2017 NAEP data also disaggregate student achievement based on racial group (see Table 1.9). For 8th-grade reading, 45% of White, 18% of Black, 23% of Latino/Latina, 55% of Asian/Pacific Islander, 23% of Native Hawaiian/Pacific Islander, 22% of American Indian/Alaskan Native, and

Table 1.7. National Student Achievement by Public School Geographic Type: Percentage at or Above Proficiency

	City (Urban)	Suburban	Town	Rural
4th-grade reading	32%	42%	31%	35%
8th-grade reading	32%	42%	30%	34%
4th-grade mathematics	35%	45%	36%	40%
8th-grade mathematics	31%	39%	29%	33%

Source: National Assessment of Education Progress (2017a, 2017b).

Table 1.8. National Student Achievement by School Type, Percentage at or Above Proficiency

	Public	Private
4th-grade reading	35%	49%
8th-grade reading	35%	55%
4th-grade mathematics	40%	47%
8th-grade mathematics	33%	44%

Source: National Assessment of Education Progress (2017a, 2017b).

Table 1.9. 8th Grade National Student Achievement Data by Race, Percentage at or Above Proficiency

	Reading	Mathematics
White	45%	44%
Black	18%	13%
Latino/a	23%	20%
Asian/Pacific Islander	55%	62%
Native Hawaiian/Pacific Islander	23%	25%
American Indian/Alaska Native	22%	18%
Multiracial	42%	37%

Source: National Assessment of Education Progress (2017a, 2017b).

42% of multiracial students were at or above proficiency in 2017 (NAEP, 2017a). For 8th-grade mathematics, 44% of White, 13% of Black, 20% of Latino/Latina, 62% of Asian/Pacific Islander, 25% of Native Hawaiian/Pacific Islander, 18% of American Indian/Alaskan Native, and 37% of multiracial students were at or above proficiency (NAEP, 2017b). These performance levels may also justify why alternative models are needed, and why a healing paradigm is needed particularly for Black students, who fare far worse in public schools. There is a disparity among all racial groups toward the ultimate goal of 100% student proficiency. This demonstrates once again that excellence, not the metric of White student achievement, should be the primary measure of student success (Perry et al., 2003). A conceptual view of how students measure against educational "excellence" is displayed in Figure 1.4.

Figure 1.4 illustrates that disparities overwhelmingly exist between all U.S. students and excellence (Darling-Hammond, 2010; Perry et al., 2003). Based on the most recent data, the U.S. public school system is underserving the majority of its students, despite the innate flaws and bias within standardized assessment measures. This is a crucial issue that must be addressed. Since it has been dispelled through research that African American students are less capable academically (Hilberth & Slate, 2014; Wilson, 1992), it is important to display successful school models that are setting "excellence," not racialized achievement, as the standard-bearer for educational success. This book highlights one of these successful school

Figure 1.4. 2017 8th-Grade U.S. Student Achievement by Racial Group: A Conceptualization of Excellence

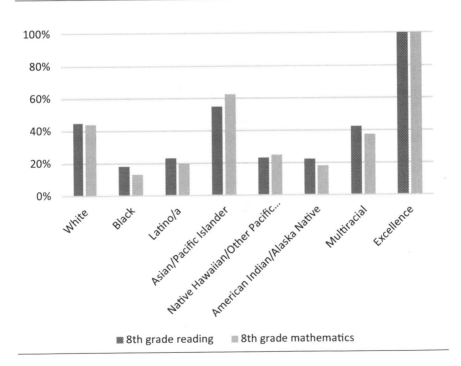

8th grade reading   8th grade mathematics

models—Afrocentric schools—and expounds on the educational and social benefits for students.

SUMMARY

This chapter described the current educational conditions of African American students and connected them to the dangers of hegemony within traditional public school curricula. This discussion took into account recent educational reform initiatives that place increased emphasis on high-stakes standardized assessments and rote memorization, which are harmful to students. Additionally, the chapter stressed the importance of inclusion and alternative curricula for all students. One alternative form of schools is Afrocentric education. The need for embedded cultural perspectives within a school design has led some educators to explore Afrocentric education as a viable alternative approach (Banks, 1998; King et al., 2014; Murrell, 2002). These schools reposition Africa at the center and as a place of importance, rather than on the margins (Asante, 1998). This approach encourages critical counternarratives that are often ignored in traditional schools (King et al., 2014).

A qualitative single case study is one of the effective ways of studying Afrocentric schools and addressing the limited recent research in the field. While research has studied Afrocentric school designs, there has been little consistency on the importance of alternative curricula for realigning right knowledge, and little to no research regarding Afrocentricity as a tool for healing and restoration. These research opportunities are unique to this book, which argues that it is important to address the needs of all students with a self-healing, alternative approach.

CHAPTER 2

Social and Historical Context of Black Education

Whatever faults and failings other nations may have in their dealings with their own subjects or with other people, no other civilized nation stands condemned before the world with a series of crimes so peculiarly national. It becomes a painful duty of the Negro to reproduce a record which shows that a large portion of the American people avow anarchy, condone murder and defy the contempt of civilization.

—Ida B. Wells, *The Red Record,* 1895

But can you expect teachers to revolutionize the social order for the good of the community? Indeed we must expect this very thing. The educational system of a country is worthless unless it accomplishes this task.

—Carter G. Woodson, 1933/1977

The purpose of this work is to explore education as a self-healing framework. In doing so, it explores the experiences and perceptions of students and teachers at an Afrocentric school. More specifically, this book aims to answer the following key questions: What are the experiences of students and teachers at a high-performing Afrocentric school? What role does education or "right knowledge" play in helping oppressed groups to heal from trauma and social, cultural, and psychological domination? Limited research has explored Afrocentric schools as models of self-healing and restoration, so this work aims to enhance the current understanding of Afrocentricity, specifically within a 21st-century educational context. Afrocentric schools have emerged in response to inadequate learning environments and/or curricula for students. Today's 21st-century public schools are guided primarily by standardized assessments and statewide curricula, which marginalize African American history into small, menial contributions (Akbar, 1998; Dei, 1996). Many parents and educators have sought alternative learning environments, such as Afrocentric schools, for a more inclusive school culture. In order to understand how these contemporary Afrocentric schools emerged, it is important to illustrate the historical trends of Pan-Africanism, Afrocentricity, and the long-term influence that Africa has had on humanity. We also need to note that before the term "Afrocentricity" emerged, there was Pan-Africanism and Black Nationalism (Pollard & Ajirotutu, 2000; Shockley & Frederick, 2010). These historical movements are important in connecting Afrocentricity as a social theory, as well as its emergence as a school model.

This chapter provides precolonial history and reviews the formations of Pan-Africanism, Black Nationalism, and Afrocentric education. In doing so, the chapter explores Afrocentricity and its self-healing power through alternative curricula and right knowledge. Again, we should underscore that Afrocentric schools do not just teach history—they teach all subject areas. This review situates Afrocentricity in a broader educational context and discusses plausible options for today's hegemonic educational system. It surveys case studies of Afrocentric schools and discusses the advantages and disadvantages of these alternative learning environments for students.

PRECOLONIAL HISTORY

The topic of Afrocentricity must start with a precolonial discussion of Africa and the origins of humanity. To begin, the conversation about humanity must start in the modern-day Ethiopian region. The word "Ethiopia" means "burnt skin" or "Black people." Ethiopia is where the oldest human fossil remains are found along with the earliest evidence of human civilization (Hilliard, 1998; Jackson, 1970; Williams, 1987). Concurrently, Egypt (originally known as Kemet) was first located in the northeastern region of ancient Ethiopia (Ani, 1994; Asante, 1990; Clarke, 1993; Jackson, 1970; Karenga, 2002; Williams, 1987). As mentioned earlier, in this book, Egypt and Kemet are used interchangeably. The first known inhabitants of Kemet date to 10,000 BCE (Clarke, 1993; Hilliard et al., 1987). Kemet's inhabitants were Black Africans:

> That means that it was a black or Africoid civilization. If one places the evidence from skeletal remains, mummified remains, carvings, paintings and ancient historical accounts into chronological order, the Blackness of ancient Kmt, ancient Ta-Seti and even more ancient Hapi (Nile) Valley cultures will be obvious to any observer. (Hilliard et al., 1987, p. 9)

This can also be confirmed through primary interaction with the Greeks, as indicated in Aristotle's *Physiognomonics* and Herodotus's *Histories*. Both accounts describe the Egyptians with Black skin and woolly hair. Herodotus wrote:

For the people of Colchis are evidently Egyptian, and this I perceived for myself before I heard it from others. So when I had come to consider the matter I asked them both; and the Colchians had remembrance of the Egyptians more than the Egyptians of the Colchians; but the Egyptians said they believed that the Colchians were a portion of the army of Sesostris. That this was so I conjectured myself not only because they are dark-skinned and have curly hair (this of itself amounts to nothing, for there are other races which are so), but also still more because the Colchians, Egyptians, and Ethiopians alone of all the races of men have [practiced] circumcision from the first. The Phenicians and the Syrians who dwell in Palestine confess themselves that they have learnt it from the Egyptians, and the Syrians about the river Thermodon and the river Parthenios, and the Macronians, who are their [neighbors], say that they have learnt it lately from the Colchians. These are the only races of men who [practice] circumcision, and these evidently [practice] it in the same manner as the Egyptians. (Herodotus, 440 BCE [2014], p. 104)

Their physical descriptions are important when distinguishing their undeniable African features. Figure 2.1 depicts Shepsesre from the 24th dynasty, which is a visual representation of a Black African.

The Greeks' invasion of North Africa in 332 BCE ushered in European involvement in the continent. The Greeks' entry into Kemet highlights another misconceived idea about ancient African history, that of an uncivilized, "contribution-less" people. The precolonial Africans were documented teachers of the Greeks (James, 2010; Williams, 1987). In fact, the oldest university in the world is the University of Wa-set (also called the Grand Lodge of Luxor), founded circa 2800 BCE in Karnak (Diop, 1987; James, 2010). Note that Luxor is in the ancient city of Thebes, which once again became a continental epicenter under Akhenaten in 1343 BCE, who

Figure 2.1. Shepsesre of the 24th Dynasty: Old Kingdom Dynasty 2500 BCE; National Museum

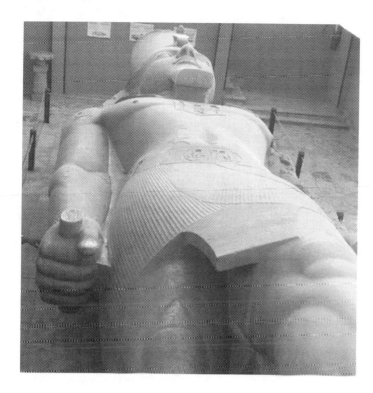

**Figure 2.2.
Ramses II
as shown in
Memphis
Museum**

introduced one of the earliest known monotheistic systems (the worship
of God Aten), centuries before the Torah (also called Pentateuch, a Greek
word meaning the first), the Bible, or the Quran (all having the same origin
stories), which generally vilify Egypt and Egyptians through their mythology. Written between 700 and 500 BCE, master scripting as a tool of social
control, these stories are incorrectly attributed to Moses (who according to
the narrative was actually born in Goshen, Egypt—and as such by national-
ity was an Egyptian), who would have lived almost 700 years before these
writings were created (Greenberg, 1996). In the narrative, Moses is said to
have married Zipporah, who was an Ethiopian. In the story, he is said to
have lived in the home of a Black pharaoh, Ramses II (Figure 2.2), and thus
could not have been a European, as no Europeans lived in Egypt at this time,
and Europe was not founded yet. The presumption that the ancient Africans
were European is thus illogical, as there were no Europeans in the region.

This is another source of healing that Blacks and African-descent
people require—to heal from negative portrayals and master scripting of
religion for enslavement purposes. This is not an invalidation of the narratives or the tradition, but they must be contextualized as such if they are
to be instruments of liberation rather than tools of enslavers, colonists,
and imperialists. In this sense, belief is not necessarily knowledge, as for

centuries Europeans used religious manipulation as a form of social control and mechanism for enslavement of oppressed groups. To this point, the University of Wa-set dates at least 3,500 years before the first university in Europe, the University of Bologna, Italy, founded in 1088 as a Roman Catholic theological school. Figure 2.3 provides a photo of a cornerstone from the University of Wa-set.

Kemet was the wealthiest and most powerful nation in the world, and the University of Wa-set attracted students from around the globe and served as the center of higher learning. The University of Wa-set did not maintain racialized admissions or discriminatory practices, as there were many non-Africans, Greeks in particular, who attended this Black institution. Later in North America, the earliest schools—in 1634, Harvard College, and including the College of New Jersey (Princeton University), the College of Philadelphia (University of Pennsylvania), the College of Rhode Island (Brown University), King's College (Columbia University), Dartmouth College, and Yale College (Yale University)—were created as seed schools to train Protestants and were founded on slavery (Wilder, 2014). Each of these institutions was funded by forced servitude and slave labor from African, African American, and Native American populations. Yet these people could not attend these institutions, as Blacks and Natives were claimed to be inferior (Wilder, 2014).

Figure 2.3. University of Wa-set Cornerstone

LOGO
IPT AST UNIVERSITY
WAST KMT 2000 B.C.E.

OLDEST UNIVERSITY IN THE WORLD IN "LUXOR" CALLED "KARNAK TEMPLE" / Egypt or Kemet is in Africa

James (2010) asserts, "the Egyptians taught Pythagoras and the Greeks, what mathematics they knew" (p. 8). When considering how Afrocentricity can realign right knowledge, it is important to note these particular historical events. Primary European sources also confirm the Greeks' presence in Egypt in the form of apprentices or students. Plutarch's *Parallel Lives* mentions:

By way of completing of his education [Plutarch] proceeded to visit Egypt. The "wisdom of the Egyptians" always seems to have a fascination for the Greeks, and at this period Alexandria, with its famous library and its memories of the Ptolemies, of Kallimachus and of Theokritus, was an important [center] of Greek intellectual activity. Plutarch's treatise on Isis and Osiris is generally supposed to be juvenile work suggested by his Egyptian travels. (Plutarch, 75 CE [2012], p. 17)

Herodotus adds that in addition to being preeminent writers and scholars, the ancient Egyptians were mathematicians and astronomers. He notes in his primary documents in 440 BCE:

But as to those matters which concern men, the priests agreed with one another in saying that the Egyptians were the first of all men on earth to find out the course of the year, having divided the seasons into twelve parts to make up the whole; and this they said they found out from the stars: and they reckon to this extent more wisely than the Hellenes . . . whereas the Egyptians, reckoning the twelve months at thirty days each, bring in also every year five days beyond the number, and thus circle of their seasons is completed and comes round to the same point whence it was set out. (Herodotus, 440 BCE [2014], p. 4)

Aristotle also mentions the Greeks' involvement in Egypt. He notes in *Metaphysics Volume 1*:

Hence when all such inventions were already established, the sciences which do not aim at giving pleasure or at the necessities of life were discovered, and first in the places where men first began to have leisure. This is why the mathematical arts were founded in Egypt; for there the priestly caste was allowed to be at leisure. (Aristotle, 350 BCE [1966], p. 3)

Aristotle confirms that mathematics was founded in Egypt. He further notes that the Greeks "discovered" the importance of science and mathematics after the Egyptians. It is important to note that over 100 books are attributed to Aristotle, but many are actually books plagiarized from the libraries in ancient Kemet (Egypt) when the Greeks invaded the country in 332 BCE. In effect, Alexander pillaged the royal libraries, took most of the books, and named them for his teacher and mentor Aristotle (James, 2010).

Figure 2.4. Ptolemaic Temple of Serapis; Alexandria, Egypt

Alexander went so far as to name a city in Egypt after himself, a city that still exists today. Figure 2.4 shows a site in Alexandria, Egypt that housed the Ptolemaic pharaoh temple. At the time of the Greek invasion, Alexandria was named as their capital city.

The Greeks were so fascinated and impressed with the ancient Kemetians (Egyptians) that they adopted Kemetian gods and attempted to make themselves into pharaohs. Similarly, the founding fathers of the United States were so enamored with ancient Kemet that they named a city in North America (Alexandria, Virginia) after this great ancient city in Africa. Figures 2.5 and 2.6 depict Greek imitation pharaohs during the period of Greek occupation in Egypt.

The images shown in the figures can be found at the Alexandria Museum in Egypt. Figure 2.5 depicts Greek imitations of Black Egyptian pharaohs, which were direct copies of the ancient Kemetians. Figure 2.6 displays the Greek imitation of Egyptian burial practices. The Greeks undeniably modeled themselves after the Kemetians (Egyptians) and adopted many of their customs. Additionally, the Greeks eventually became students of the Egyptians, as discussed later in the chapter.

In order to teach the Greeks, the ancient Kemetians had to possess knowledge of the world order and the cosmos. Africans were producers of science, mathematics, philosophy, religion, and literature long before the Western world came in contact with the region (Asante, 1990; Clarke, 1977; Diop, 1974, 1981, 1987; Kunjufu, 2002; Obenga, 2004). These Kemetians showed evidence of:

> The burial of the dead, the existence of a highly developed monotheistic religious system, the existence of a pharaonic led political system, the existence of a highly developed science of astronomy and many other things associated with cooperative and intelligent human society proved the existence of early civilization in the Hapi Valley, more developed than anywhere else in the world at that time. (Hilliard et al., 1987, p. 9)

Figure 2.5. Greek Imitation of Egyptian Pharaohs

Figure 2.6. Greek Imitation of Egyptian Burial Practices

Herodotus also acknowledges the ancient Egyptians' spirituality. He notes in his primary work *Histories*:

> Moreover, it is true also that the Egyptians were the first of men who made solemn assemblies and processions and approaches to the temples, and from them the Hellenes have learnt them, and my evidence for this is that the Egyptian celebrations of these have been held from a very ancient time, whereas the Hellenic were introduced but lately. (Herodotus, 440 BCE [2014], p. 58)

The high level of organization within this ancient culture has dumbfounded scholars for centuries and remains a model for replication today. Hilliard and colleagues (1987) note:

> Ancient Egypt's Middle Kingdom must be regarded as one of the most remarkable epochs in the long history of African people. From 2050–1786 BCE, the Middle Kingdom contributed some of Africa's most significant literary and religious innovations. Its literature set the standard of future generations. Its art was held in such esteem that it was used as a model in the Egyptian renaissance of the last native dynasties. In the fields of scientific and technical proficiency, the Blacks took giant steps and left a record of genius that continues to amaze modern scholars. Its colossal, yet precise, construction projects have few parallels, past or present. (p. 49)

This positions the land of Kemet (known today as Egypt) as the center of world formation, world thought, and education. This is an example of generally omitted information from the traditional Western curriculum, material that helps promote right knowledge and healing.

Kemetians created this high civilization before invaders arrived (Williams, 1987). The most influential scholar during the Kemetic period was Imhotep, who lived in 2650–2600 BCE and was "[the] builder of the first pyramid, architect, prime minister, philosopher-teacher, [and] father of medicine" (Karenga, 2002, p. 96). Figure 2.7 is a depiction of Imhotep at the Museum of Imhotep in Saqqara, Egypt.

Today, Imhotep is an ancestor of distinction. He resides on the human record as the world's first multi-genius:

> [Imhotep] is the earliest personality recorded in history who dealt with questions of space, time, volume, the nature of illness, physical and mental disease, and immortality. There was no situation during his lifetime that did not cause Imhotep to reflect on the meaning and significance of its origin, development, and conclusion. He was the first philosopher in human history. In this sense, he is the true father of medicine, architecture, politics, and philosophy. (Asante, 2000, p. xiii)

Figure 2.7. Imhotep: Architect and Scientist: Imhotep Museum in Saqqara, Egypt

Imhotep's knowledge of astronomy, architecture, and physics are manifest today through the great pyramids. Yet this historical fact is often unknown to mainstream Western audiences. For many African American students, the lack of cultural representation in curricula falsely placates Europeans as the sole contributors to world achievement.

Africans demonstrated their brilliance again when they used trade winds to cross the Atlantic Ocean, formerly called the Ethiopian Ocean, and settled in La Venta, Mexico, known as Olmec city. Van Sertima (1976 [2003]) asserts the Olmecs were Black Africans who migrated into the Americas as early as 800 BCE, and created a civilization in present-day La Venta, Mexico. While some contest Van Sertima's findings and suggest that the Olmecs were additionally influenced by indigenous or Chinese cultures (Anderson, 2016; de Montellano et al., 2015; Haslip-Viera et al., 1997), it is well established that precolonial African explorers influenced other regions. Greek historian Herodotus (440 BCE [2014]) confirms these findings in his book *Histories*, when he mentions the exquisite maritime skills of ancient Egyptians under the leadership of Sesostris [Egyptian]:

[Sesostris] first of all set out with ships of war from the Arabian gulf and subdued those who dwelt by the shores of the Erythraian Sea, until as he sailed he came to a sea which could not further be navigated by reason of shoals: then secondly, after he had returned to Egypt . . . He [Sesostris] traversed the continent, until at last he passed over to Europe from Asia and subdued the Scythians and also the Thracians. These, I am of the opinion, were the furthest people to which the Egyptian army came . . . (p. 103)

Historians have discovered evidence that suggests Africans were master shipbuilders and possessed maritime skills prior to European colonization (Barton, 2001; Law, 1989; Whitewright, 2018).

The civilization of the Olmecs in the ancient city of La Venta is, in effect, the site of the oldest known civilization in the Americas. The Olmecs built the first pyramids in the Americas in this city. They were step pyramids like the ones found around continental Africa in places such as Egypt (Kemet), Niger, and Sudan (known as Kush or Nubia, meaning Black), which has the most pyramids in the world. In the case of the Americas, as proof, the Olmec pyramids remain there today (see Figure 2.8). Note that African influences on the Mesopotamian region do not invalidate or undermine indigenous cultures. Rather, this is important contextualization to showcase the presence of African exploration across the world, which is often ignored in U.S. history textbooks.

The Olmecs (see Figure 2.9) brought with them the knowledge of building pyramids, which was widespread across continental Africa (Van

Figure 2.8. View of the Great Pyramid at La Venta

Source: Wikimedia Commons (2010).

Figure 2.9. Olmec Head, Cabeza Olmeca

Source: Wikimedia Commons, 2007 (National museum für Anthropologie, Mexiko-Stadt).

Sertima, 1976/2003). The Olmecs also left behind writings, which would suggest that this is the oldest writing system in the Americas. The Olmec civilization is the cradle of civilizations in the Americas. This civilization later influenced the Teotihuacan city, the site of a later civilization in Mexico where they emulated the buildings and pyramids of the Olmecs at La Venta, a pioneering city in the Americas.

Excerpts from Columbus's third voyage suggest that he and his crew were sent to "investigate the report of the Indians of this Española who said that [they] had come to Española from the south and south-east, a black people who have the tops of their spears made of a metal which they call *guanine*" (Olson & Bourne, 1906 [2006], para. 327). These evidences of early African presence in the Americas connect African contributions to world history. This is a major contribution that all students and teachers should know, but due to the pervasive force of cultural hegemony, it is often omitted from traditional public schools, and not even noted in history curricula or the revised social studies standards. These are shameful and glaring

omissions, as students are often taught the history of the Americas beginning with Columbus. This is another case in which right knowledge can
promote healing from miseducation.

In regard to continental Africa, Sir William Osler's Yale University lec-
ture entitled the *Evolution of Modern Medicine* (1913 [2013]) positions
Imhotep as "the first figure of a physician to stand out clearly from the
mists of antiquity" (para. 34). Imhotep's influence on Kemetian royalty was
so great that he became one of the few citizens outside of the royal lineage
promoted to the status of a god, known as Asclepius/Asclepios/Asklepios
(Osler, 1913/2013; Peltier, 1990; Pinch, 2002). These findings are confirmed
in Imhotep's manuscript, which was in 1862, paradoxically, renamed the
"Edwin Smith Surgical Papers" after antiquities collector Edwin Smith.
Here again, White supremacy cultural domination is at work, with Imhotep's manuscript being renamed for a European. Regarding Imhotep's work
and writing, Breasted (1930) states:

> In the history of medical science in particular, it was no accident that the leading
> patron god of medicine in early classical Europe—he [Imhotep] who was called
> Asclepios by the Greeks and Aesculapius by the Romans—was originally an
> historical personage, an ancient Egyptian wise man and physician called Imho-
> tep by the Egyptians, grand vizier, chief architect, and royal medical advisor of
> the Pharaoh in the Thirtieth Century [BCE], the earliest known physician in
> history. (p. 3)

The Centre for Biomedical Egyptology suggests that Kemetian [Egyp-
tian] doctors were practicing credible medicine over 1,000 years before
Hippocrates was born (El-Gammal, 1993; Serageldin, 2013). Additionally,
Hippocrates mentions Imhotep in the beginning of his Hippocratic Oath in
400 BCE (National Library of Medicine, 2002). This oath is still used by
doctors today, and honors the god Asclepius [Imhotep]:

> I swear by Apollo the physician, and Asclepius, and Hygieia and Panacea and
> all the gods and goddesses as my witnesses, that, according to my ability and
> judgment, I will keep this Oath and this contract . . . (National Library of Med-
> icine, 2002, para. 3)

While Western science often cites Hippocrates as the father of modern
medicine, research shows that Egyptians were the original archetypes (Diop,
1974; El-Gammal, 1993; Hilliard et al., 1987; James, 2010; Williams,
1987). Imhotep's existence is imperative in recasting African American
historical discourse. His legacy debunks Western myths suggesting Hippocrates was the father of medicine and Socrates, Plato, and Aristotle were the
originators of ancient philosophy (Asante, 2000). His legacy also recasts the
significance of precolonial African intellect. Additionally, C. B. Hilliard's

(1998) *Intellectual Traditions of Pre-Colonial Africa* substantiates the presence of scientific, religious, historical, and philosophical thought throughout the Pharaonic Kemet [Egypt] and Nubian [Southern Egypt and Sudan] regions. In a comprehensive outlining of precolonial texts, Hilliard provides a histography of intricate languages and complex philosophical understandings on the African continent long before outside invaders. Hilliard (1998) further contends that ancient European philosophers and theologians, such as Augustine, Cyprian, and Tertullian, should always be analyzed within the contextual understanding of their relationships with Africa. These facts also promote healing from racist White supremacy discourse, which claims that Africans and Blacks made no major contributions of subsequence.

Mathematics, as we previously stated, was created by Africans and later taught to the Greeks. One well-known student who attended the ancient University of Wa-set was Pythagoras. He learned teachings from "[the] *Rhind Papyrus* and the *Moscow Papyrus* [which] predate anything else in the word in mathematics" (Asante, 2003, p. 223). The *Rhind* was written by Ahmes (or Ahmose) around 1550 BCE (see Figure 2.10).

Figure 2.10. Head of Ahmose I, ca. 1550–1525 BCE.

Source: The Metropolitan Museum of Art, New York.

Ahmes provides the first evidence of advanced mathematics and analytics (Zaslavsky, 1973). Scottish antiquarian Alexander Henry Rhind eventually purchased the papyrus in 1858, hence denoting the manuscript's name. Similar to the case of Imhotep, Ahmes's manuscript is attributed to a White antiquities collector, once again demonstrating the power of hegemony. Mathematician Arnold Buffum Chace translated the *Rhind* and confirmed the origins of the manuscript's authorship as Ahmes. This excerpt is from the manuscript's opening page:

> This book was copied in the year 33, in the fourth month of the inundation season, under the majesty of the king of Upper and Lower Egypt, A-sure-Re, endowed with life, in likeness to writings of old made in the time of the king of Upper and Lower Egypt. Ne-ma'et-Re. It is the scribe A'h-moses who copies this writing. (Chace, 1927, p. 48)

To date, the *Rhind* is documented as the oldest mathematical manuscript in the world. Several significant concepts appear in the Rhind manuscript, including arithmetic, measurement, geometry, the Egyptian calendar, and food science (Chace, 1927; Zaslavsky, 1973). Figure 2.11 shows a section of the original manuscript and Figure 2.12 shows a translated version.

Whereas the Greeks and Romans are often considered the inventors of classical education, including philosophy, mathematics, and civics, primary sources such as the *Rhind* indicate that Egyptians predate both empires (Asante, 1990; Diop, 1974). This is important to consider when revisiting the significance of Africa in human history.

Figure 2.11. The Rhind Mathematical Papyrus from the British Museum

Source: Wikimedia Commons (2018).

Figure 2.12. Excerpt from the Rhind Mathematical Papyrus, problem 81 (translated).

heqat expression	+ ro	= hinu	= heqat
$(\frac{1}{2} + \frac{1}{4} + \frac{1}{8})$ heqat		$= (8 + \frac{1}{2} + \frac{1}{4})$ hinu	
$(\frac{1}{2} + \frac{1}{4})$ heqat		$= (7 + \frac{1}{2})$ hinu	
$(\frac{1}{2} + \frac{1}{8} + \frac{1}{32})$ heqat	$+ (3 + \frac{1}{3})$ ro	$= (6 + \frac{2}{3})$ hinu	$= \frac{2}{3}$ heqat
$(\frac{1}{4} + \frac{1}{8})$ heqat		$= (6 + \frac{1}{4})$ hinu	$= (\frac{1}{2} + \frac{1}{8})$ heqat
$(\frac{1}{4} + \frac{1}{8})$ heqat		$= (3 + \frac{1}{2} + \frac{1}{4})$ hinu	$= (\frac{1}{4} + \frac{1}{8})$ heqat
$(\frac{1}{4} + \frac{1}{16} + \frac{1}{64})$ heqat	$+ (1 + \frac{2}{3})$ ro	$= (3 + \frac{1}{3})$ hinu	$= \frac{1}{3}$ heqat
$\frac{1}{4}$ heqat		$= (2 + \frac{1}{2})$ hinu	$= \frac{1}{4}$ heqat
$(\frac{1}{8} + \frac{1}{16})$ heqat	$+ 4$ ro	$= 2$ hinu	$= \frac{1}{5}$ heqat
$(\frac{1}{8} + \frac{1}{32})$ heqat	$+ (3 + \frac{1}{3})$ ro	$= (1 + \frac{2}{3})$ hinu	$= \frac{1}{6}$ heqat
$(\frac{1}{8} + \frac{1}{16})$ heqat	$+ 4$ ro	$= 2$ hinu	$= \frac{1}{5}$ heqat
$(\frac{1}{16} + \frac{1}{32})$ heqat	$+ 2$ ro	$= 1$ hinu	$= \frac{1}{10}$ heqat
$(\frac{1}{32} + \frac{1}{64})$ heqat	$+ 1$ ro	$= \frac{1}{2}$ hinu	$= \frac{1}{20}$ heqat
$\frac{1}{64}$ heqat	$+ 3$ ro	$= \frac{1}{4}$ hinu	$= \frac{1}{40}$ heqat
$\frac{1}{16}$ heqat	$+ (1 + \frac{1}{3})$ ro	$= \frac{2}{3}$ hinu	$= \frac{1}{15}$ heqat
$\frac{1}{32}$ heqat	$+ \frac{2}{3}$ ro	$= \frac{1}{3}$ hinu	$= \frac{1}{30}$ heqat
$\frac{1}{64}$ heqat	$+ \frac{1}{3}$ ro	$= \frac{1}{6}$ hinu	$= \frac{1}{60}$ heqat
$\frac{1}{2}$ heqat		$= 5$ hinu	$= \frac{1}{2}$ heqat
$\frac{1}{4}$ heqat		$= (2 + \frac{1}{2})$ hinu	$= \frac{1}{4}$ heqat
$(\frac{1}{2} + \frac{1}{4})$ heqat		$= (7 + \frac{1}{2})$ hinu	$= (\frac{1}{2} + \frac{1}{4})$ heqat
$(\frac{1}{2} + \frac{1}{4} + \frac{1}{8})$ heqat		$= (8 + \frac{1}{2} + \frac{1}{4})$ hinu	$= (\frac{1}{2} + \frac{1}{4} + \frac{1}{8})$ heqat
$(\frac{1}{2} + \frac{1}{8})$ heqat		$= (6 + \frac{1}{4})$ hinu	$= (\frac{1}{2} + \frac{1}{8})$ heqat
$(\frac{1}{4} + \frac{1}{8})$ heqat		$= (3 + \frac{1}{2} + \frac{1}{4})$ hinu	$= (\frac{1}{4} + \frac{1}{8})$ heqat
$(\frac{1}{2} + \frac{1}{8} + \frac{1}{32})$ heqat	$+ (3 + \frac{1}{3})$ ro	$= (6 + \frac{2}{3})$ hinu	$= \frac{2}{3}$ heqat
$(\frac{1}{4} + \frac{1}{16} + \frac{1}{64})$ heqat	$+ (1 + \frac{2}{3})$ ro	$= (3 + \frac{1}{3})$ hinu	$= \frac{1}{3}$ heqat
$\frac{1}{8}$ heqat		$= (1 + \frac{1}{4})$ hinu	$= \frac{1}{8}$ heqat
$\frac{1}{16}$ heqat		$= (\frac{1}{2} + \frac{1}{8})$ hinu	$= \frac{1}{16}$ heqat
$\frac{1}{32}$ heqat		$= (\frac{1}{2} + \frac{1}{16})$ hinu	$= \frac{1}{32}$ heqat
$\frac{1}{64}$ heqat		$= (\frac{1}{4} + \frac{1}{32})$ hinu	$= \frac{1}{64}$ heqat

RHIND MATHEMATICAL PAPYRUS, PROBLEM 81: The Rhind Mathematical Papyrus is an ancient Egyptian document which is a record of elementary mathematics. Its so-called Problem 81 is a large table of equalities among various quantities, using physical units of volume. The heqat is a unit of volume which is equal to ten hinu, and the hinu is a unit of volume which is equal to 32 ro, another much smaller unit of volume. In other words, 1 heqat = 10 hinu = 320 ro. Note that at either side of the table, the "heqats" are sometimes given in the same terms, or sometimes in different terms. This presentation of Problem 81 is based upon the translation of Arnold Buffum Chace, who published a translation of the Rhind Papyrus in 1927 and 1929.

The table expresses quantities using Egyptian fractions, which were a common convention for expressing numbers in ancient Egypt. Egyptian fractions are series of unit fractions having natural denominators — that is, fractions having a numerator equal to one, and a denominator equal to a positive whole number. A "special exception" which the Egyptians allowed to this convention, was the fraction 2/3, which is used here. A special case of unit fractions are the so-called "Horus eye" fractions, which are used frequently throughout the rest of the Rhind papyrus. The "Horus eye" fractions are the fractions 1/2, 1/4, 1/8, 1/16, 1/32, and 1/64 — that is, Egyptian fractions where the denominator is a low power of two.

Source: Wikimedia Commons (2016).

In addition to being the first preexisting civilization with an incomparable command of mathematics, ancient Kemetians had the oldest writing system and language. Mdw Ntr (or Mdw Netcher) was the name of their sacred writing system. The Greeks later called this *hieroglyphics*. "The existence of this writing alone is testimonial to the development of early civilization in the ancient [Nile Valley]" (Hilliard et al., 1987, p. 8). The evidence of this writing system along with archeological artifacts has solidified the importance of Kemetians throughout world history (Diop, 1981).

Mdw Netcher's significance is important for the realignment of historical timelines. It is perhaps most important for signifying the ancient Kemetians' acknowledgment of God:

> The earliest Mdw Netcher writings described Offering lists to the deity or to its manifestations and powers. Later prayers of offerings were substituted for the Offering list. These writings as with almost all writings in ancient Kmt emerged out of a profound religious orientation toward the world. This religious orientation found its expression in preparations for life after death or for the resurrection. However, lost to many analysts is the fact that in the preparation for life after death or for the resurrection, the supplicant was actually articulating a set of values and a code of behaviors by which to live one's life in the world before death. No higher human behavioral code has been found anywhere in human history than the earliest code of the ancient Kamites. (Hilliard et al., 1987, p. 11)

The evidence of Mdw Ntr is found in *The Teachings of Ptahhotep*, which is the oldest book in the world, dating to 2,300 BCE. An opening excerpt of this book reads:

> And so it begins the formation of Mdw Ntr, *good speech*, to be spoken by the Prince, the Count, God's beloved, the eldest son of the Pharaoh, the son of his body, Mayor of the City, and Vizier, Ptahhotep, instructs the ignorant in the knowledge and in the standards of *good speech*. It will profit those who hear. It will be a loss to those who transgress. (Hilliard et al., 1987, p. 17)

This book, along with *The Book of the Coming Forth*—the oldest religious book in the world—corrects misconceptions regarding African origin and intellectual thought. Most importantly, it redefines thoughts concerning African spirituality (Karenga, 1984). Figure 2.13 presents a depiction of Ptahhotep, taken at the Imhotep Museum in Saqqara, Egypt.

The Book of the Coming Forth is the oldest holy book in the world. Africans were the first known people to acknowledge a higher power and a monotheistic God. Figure 2.14 displays the ancient Kemetian (Egyptian) holy trinity, including Asar, Aset, and Heru. These were later renamed by the Greeks as Osiris, Isis, and Horus. Below is an image of Aset with the virgin-born child, Heru. She is venerated in the Greco-Roman Catholic tradition in the image of Mary. For historical reference, this eventually made its way into Catholicism by way of the Greeks, followed by the Romans. As further evidence, the Black Madonna and child image was popularized around Europe and ultimately in the Vatican, its museum, and Catholicism,

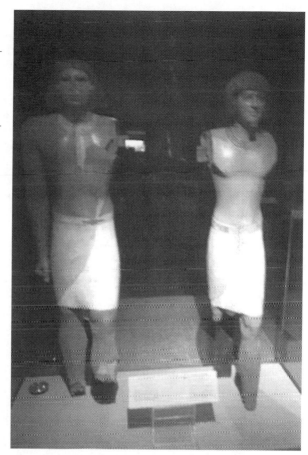

Figure 2.13. Two Images of Ptahhotep: Imhotep Museum in Saqqara, Egypt

Figure 2.14. Aset (Isis) With Heru (Horus): Museum of Egyptian Antiquities

as Mary and Jesus (Yeshua) images. Mary is also made into a deity, as Goddess Aset was worshiped in Greece and Rome. This helps to provide a context to understand the appropriations used by the Greeks and Romans. However, it does not invalidate or undermine the benefits of the religious traditions. Still, this is the kind of important contextualization that enslaved and colonized people were denied, as they were being conditioned for dehumanization and servitude.

Much like the worship of the Black Madonna and child (Aset and Heru) of Egypt, it is also important to note that in the 4th century CE, Constantine commissioned the removal of the largest obelisk in Egypt and had it transported and erected in Rome, Italy. It stands there today, called the Lateran obelisk, the tallest obelisk in the world—and taken from Egypt. This particular obelisk was originally built under the reign of Thutmoses III in the 15th century BCE, and was the largest standing obelisk in ancient Egypt. Constantine followed the tradition of Roman Emperor Augustus Caesar, who, under his reign (62 BCE–14 CE), had several large obelisks removed from Egypt and placed in Rome. The Romans' fascination with Egyptian culture is undeniable, yet hardly admirable, as they often looted the country and gave no proper attribution for things they stole and ideas they took directly from Egypt.

In the case of the spiritual system of Kemet or Egypt, within the Kemetian culture, spirituality is embedded and evidenced in *The Teachings of Ptahhotep*, written during the 5th dynasty, long before any invaders or cultural influencers came to the region (Hilliard et al., 1987; Karenga, 1984).

The university, or higher education system, was also well established in the Kemetian region. "[In] the peak of Kemetic civilization there were actually more than 80,000 students . . . studying" (Akbar, 1998, p. vi). Universities such as Wa-set (also called the Grand Lodge of Luxor), the University of Sankore, Al-Azhar University, and the University of Fez were home to geniuses who have permanently shaped world history (Rodney, 2011). The existence of these universities is well-established. "Students from all over the Moslem world came to [Timbuktu] to study grammar, law and surgery at the University of Sankore; scholars came from North Africa and Europe to confer with learned historians and writers of this Black empire" (Clarke, 1993, p. 42). Clarke (1977, 1993) further describes the University of Sankore as the epicenter of African intellectual thought prior to colonialism. Clarke notes:

> During the period in West African history—from the early part of the fourteenth century to the time of the Moorish invasion in 1591—the city of Timbuctoo and the University and Sankore in the Songhay Empire were the intellectual centers of Africa. Black scholars were enjoying a renaissance that was known and respected throughout most of Africa and in parts of Europe. At this period in African history, the University of Sankore was the educational capital of the Western Sudan. (1977, p. 142)

The ruins of the University of Sankore, for example, can still be seen today (Clarke, 1977). Thus, it must be acknowledged that "[the] colonizers did not introduce education into Africa: they introduced a new set of formal educational institutions which partly supplemented and partly replaced those which were before" (Rodney, 2011, p. 240). This is important to note when situating this discussion within 21st-century contexts.

After the conquest of Kemet (later called Egypt by the Greeks) by Alexander the Great in 332 BCE, the Greeks looted and burned the Royal Library at Alexandria (Hilliard et al., 1987; James, 2010; Williams, 1987). This library originally housed the teachings of African professors and teachers who instructed the Greek philosophers on mathematics and theory. What was left after the disastrous fires became home to many of the well-known scholars of Grecian history. Parts of the library were destroyed again in 48 BCE by Julius Caesar. According to Hilliard and colleagues (1987), the subsequent colonization and enslavement of Africans across the Diaspora was:

accompanied by a wholesale, systematic falsification of the human record. It left the descendants of Africans and others throughout the world in almost total darkness, regarding the contributions of African people to the population of the world and to world civilization. (p. 9)

Even after the Kemetian rule and the Hellenistic period, there were evidences of Black civilizations prior to colonialism (Understanding, 2013). Black Moors in Spain, for example, were integral in introducing algebra and calculus to the Middle Ages in 500–1100 CE (Williams, 1987). These events are important for understanding later concepts of Afrocentricity. In the aforementioned historical overview, precolonial Africans are described as leaders in education. Their scholarly contributions to world history helped buttress subsequent European classical movements. In this regard, it is important to realign Africa's history with the aforementioned historical facts. This is the premise of education as self-healing power. Whereas students typically learn solely about the nightmares of slavery and colonialism, for healing and restoration, the triumphant moments of Black history should be part of the curriculum as well.

PRECURSORS TO PAN-AFRICANISM

The damages from the African Diaspora, known as the MAAFA, dislocated African Americans from Africa. Ever since, deliberate processes have been needed to promote healing and wholeness. In the early to mid–19th century, Northern Black abolitionists—such as Bishop Richard Allen—congregated, and in 1817 formed the National Negro Convention Movement

(Karenga, 2002). Almost a century before formal Pan-Africanism, and at the height of American slavery, Black activists in the North expressed a concerted effort toward the unification of Blacks. The Convention's aim was to unify Blacks to migrate to Canada (Karenga, 2002). The National Negro Convention Movement expanded beyond just the northern United States, moving also into the Midwest. The looming Fugitive Slave Act of 1850 crystallized the group's efforts to unify Blacks in the North and the South. This represents an inseparable connection to the eventual Pan-African movement.

Later, clergymen such as Alexander Crummell, Martin Robinson Delany, and Robert Campbell recognized this dislocation nearly 50 years before there was organized Pan-African unity (Okafor, 1998). Afrocentricity today rests on the intellectual heritage of these three thinkers. In 1831, Delany wrote of the need to establish a sense of community within the African American experience. These efforts created solidarity among African Americans decades before Emancipation (Adeleke, 1994; Pollard & Ajirotutu, 2000; Ratteray, 1994). Delany, an abolitionist who lived from 1812 to 1885, argued:

> Education should both liberate the mind and teach people the skills needed for economic survival. He also postulated that education could be used as a means of "moral suasion" to change the attitudes whites held toward African Americans. . . . He began to argue that Blacks needed to control their children's education and that race and ethnicity should be the central constructs for the study of the African American experience in the United States. (Pollard & Ajirotutu, 2000, p. 17)

Delany was a free man born in West Virginia who resisted racism and colonialism, holding views similar to Afrocentric theorists of today (Adeleke, 1994; Pollard & Ajirotutu, 2000). After visiting Sierra Leone and Liberia, Delany's views became grounded in African unity. He was, in fact, associated with the African Settlement Movement in Liberia, which predates Marcus Garvey's "back to Africa" movement. The African Settlement Movement aimed to facilitate a migration back to Africa post-emancipation in the 19th century, whereas Garvey's movement is usually associated with Black Nationalism of the 20th century. Delany's beliefs surrounding the need for self-sufficiency and Black unity within the community heralded subsequent theories such as Black Nationalism and Pan-Africanism. We should mention that each of the aforementioned Black unification movements promoted the importance of education. In this regard, education as self-healing power was recognized and promoted for generations. Additionally, although each of the respective movements was distinctive in some ways, there were common underlying foci on Black unity, empowerment, and right knowledge. Afrocentric schools today are extensions of these precursory movements.

Alexander Crummell was another historical Pan-African pioneer. Like Delany, Crummell was a clergyman who spent time in Africa during the 19th century. He received his formal training through the Evangelical church, but spent time in Liberia from 1853 to 1873 (Crawford, 2003). While his original intent was to convert Africans to Christianity (Appiah, 1990), Crummell also pushed for political independence and liberation. At the core of his concern was the topic of race (Appiah, 1990). He saw himself as a "Negro" and understood the connection between his heritage and Africa. More important, he identified with the plight of Black people. His writings "effectively inaugurated the discourse of Pan-Africanism" (Appiah, 1990, p. 388). Crummell played an important intellectual role in the founding of the American Negro Academy. The American Negro Academy (ANA) was a scholarship society that promoted literacy among Black people (Moss, 1981). The promotion of Black education during Reconstruction was a revolutionary idea supported by other ANA members, such as W.E.B. Du Bois, James Weldon Johnson, and Carter G. Woodson (Moss, 1981). This organization was responsible for publishing prominent African American scholarship during this time. Both Delany and Crummell were religious leaders by trade, but they used their occupations as vehicles to disseminate information about Africa (Crawford, 2003).

Robert Campbell should also be included in the precursory Pan-African conversation. Campbell was a Jamaican man who, along with Delany, helped form the Niger Valley Exploring Party (Blackett, 1977). He visited Africa in 1859 and argued for the creation of an independent Black settlement in Liberia. Campbell distinctively opposed accepting support from White philanthropists, while Delany accepted their support (Adeleke, 1994; Blackett, 1977). In spite of their minor differences, Campbell and Delany worked together to establish a treaty with the Alake [king] of the Abeokuta Nation in Nigeria, in hopes of establishing an independent Black nation in Africa. The treaty was ratified on December 28, 1859. In 1860, Campbell and Delany recruited other abolitionists in England and formed the African Aid Society to support the efforts of immigration to Nigeria (Blackett, 1977). They heralded support from both White and Black businessmen to fund an independent Black settlement in Africa. Lancashire and Scottish cotton manufacturers supported their efforts in hopes of building a slavery-free cotton plant in Africa, rather than supporting the South's plantation economy (Blackett, 1977). Campbell and Delany went on advocacy tours in Europe, Canada, and the Caribbean in order to galvanize additional support from the Black community. They received little, as many Blacks in the United States were preoccupied with the Civil War. While away from Africa on tour, the previously signed 1859 treaty became ensnarled with various political particularities. Campbell and Delany's efforts to establish an African nation "fell prey to the opposition of English missionaries in Abeokuta, English imperialist expansion and the outbreak of the Civil War in

America" (Blackett, 1977, p. 24). As a result, their plans for an independent African nation were delayed, but their efforts were not in vain.

Similarly, Henry McNeal Turner was also a pioneer in the struggle for racial liberation. Turner was a bishop in the African Methodist Episcopal (AME) church from 1880 to 1915 (Angell, 1992). During the Civil War, Turner was appointed the first Black chaplain for the African American troops and eventually became a politician and Georgia legislator during Reconstruction (Spigner, n.d.). Turner promoted the liberation of African Americans and was one of the early supporters of the Back to Africa movement. These initial ideological stirrings united Africans and African Americans over 40 years before the Pan-African movement officially started. It must be acknowledged that Crummell, Delany, Campbell, and Turner's efforts led directly to what Pan-Africanism and Afrocentricity of later years eventually achieved.

Even prior to the formation of Pan-Africanism in the late 19th century, Delany, Crummell, Campbell, and Turner recognized the importance of restoring Black communities. These men spearheaded initial conversations regarding African unification over 40 years before formalized movements began. In essence, Delany, Crummell, Campbell, and Turner recognized the importance of Africa decades before a large-scale unification movement began.

Delany, Crummell, Campbell, and Turner have secured their place in the intellectual genealogy of Pan-Africanism, which later led to Afrocentricity. It is important to acknowledge their transition as European-trained clergymen to Pan-African activists. Their contributions serve as an appropriate foundation for this book. Arguably, Afrocentric schools have a direct connection to these revolutionaries.

THE FORMATION OF PAN-AFRICANISM

The official formations of Pan-Africanism came 2 years after Alexander Crummell's passing in 1898. The term "Pan-Africanism" was eventually created by three Trinidadians: Henry Sylvester-Williams, C.L.R. James, and George Padmore (Clarke, 1993). Pan-Africanism can be defined as an attempt to establish "a common cultural and political community by virtue of [origin] in Africa and common racial, social and economic oppression" (Adogamhe, 2008, p. 7). As early as 1900, Sylvester-Williams organized a group in hopes of unity within the confines of "Pan-Africanism," known as the Pan-African Congress (Adogamhe, 2008). Six distinct meetings—in 1900, 1919, 1921, 1923, 1927, and 1945—solidified Pan-African's place in world history.

There were two initial goals of the Pan-African Congress. The first was the unification of Africa toward a central government (Adogamhe, 2008).

This revolutionary idea would essentially change the structures of world government and economics, all while promoting African unity and economic stability. A second goal was self-reliance and independence. Many African and Caribbean countries during the formation of the Pan-Africanist movement were being colonized, while concurrently all remaining continental African nations were being placed in bondage as a direct dictate of the Berlin Conference of 1884–1885. Decolonization was an essential aim of Pan-Africanism, through the methods of African unity and empowerment.

Pan-African ideas were disbursed through varying political organizations, such as the United Negro Movement, International African Services Bureau, and Pan-African Federation. In 1936, Padmore and James organized the International African Services Bureau and the Pan-African Federation to secure civil rights for African people (Okafor, 1998). Padmore had a political stage "wide opened" from precursor Pan-Africanists (Lemert, 2010). From here, Padmore united with Kwame Nkrumah to organize the Fifth Pan-African Conference.

The Fifth Pan-African Congress of 1945 hosted leaders such as W.E.B. Du Bois, George Padmore, and Kwame Nkrumah, who began to shift focus specifically to continental Africa and the decolonization process. The liberation of African nations was directly tied to this Pan-African Congress. During the height of African decolonization, Haile Selassie I of Ethiopia founded the Organization of African Unity (OAU) in 1963. Selassie's aim was to unify individual nation-states across Africa. Fifty-three of the 54 countries—with the exception of Morocco—joined the organization. This was a substantial accomplishment, especially considering that South Africa was the last African nation to receive its independence and freedom from apartheid, which did not happen until 1994 (Adogamhe, 2008). Selassie's organization was eventually transformed into the African Union in 2002.

BLACK NATIONALISM

The key distinction between Black Nationalism and Pan-Africanism is their respective origins. Pan-Africanism emphasized the unity of all Africans, continental and Diasporic, for the advancement of Africa as its central theme, while Black Nationalism focused on the fight for self-governance and ending discrimination, and later connected to the struggle for the "upliftment" of Africa. Whereas Pan-Africanism aimed to unite African countries with a concerted effort on continental Africa, Black Nationalism was initially more concerned with the Black experience and day-to-day experiences of Black people in the Diaspora. Black Nationalism is defined as "a thrust to build alternative structures, which . . . advance Black aspirations and interest" (Karenga, 2002, p. 383). Well-known Black Nationalists include Malcolm X, Stokely Carmichael, Maulana Karenga, and Marcus Garvey. In the case of Garvey, he is also duly noted as the greatest Pan-Africanist. Each of these men placed a concerted effort on uplifting Blacks from their current social conditions. In this same respect, the "upliftment" of Africa helps to promote education as self-healing power.

Marcus Garvey's Universal "Negro" Improvement Association (UNIA) called for the advancement and unification of Africans across the Diaspora (see Figure 2.15). Garvey is known as both a Black Nationalist and Pan-Africanist because of his efforts to unite all Africans, both Diasporic and continental. As noted earlier, this was not an entirely new concept due to the efforts of Delany, Crummell, and Campbell. Garvey's concern with the unification of Africa led to plans of relocating in Africa (Adogamhe, 2008). Garvey's program had a concerted interest in character-building and education, rooted in the belief that African culture and heritage were "necessary for true liberation of Diaspora Africans" (Asante, 2003, p. 17).

There are noticeable overlaps of Black Nationalism and Pan-Africanism. Although continental origin is a key difference, both Black Nationalist and Pan-African movements worked toward unity in Africa. Black Nationalism aimed for Blacks to "see themselves as connected by their common position in America relative to Whites" (Tauheed, 2008, p. 699). Black Nationalism is similar to Pan-Africanism in regard to its critiques of racism. Black Nationalism also urges for complete economic independence and self-separation

Figure 2.15. Marcus Garvey's Organizations

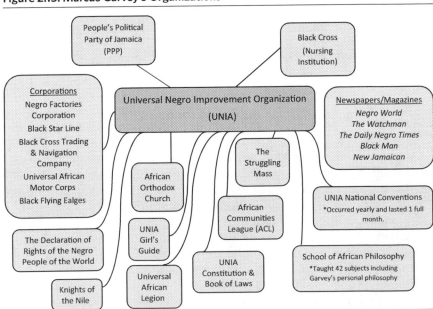

(Karenga, 2002). Although many viewed the Black Nationalism model as flawed and dangerous, some commendable efforts spawned from its conception. For example, the idea of *cooperative commonwealth* during the political periods of segregation and inequality included "efforts in education through school and church, and economic cooperation in the arts, health care, trade unionism, banking, law, and insurance, among other aspects of economic and social life" (Tauheed, 2008, p. 699). The separation of Blacks from Whites was seen as a viable option for the economic and social independence of Blacks.

As mentioned, the Pan-African and Black National movements were distinctive, yet they both attempted to address the historical trauma of dislocation and separation caused by the MAAFA. Within the core tenets of these respective movements was a primary focus to reestablish Black contributions and significance in African American communities. This, in essence, is a historical example of education as self-healing power. This often took form through African American community schools, as discussed in the following section.

PAN-AFRICANISM AND EDUCATION

W.E.B. Du Bois's early career advocated for integration and equality, which led him to consider Marcus Garvey's views as wayward (Asante, 2003; Wiggan, 2010). Years later, through his intermixing with the Communist Party and subsequently being placed under surveillance by the Federal Bureau of Investigation (FBI) (Wiggan, 2010), Du Bois was ousted from the same America he once advocated for. Later in Du Bois's life, he resided in Ghana and adopted an Africanist outlook. This is where he began writing the *Encyclopedia Africana*, which is undoubtedly Pan-African. Meanwhile, although Garvey is usually heralded under the category of Black Nationalist, he is arguably the greatest Pan-Africanist in history (Asante, 2003). Asante (2003) notes:

> [Garvey] saw clearly the relationship of Africans on the continent and in the Diaspora as variations of one people, one giant cultural project. The complete name of his organization emphasized his Pan-African commitment, the *Universal Negro Improvement Association and African Communities League* ... The complete Garvey was a Pan-African nationalist whose entire life was consumed with seeing oppressed and downtrodden Africans respected and respecting themselves. (p. 18)

Aside from political efforts, Pan-Africanism also placed a concerted focus on education. The need for alternative education for African Americans was central to the argument of early and formative Pan-African movements. Early scholars such as Du Bois, Edward Wilmont Blyden, and Carter G. Woodson recognized that education was the impetus for freedom, which is important to acknowledge in our discussion of the need for Afrocentric schools. Blyden—like Delany, Crummell, and Campbell—was a clergyman who eventually helped to unify Africans and African Americans across the Diaspora. Blyden worked alongside Crummell to begin Liberia's modern system of education (Appiah, 1990). Blyden and Crummell believed the proper home for African Americans was in Africa. In another sense, Carter G. Woodson also believed education was critical to the plight of African Americans. Woodson's (1933/1977) iconic *The Mis-Education of the Negro* recognized that education was essential for African American uplift and social mobility. Joyce (2005) asserts:

> [Woodson] made the connection between laws that forbade the teaching of reading and writing to slaves and the deliberate sparsity of information on Black history and the contribution of Blacks to world society. He was also clear on how this lack of information affected Black consciousness and impeded Black determination for independent educational, social, economic, and political progress. (p. 111)

As Joyce (2005) notes, Woodson made a connection between the deliberate subjugation of Blacks and the scarcity of African American history in schools. Woodson is not usually associated with Black National politics, but his views as presented in *The Mis-Education of the Negro* and *The African Background Outlined, or Handbook for the Study of the "Negro"* are undoubtedly centered on African unity (Wiggan, 2010).

It is important to recognize that a systemic suppression of knowledge was not unique to the United States in the early 20th century. T. Albert Marryshaw (2017), a Grenadian scholar, also observed cultural suppression and inadequate education in the Caribbean. He notes:

> The only obstacle to the full realization of our heritage being that so many of us are blind to the value of unity of purpose and direction, and prefer loose and easy compromises which do not make for race identity and dignity. (p. 2)

Marryshaw describes the observable lack of positive racial awareness among Black people. This is most notably due to the systemic removal of African precolonial contributions from mainstream thought. Within Marryshaw's (1917) argument is the unveiling of how scientific racism has helped to undermine African achievement. The critique of Cecil Rhodes and the deforestation of Africa is just one example of how African history and accomplishments have been compromised. Marryshaw continues by critiquing the Western academy's role in the widespread exploitation of the African diaspora, as observed in the Caribbean, South America, and indigenous lands. In response, Marryshaw called for the unification of Caribbean islands and Africa in a federated union. In relation to education as self-healing power, it is important to acknowledge the larger Diaspora. The traumas from the transatlantic slavery extended the MAAFA to the Caribbean, to Central and South America, and to continental Africa. Marryshaw's critique of inhumane European expansion and colonialism was offered in relation to the compromising of African achievements. These moments in history are important when identifying the chronological steps toward developing Afrocentricity and, later, Afrocentric education.

THE IMPACT OF PAN-AFRICANISM AND BLACK NATIONALISM

Education is just one focus that Pan-Africanism and Black Nationalism share. There is substantial overlap in these social movements because of their overall concern with Africa and the African Diaspora. Although Black Nationalism and Pan-Africanism originated in different places, their end focus was the same. The ideological and sociopolitical forces of Pan-Africanism and Black Nationalism have essentially changed the world. For example, many praise Kwame Nkrumah for helping Ghana reach its independence in 1957 (Drake, 1959). However, decolonization was not without consequence. When African nations reached independence, they experienced financial turmoil and debt caused by years of being under colonial rule (Stiglitz, 2002). The International Monetary Fund (IMF) and World Bank granted loans to these newly independent African nations in order to "stabilize" their economies. Stiglitz (2002) notes, "the high aspirations following colonial independence have been largely unfulfilled. Instead, the continent plunges deeper into misery, as incomes fall and standards of living decline" (p. 5). These faulty attempts at stabilization actually contributed to the destabilization of Africa's economy. The African Economic Community Treaty in 1991 (and later the Constitutive Act) aimed to save thousands of refugees displaced by religious and political wars within Africa. Along these lines, one could argue that achieving collective empowerment among African people across the Diaspora, through Pan-Africanism and Black Nationalism, has been a positive response to the negative effects of the transatlantic slave trade, colonialism, and imperialism. Despite millions of Africans being displaced, Pan-Africanism teaches the consciousness of still "belonging" to Africa, which reinforces the connection between global and continental Africanisms (Adogamhe, 2008, p. 10).

One might also argue that the proliferation of Black scholars and world leaders, including Garvey, Malcolm X, James, Padmore, Williams, and many others, evidenced Pan-Africanism's success within itself. Each of these scholars and world leaders were influential during a tumultuous time in academic world history. They emphasized the importance of Black identity, equality, and unification, each of which is a tenet of Pan-Africanism (Clarke, 1977; Lemert, 2010). The emergence of James, Padmore, and Williams as scholars interested in Black collectivity was in itself enduring proof of the effectiveness of Pan-Africanism. The political and educational courage it took to demand change for the social plight of African people across the Diaspora was especially noble when considering the segregation era in which Pan-Africanism developed.

The scholarship resulting from the Pan-African movement helped foster the initial formations of Africana, Pan-African, Africology, and Diaspora Studies departments in postsecondary universities worldwide. These historical movements laid the foundation for education as self-healing power. The first evidence of Pan-African curriculum was written by William Leo Hansberry, who taught the first African studies course at Howard University in 1922. Hansberry went on to form the first Black Studies department at Howard University (Alford, 2000). The formalization of Africana Studies, Africology, and African American Studies across postsecondary institutions helped to provide spaces for counterhegemonic learning. For many students of African descent interested in cultural history and heritage, this is a common access point. The self-healing power of education connects the inaugural steps taken in the 19th and 20th centuries toward African unification. The book you are holding is itself an extension of the foundational works of Black Nationalism and Pan-Africanism.

PAN-AFRICANISM AND BLACK NATIONALISM TODAY

Pan-Africanism and Black Nationalism are frameworks with varying degrees of similarity and differences. Some debate the currency of these frameworks in what is considered a post-racial, 21st-century society (Ravitch, 1990; Schlesinger, 1998). Although notions of post-racialism or colorblindness are quickly debunked (Ito & Urland, 2003; Rattan & Ambady, 2013), the argument still stands on whether Pan-Africanism and Black Nationalism are effective frameworks for future development plans in the Africana world. As noted, Pan-Africanism was developed as a response to White supremacy across the Diaspora and throughout the decolonization movement in Africa (Mohan & Zack-Williams, 2002). Many early Pan-Africanists believed that the Diaspora created racial conditions that were damaging to African descendants, so they sought to unify.

According to early Pan-Africanists like Marcus Garvey and Kwame Nkrumah, one of the key problems within the Diaspora was the condition of disconnectedness and lack of rootedness to Africa. Pan-Africanism frames a central "homeland" within a conceptual place or continent, versus a nation-state or specific country. According to Asante:

> This "place" perspective [is] a fundamental rule of intellectual inquiry because its content is a self-conscious obliteration of the subject/object duality and the enthronement of an African wholism . . . "place" remains a rightly shaped perspective that allows the Afrocentrist to put African ideals and values at the center of inquiry. (1990, p. 5)

The same is true for the physical locale of Africa and concepts of "home." Many critics discredit the existence of a common "homeland" because of the lack of cultural congruency across continental Africa (Adeleke, 2009); yet Pan-Africanist researchers assert that African retentions across the Diaspora are incontestable (Akbar, 1998; Asante, 1998; Asante & Karenga, 2006; Clarke, 1993; Karenga, 2002).

SCIENTIFIC RACISM

Despite early movements of Pan-Africanism and Black Nationalism, European research consistently attempted to undermine the humanity of African Americans in the 19th and 20th centuries. Thus, before proceeding with the rest of the treatment on Afrocentricity in the 21st century, it is important to address vehement research that was promoted and propagated in relation to Black education and inferiority claims. This helps to later substantiate the need for Afrocentric schools in the 21st century.

An efflorescence of scientific racism and pseudoscience promoted such concepts as craniometrics, phrenology, eugenics, and social Darwinism (Dennis, 1995; Gillham, 2001). Chase (1977) defines scientific racism as the perversion of scientific truth to create historical myths about distinct races. In 1839, Samuel Morton's *Crania Americana* posited that different racial groups had different skull sizes. His "research" suggested that Whites had larger skulls than Blacks, and therefore larger brains (Washington, 2008). This helped to undergird White superiority claims, including those of Samuel A. Cartwright, who published several papers on African American health and medicine to justify slavery based on Black inferiority. Cartwright suggested that because of Black inhumaneness and unintelligence, there must be White oversight and caretaking, best achieved through plantation slavery (Washington, 2008). Later, Darwin's *Origin of Species* (1859) inspired Herbert Spencer's (1874) racist ideologies that concluded that humans' natural selection processes were based primarily on power and innate abilities (Dennis, 1995). Social Darwinists such as Karl Pearson and Benjamin Kidd later used these theories to justify colonialism and imperialism in the 19th century (Dennis, 1995).

Colonialism and imperialism were especially prevalent in Africa during the late-19th and 20th centuries. The Berlin Conference of 1884–1885 helped to solidify regional political states in Africa. As a result, Europeans gained primary control of the continent. As mentioned, a heinous byproduct of scientific racism was colonialism and global imperialism. One exigent example was the Congolese genocide of the late 19th and early 20th centuries, where King Leopold II led efforts that killed at least 10 million Africans in the Congo. Stapleton (2017) asserts that the death in the Congo was of Holocaust proportions, yet this is only *one* reported country in Africa. Stapleton (2017) asserts that similar atrocities were evident in Namibia, Rwanda, Burundi, Sudan, and Nigeria. Several scholars have found links between German colonists in Namibia and Nazi soldiers of the 20th century. During the Namibian genocide, most natives died from migration through the desert or being imprisoned in concentration camps (Stapleton, 2017). German Kaiser Wilhelm II, in an "extermination order," was responsible for the slaughter of over 75,000 Namibian people (Mumbere, 2018). The results of German occupation in Namibia remain evident today. As recently as 2018, Germany finally returned dozens of Namibian skulls taken to Germany as scientific specimens (Mumbere, 2018). Today it is estimated that the Herero population was reduced from 40% to 7% due to the Namibian extermination. Acts of oppression such as these call for a degree of healing that only focused education can supply.

The Rwandan genocide is perhaps among the most widely known cases in modern history. In 1994, over 800,000 people died in 100 days. Although many people in the West reduced the Rwandan conflict to a mere tribal dispute between the Hutus and Tutsis, Ledwith (2014) suggests that colonialism played an integral role. After Germany's defeat in World War I, Belgium overtook many of the colonized lands once occupied by Germans. Belgians then synthetically created Hutu/Tutsi racial classifications and subsequently instituted an apartheid system (Mamdani, 2001). The Tutsis were described as having a "distant, reserved, courteous, elegant manner," while the Hutus were considered "Negroes" with "brachycephalous skull[s]" who were "childish in nature both timid and lazy, and as often not, extremely dirty" (Peterson, 2001, p. 269). Similar to Western colonialism, Tutsis were favored by Belgians, while Hutus were denied access to any education outside of Catholic priesthood training. In the 1960s, the Tutsis constituted 14% of Rwanda's population, whereas Hutus represented over 85% (Peterson, 2001). Since the power dynamics between the two ethnic groups grew, extremism ensued, and "Hutu Power" was born (2001, p. 260). As stated earlier, researchers implicate colonialism as the inception of ethnic superiority claims in Rwanda (Mamdani, 2001; Peterson, 2001).

In the West, the late 19th century helped to produce the eugenics movement, spearheaded by Sir Francis Galton (Gillham, 2001). Black (2012) describes the racist and systematic eugenics movement that targeted communities of color in the United States. The primary aims were population control, racial purity, and the eradication of "inferior" people (Gillham, 2001). These methods emulated the ethnic sterilization practices of Hitler's

Nazi extermination. Most eugenics research aimed to reproduce persons of Nordic or Aryan descent (Black, 2012). To accomplish this, inhumane scientific testing was conducted on people of color (Chase, 1977). William Ripley's skull size studies helped to solidify racist and misguided research on the psychological and physiological differences between races (Hartigan, 2010).

Another example of evidence of scientific racism is the exploitation of Ota Benga, a young Congolese man displayed at the 1904 St. Louis World Fair and in the Monkey House at the Bronx Zoo in 1906 (Newkirk, 2015) (see Figure 2.16).

Figure 2.16. Ota Benga

Source: Library of Congress.

Samuel Phillips Verner purchased Ota Benga with the support of Madison Grant, a leader in the eugenics movement (Keller, 2006). Records indicate that hundreds of thousands of people gathered to gawk at Benga, who was billed as subhuman (Newkirk, 2015). After Benga's eventual release to an asylum, and later to a Virginia farm, he committed suicide following an extended battle with depression (Newkirk, 2015). This 20th-century astonishment illustrates clearly the shameful and vehement spectacle of scientific racism in the United States. Unfortunately, this type of public display had precedence in modern history. Nearly a century earlier, at least two South African Khoikhoi women, one of them Sartjee (Sarah) Baartman, were put on public display in Europe (see Figure 2.17).

Figure 2.17. Sartjee (Sarah) Baartman (1811)

Source: Library of Congress. Published by Christopher Crupper Rumford (England).

Baartman was made a spectacle throughout Europe when she was showcased alongside animals in London and Paris (Parkinson, 2016). The derogatory name she was tagged with, *Hottentot Venus*, was intended to degrade Khoikhoi (South African) people. After Baartman's death, George Cuiver dissected her body and used it for scientific research (Daley, 2002). Her genitals and body parts were put on display in glass jars at the Musée de l'Homme in Paris. Her body was not properly buried until 2002 (Parkinson, 2016). The stories of Benga and Baartman were not uncommon, as hundreds of South African children were displayed in European circuses, menageries, and "freak shows" in the 19th century.

But the atrocities committed against Black (African) bodies were only one component of scientific racism. Intellectual and psychological testing became one of the most influential ways that science reified racism. For instance, Herrnstein and Murray's *The Bell Curve* reintroduced racist arguments about innate human abilities (Dennis, 1995). Intelligence testing and ideas such as the bell curve promoted pseudoscience that helped to affirm racial superiority (Chase, 1977). Later, Alfred Binet's research on intelligence testing helped to substantiate immigration, segregation, and eugenics policies (Evans, 2018). However, 21st-century researchers have widely debunked these sorts of assessments due to their lack of validity and reliability (Dennis, 1995). The narrow presuppositions toward White, middle-class ethos help to discredit intelligence testing.

Unfortunately, the 21st century has seen a resurgence of race science based on intelligence testing (Evans, 2018), as demonstrated by the growing popularity of alt-right (alternative-right) and White supremacy movements. Similar to centuries prior, scientific racism of the 21st century has shaped public perception of knowledge and racial differences in human ability. Bachynski (2018) revealed in a 2016 survey that almost 50% of White medical students and residents believed there were biological differences among races. Moreover, over 25% of these students believed in skull research, as referenced by the 19th- and 20th-century psychology studies (Bachynski, 2018). Unmistakably, the pervasive damage of scientific racism continues to plague communities and people of color—thus the urgent need to promote right knowledge and self-healing in both the public and political spheres.

STORIES OF RESISTANCE: WARRIOR QUEENS

Next to God we are indebted to women, first for life itself, and then for making it worth living.
—Mary McLeod Bethune

During the pinnacle of scientific racism in the 19th century, civil rights leader and school desegregationist Mary McLeod Bethune appropriately venerated women in relation to social and political rights. In that same regard, many of the greatest historical omissions in K–12 curricula are those involving Black women, particularly those who defied the status quo. This section illuminates some of their stories, offering their narratives to promote education as healing power.

Some of the most important omissions in Western history books are the stories of Maroon societies and other luminary personalities that fought for freedom. Maroons were runaway slaves who formed separate enclave communities (Gottlieb, 2000). Numerous Maroon societies resided in the mountains or other remote areas, where they trained to fight plantation owners and help to free slaves (Campbell, 1988). Many people do not know that some of the first known free Black communities in the United States were located in Florida (Giddings, 2015). Most notably, the Maroon societies in Jamaica were known for their defeat of the British government. Queen Nanny, who was a descendant of Ashanti (Ghanaian) lineage, spearheaded efforts to fight the British in Jamaica (Gottlieb, 2000) (see Figure 2.18).

These efforts were so successful that the British government was defeated multiple times before the Maroons were "tricked," captured, and eventually sent to Sierra Leone (Wiggan et al., 2014). Today, Queen Nanny's significance to world history is recognized, as she is credited with freeing hundreds of slaves from British colonial rule (Campbell, 1988).

**Figure 2.18.
Queen Nanny
of the Maroons**

Source: FreeSVG.org

Figure 2.19. Achille Devéria's lithograph of Queen Ana Nzinga Mbande of Ndongo and Matamba (1583-1663)

In addition to Nanny, other warrior queens were committed to freedom and justice. A notable example was Queen Ana Nzinga, who was prominent in preventing the overtaking of Angola by Portugal (Engel, 2012) (see Figure 2.19). Nzinga rose to power for her military acumen and tactical prowess against the Portuguese (Bortolot, 2003). She eventually offered sanctuary to runaway slaves and united with the Dutch to combine forces against the

Portuguese (Engel, 2012). It was not until her death in 1671 that Portugal was able to fully inhabit and overtake Angola. Nzinga consistently fought against slavery and is revered today as a heroic woman committed to resistance, cultural preservation, and the advancement of Black people.

Another warrior of distinction was Queen Muhumusa (aka Muhmumusa), who is also believed to be a spiritual leader of the Nyabinghi (Ayeko-Kümmeth & Sandner, 2018) (see Figure 2.20). Over a century ago, Queen Muhumusa led a rebellion army against the colonial establishments in Rwanda (Ayeko-Kümmeth & Sandner, 2018). She is considered especially powerful because of her aggressive confrontations with three different European rules: Germany, Great Britain, and Belgium. She led an anticolonial struggle in both Uganda and Rwanda and is known for spearheading women's rights in this region.

Similarly, Queen Mother Yaa Asantewaa was another woman of distinction (see Figure 2.21). Born in present-day Ghana, Yaa Asantewaa fervently resisted British rule. Due to her unwavering persistence, she was eventually elevated to the role of war leader for the Ashanti Nation (McCaskie, 2007).

Figure 2.20. Muhumusa ("Sultanin Mumusa" in the Original), ca. 1904

Source: Wikimedia Commons (2017a).

Figure 2.21. Yaa Asantewaa (Mid-1800s-1921)

Source: West (2019).

Under Yaa Asantewaa's leadership, the Ashantis were able to fight 5,000 British troops for the infamous "golden stool," a symbol of political power in the region. During her war efforts, she challenged gender roles and British occupancy by asserting the power of the Ashanti women to defend themselves (Pulsipher, 2019). Queen Mother Yaa Asantewaa's leadership was so profound in Ghanaian history that a museum was dedicated to her in the Ejisu-Juaben District of Ghana (Pulsipher, 2019).

The life of Yaa Asantewaa can help to inspire students and nurture healing from negative self-concept among all students, but particularly Black women, as numerous negative portrayals, stereotypes, and tropes continue to be perpetuated through social media. Each of these queen warriors can be viewed as early Pan-Africanists fighting for the freedom of Africa and the people of African descent.

Of course, famous (or infamous) women of distinction also operated in the United States. These warrior queens include Harriet Tubman, Sojourner Truth, and Amy Jacques Garvey. For her achievements, Tubman, also known as Araminta Ross or "Moses," is unequivocally one of the most important figures in U.S. freedom discourse (Harriet Tubman Historical Society, 2019) (see Figure 2.22). Born a slave, Tubman is estimated to have led over 300 people to freedom on the Underground Railroad (Larson, 2004). She also helped Union soldiers lead a military raid of a rice plantation and served as an infiltrator for the North, using her "invisibility" as a slave to spy on

**Figure 2.22.
Harriet
Tubman
(1911)**

Source: Library
of Congress.

the Confederates (Little, 2016). Her tactical prowess and courage are often omitted from the Tubman narrative.

Another strong woman of great historical significance is Sojourner Truth (see Figure 2.23). Born Isabella Bomfree, Truth was an established abolitionist and women's rights advocate in the 19th century. Truth was born into slavery, was sold four times, and eventually gained freedom. Her famous speech delivered at the Women's Convention in Ohio, entitled "Ain't I a Woman?," incited new racial perspectives within the predominantly White suffrage movement (Truth, 1851). In this speech she recounted her story of bearing 13 children, most of whom were sold into slavery (Halsall, 1997). Truth saw the indistinguishable relationship between race and gender. As a result, many would consider her speech as part of the earliest beginnings of intersectionality research (Crenshaw, 1991; Smith, 2014).

In addition to her advocacy work in the suffrage movement, Truth helped other slaves achieve their freedom. Her abolitionism included advocacy for her own son, who was illegally sold in Alabama after the New York State Emancipation Act was passed. She won the case and successfully secured her son's return (Painter, 2000). Along with the numerous accolades

Figure 2.23. Sojourner Truth (1864)

I Sell the Shadow to Support the Substance

SOJOURNER TRUTH.

Source: Library of Congress.

awarded to Truth, many acclaim her role in upsetting and challenging both mainline early feminist movements and gender movements of the 20th and 21st centuries. Truth disrupted the image of passive Victorian women in early feminist movements (Minister, 2012), and instead operated as a legal actor (Accomando, 2003) and promoted the inclusion of *all* women. Today, McQueen (2014) notes that Truth considered the axis of enmeshed identities, including race, gender, class, and citizenship (slave) status.

Holding a commitment to racial and gender equality similar to Sojourner Truth's, Amy Jacques Garvey was a leading Pan-Africanist and Black Nationalist in the 20th century (see Figure 2.24). Although Garvey is probably best known for her husband, Marcus Garvey, she was a prominent feminist, orator, editor, and race activist at the height of the Black Nationalist movement (Adler, 1992). She was a leader in the Universal Negro Improvement Association (UNIA) from 1925 to 1927. In the early 1920s, this organization was the most powerful organization of Black people in the world, with over 800 chapters in 40 countries (Adler, 1992). While her husband was away on tour or being falsely imprisoned, Amy published his

Figure 2.24. Amy Jacques Garvey, with husband Marcus (1922)

Source: Wikimedia Commons (2017b).

writings and created her own column devoted to Black women's issues (Taylor, 2000). She recognized the interconnections among race, gender, and class issues at a time when the United States witnessed widespread economic disparities. To that end, Amy Garvey believed that problems such as poverty, health care, violence, workers' rights, and segregation were women's issues, just as much "as women's suffrage and women's higher education were strategies of racial advancement" (Adler, 1992, p. 357). At the height of widespread division within the United States, Amy Garvey sought to unify African-descent people across the Diaspora. Her contributions to history are significant, as she was among the frontrunners in the quest for Black unity and Pan-Africanism.

The above sections highlight some of the vitriolic research done in the name of empiricism and science, along with forgotten stories of African warrior queens in world history as counterhegemonic movements. This information helps to shape the forthcoming section on Afrocentricity in the 21st century, especially in relation to school curricula and social control.

AFROCENTRICITY IN THE 21st CENTURY

Afrocentricity stands on the shoulders of Pan-Africanism and Black Nationalism (Shockley & Frederick, 2010). In fact, it should be noted that Kwame Nkrumah, organizer of the Fifth Pan-African Congress and former president of Ghana, first used the word "Afrocentricity" in the 1960s, before the term was popularized in the 1980s by Molefi Kete Asante (Asante, 2009b; Shockley & Frederick, 2010). Today, Molefi K. Asante is known for developing Afrocentricity into a social and theoretical framework. Asante (2010) contends:

> Afrocentricity finds its grounding in the intellectual and activist precursors who first suggested culture as a critical corrective to the displaced agency among Africans. Recognizing that Africans in the Diaspora had been deliberately de-cultured and made to accept the conqueror's codes of conduct and modes of behavior, the Afrocentrist discovered that the interpretive and theoretical grounds had also been moved. (p. 37)

Afrocentricity can be defined as the recentering of African agency from *objects* to *participants* in history. Today, Afrocentricity is a framework that confronts hegemony (Asante, 2010). Asante argues, "Many today find it difficult to stop viewing European/American culture as the center of the social universe" (1998, p. 4). Afrocentricity's role is to disrupt the hegemonic centrality of Europe into a more diversified outlook. Because Eurocentric ethos has been widely accepted for so long, "[people] often assumed that their 'objectivity,' a kind of collective subjectivity of European culture, should be the measure by which the world marches" (p. 1). Recognizing and becoming familiar with historical truths are the premise of Afrocentric views. Asante and Karenga (2006) postulate that these forms of oppression have been falsely indoctrinated throughout history. Ignoring historical truths that center Africa as the starting place of humanity undermines society's view of Black people and Black culture. As a result, African Americans and other oppressed groups now view their own culture through Eurocentric lenses.

Afrocentricity, although heavily grounded in research, is not without strong contention. Ravitch (1990), Schlesinger (1998), and Lefkowitz (1997) each have castigated the claims of Afrocentricity and disagreed with Pan-Africanists such as Molefi Asante, John Henrik Clarke, and Théophile Obenga (Asante, 1993). Even some African American researchers, such as Tunde Adeleke (2009), take issue with Afrocentric theory. Gates (1991) skeptically dismisses Afrocentricity's utility in general, asserting in a *Newsweek* article entitled "Beware of the New Pharaohs" that "too many people still regard African-American studies primarily as a way to rediscover a lost cultural identity—or invent one that never quite existed" (p. 47). Adeleke

(2009) asserts that Afrocentricity is essentialist and monolithic. However, the very basis of Afrocentricity dispels theories that perpetuate essentialist and monolithic views of history. Asante (2003) argues:

> Afrocentrists have never opposed any racial group or supported any type of discrimination . . . true Afrocentrist[s] cannot support any racist doctrine but must insist on diversity of cultural positions and experiences without hierarchy—that is, without saying one is better than another or more advanced than the other. (p. 268)

Critiques such as Adeleke's help shape the political misconceptions surrounding Afrocentricity and Afrocentric education even today. In response to this opposition, it is important to note that the hostilities and oversights of European hegemony are the primary culprits against which Afrocentricity contends, not any specific persons or racial group.

AFROCENTRIC EDUCATION

As mentioned, Afrocentricity is defined as the recentering of African perspectives toward the center of analysis (Asante, 1991). Additionally, Afrocentric education centers the African perspective to inform students' learning. Afrocentric education generally encourages the following objectives for students, teachers, and school structures:

- Legitimizes African stores of knowledge
- Positively scaffolds productive community and cultural practices
- Extends and builds on the indigenous language
- Reinforces community ties and idealizes service to one's family, community, nation, race, and world
- Promotes positive social relationships
- Imparts a worldview that idealizes a positive, self-sufficient future for one's people without denying the self-worth and right to self-determination of others
- Supports cultural continuity while promoting critical consciousness (Lee et al., 1990, p. 50)

Lee and colleagues (1990), along with Dei (1994), Asante (2009a), and Karenga (1966) propose that Afrocentricity is a unified educational effort that encompasses much more than simply learning about Africa. Afrocentric school curriculum focuses on heritage, community, and African-centered pedagogy.

Today, the idea of Afrocentric education is often misunderstood to simply involve adding African facts and history into the curriculum (Dei, 2012; Joyce, 2005; King et al., 2014; Murrell, 2002). Some key preliminary Afrocentric curriculum planners include John Henrik Clarke, Asa Hilliard, Molefi Asante, Wade Nobles, and Leonard Jeffries, among many others, who have left an undying legacy through their contributions to the pedagogical conversation (Asante, 1998). Although they are noted for their unique contributions in Afrocentric curriculum development, their undeniable purpose was to unveil accurate historical information.

Dei (1996) found that Afrocentricity is an effective way of implementing an antiracist curriculum. Dei (1996) pioneered the bridging of antiracist education and Afrocentricity. More specifically, he examined the intersectionality of Afrocentricity and anti-racism for students. Dei notes that:

> Although Afrocentricity is a world-view embraced in opposition to the subjugation of non-White peoples by Eurocentrism, it is not an attempt to replace one form of hegemony with another. Knowledge of indigenous African cultural values is important for the personal development and schooling of all students. A critical reading of the history of colonialism and neo-colonialism in Africa, and an acknowledgement of the achievements of peoples of African descent, both in their own right and in broader human development, will be helpful to the progressive politics of educational and social change. (1996, p. 181)

Dei (1996) and Joyce (2005) further assert that a focus on Afrocentricity is not oppositional to other forms of knowledge. In fact, it welcomes a plurality of varying perspectives and cultural experiences. A demonstration of Afrocentricity's utility is found in a sample Afrocentric biology curriculum presented in Table 2.1. In an Afrocentric curriculum, concepts such as the MA'AT are centered in the curriculum. Race is not necessarily the center of discussion. Even in a laboratory science like biology, the alignment of curriculum with an Afrocentric perspective is plausible and implementable.

Dei asserts that through antiracist research, Afrocentricity also requires reciprocal respect among students and teachers. "This proceeds from an understanding that each individual stakeholder has something to offer and that diverse viewpoints, experiences, and perspectives strengthen the collective bonds of the school" (Dei, 1996, p. 181). Instead of traditional methods of education where the teacher is the sole expert (Freire, 2000), students also bring to the classroom a useful skill set of their ethnicity, heritage, and culture (Jackson, 1994). This broadens the usefulness of Afrocentricity for all students.

Within schools, Afrocentricity critiques European hegemony and the adaptation of one grand narrative for the application of all students. The world's history and cultural diversity yields opportunity for critical cultural conversations, not common in traditional school environments. Dei's (1996)

Table 2.1. McClymond High School's Afrocentric Biology Curriculum

MA'AT Principles	Example Biological Concepts
Truth	Learning about truth through true scientific evidence (as opposed to pseudoscience) and reason
Justice	Understanding cell equilibrium and functions
Harmony	Understanding transportation through cell wall and surrounding environment of the cell
Balance	Understanding basic cell structure
Order	Understanding the proper function of a healthy cell (discuss viruses, cancer, steroids)
Reciprocity	Understanding the proper environment for the cells to grow
Propriety	Understanding how cells try to self-correct from an imbalance or outside influence

Source: Ginwright (2004, p. 92)

research substantiates the need for critical perspectives in education, in the form of Afrocentricity, to respond to the lack of Black and African perspectives in the curriculum. Dei (1996) found that the "perspectives, histories, and experiences; the absence of Black teachers; and the dominance of White, Eurocentric culture in the mainstream school system are shared by all Black youth" (p. 178). As noted in the previous chapter, student achievement, both nationally and internationally, demonstrates widespread inadequacies within the current curriculum. The disservice of traditional mainstream education toward African American students is just one of the primary reasons for curriculum and pedagogy that are *healing* and restorative. Without correction, the mainstream curriculum will continue to fallaciously perpetuate inaccurate narratives. This reifies psychological and emotional trauma from the MAAFA.

One model of an inclusive cultural framework was the *Portland Baseline Essays*, published in 1987. This geocultural curriculum project was led by Dr. Asa G. Hilliard III, who took the historical contributions of four cultures to promote the use of multiculturalism in mainstream curricula (Portland Public Schools, 1987). The cultures explored in the study include African American, American Indian, Asian American, and Latino/Latina American. This multiethnic/multicultural project was the first of its kind, servicing a large public school district—Portland, Oregon Public Schools. The purpose of this project was to demonstrate the cohesive nature of multiculturalism and show the interdependence of all cultures on one another (Portland Public Schools, 1987). The Portland essays eventually were adapted by school districts in Atlanta, Milwaukee, and New York (Binder, 2000; Leake & Leake, 1992b). Like Afrocentric schools today, the

Portland essays covered all subjects, not just African American history. For each academic subject, including art, language arts, music, social science, physical education and health, mathematics, and science and technology, scholars contributed extensive ethnic and cultural research. This curriculum was not only culturally enriched but also helped to promote healing from curriculum violence (Ighodaro & Wiggan, 2011). The basis of this project advocated for cultural inclusion within the curriculum. Although the essays were written over 30 years ago, they remain relevant in 21st-century contexts (Kunjufu, 2002; Ladson-Billings, 1994; Murrell, 2002; Nieto, 1992).

Engaging pedagogical approaches are imperative, arguably, now more than ever (Delpit, 2006a; Emdin, 2016; Gay, 2000; Ladson-Billings, 1994). Afrocentric curriculum is encouraged for implementation in order to counter systemic methods of curricular hegemony. Current models of education focus on White, middle-class ethos (Kunjufu, 2002). In fact, many Black students experience dissonance and marginality in educational public schools (Dei et al., 2000). Their experiences are typically directly related to cultural exclusion, racism, or prejudice. Afrocentricity, however, places importance on Black cultural contributions within the school curriculum (Asante, 1998, 2009b).

SUMMARY

This chapter has discussed the connections among precolonial history, Black Nationalism, Pan-Africanism, resistance of the queen warriors, and Afrocentricity. Each of these developments is influential toward the development of Afrocentric schools today. Precolonial research on ancient Egypt demonstrates that its inhabitants were undoubtedly Black and possessed a highly functioning society long before invaders arrived (Ani, 1994; Asante, 1990; Clarke, 1993; Jackson, 1970; James, 2010; Karenga, 2002; Williams, 1987). These societies consisted of mathematicians, philosophers, and religious leaders, which debunks the myths of African origins being primitive or beastly (James, 2010). Awareness of this knowledge is the precondition for Afrocentric philosophy and subsequent Afrocentric school models. Contemporary examples of Afrocentric education are made possible not only through ancient Kemetian influences, but also through the Pan-African and Black Nationalist movements of the late 19th and early 20th centuries. Pan-African and Black Nationalist scholars such as Martin Delaney, Alexander Crummell, Robert Campbell, W.E.B. Du Bois, Marcus Garvey, Malcolm X, C.L.R. James, George Padmore, and H. Sylvester Williams bravely influenced the political and social connection between Africa and African Americans, which was severely damaged during colonialism and slavery. It is because of their efforts that contemporary Afrocentric studies, such as those explored in this book, are possible.

CHAPTER 3

Overview of Afrocentric Schools in the 20th and 21st Centuries

The most potent weapon in the hands of the oppressor is the mind of the oppressed.

—Steve Biko, 1978

Excellence in education is much more than a matter of high test scores on standardized minimum or advanced competency examinations. We expect the schools to expand the scope of knowledge and develop the rational reflective and critical capacities of our children. We have every right to expect that, upon completion of public school work, our children will have the general skills to enter the world of work and to be fully functional members of the society. But more than this, we want the content of education to be true, appropriate, and relevant. We want the educational processes to be democratic and humane. We want the aim of education to be the complete development of the person, and not merely preparation for the available low-level jobs, or even for high-level jobs, that may serve no purpose beyond individual enhancement. Among other things, excellence in education must prepare a student for self-knowledge and to become a contributing problem-solving member of his or her own community and in the wider world as well. No child can be ignorant of or lack respect for his or her own unique cultural group and meet others in the world on an equal footing. We believe that this type of excellence in education is a right of the masses and is not merely for a small elite.

—Hilliard et al., 1984

The previous chapter detailed important moments in precolonial African history and their relation to historical fact and right knowledge. This, in essence, is the bedrock of education as self-healing power. The subsequent time periods of Black Nationalism, Pan-Africanism, and Afrocentricity of the 20th century are foundational to the formation of Afrocentric schools. This chapter highlights in more detail the history of Afrocentric education in the 20th and 21st centuries. Even with current research on Afrocentric schools, it remains unclear to many how Afrocentricity can be used in the 21st century to systemically combat cultural, social, and psychological domination for *all* students. While many Afrocentric schools are effective in providing right knowledge for students, the majority of U.S. students do not attend these schools. Additionally, there is limited research on the connectivity between education and other institutions such as family, religion, and social organizations. Thus, this chapter provides an overview and analysis regarding the trajectory of Afrocentricity and its utility within 21st-century contexts. Note that the chapter is not intended to be a comprehensive list of Afrocentric schools, but rather an overview of the development and current status of Afrocentric education in the United States. This includes an in-depth analysis of curriculum and pedagogy in these schools. The chapter is organized into the following subsections: Early Afrocentric School Models, Afrocentric Schools in the 1990s, 21st-Century Afrocentric Schools, Afrocentric Curriculum in the 21st Century, Afrocentric Schools: Where Are We Now?, and Status of Afrocentric Education Today.

EARLY AFROCENTRIC SCHOOL MODELS

As early as 1789, there was evidence of formalized and institutionalized Black education in the United States (Rury, 1983). The African Free School in New York was one example of formal education for free Blacks in the 18th and 19th centuries (Rury, 1983). In 1829, abolitionist minister Samuel Cornish declared that African Americans must bind together for the sake of justice. His approach was to actively seek educational improvement (Gross, 1932). Involved parents and community members ensured that teachers in the African Free School were Black and culturally immersed in the surrounding community (Rury, 1983). By 1834, enrollment reached over 1,500 children, including prominent student Martin Delany. Many researchers suggest that the formation of the African Free School helped to disrupt misconceptions about African Americans' unwavering commitment to education and social autonomy.

In the 20th century, one of the earliest evidences of an U.S. Afrocentric school was the Nairobi Day School in East Palo Alto, California, which operated between 1966 and 1984, proclaiming to teach "African and African American history, culture, and language as the basis of its curriculum and [make] use of pedagogical techniques that respond to African American children's learning styles" (Pollard & Ajirotutu, 2000, p. 17). The formation of the Nairobi Day School stemmed from community efforts to control and govern the neighborhood's education in East Palo Alto. When the school opened in 1966, it operated primarily as a supplementary program on Saturdays. Four years into existence, Nairobi expanded to a full-time school for students (Hoover, 1992). Nairobi's pedagogical approach required teachers to hold high expectations for students. Teachers were required to modify their lesson plans to incorporate an African perspective. Nairobi outperformed neighboring schools in literacy. In fact, Nairobi's administration guaranteed that each student would read on grade level after one year of attendance at Nairobi (Hoover, 1992). Nairobi was so successful that the Institute for Black Child Development described the school as "one of the best educational programs for Black children in the country" (Blakeslee, 1975, p. 30). The school closed in 1984 because of financial challenges, but findings from Nairobi demonstrate that high student achievement is possible when implementing corrective Black history, positive self-concepts, and restorative and healing education (Hoover, 1992).

Other Afrocentric schools were active during the late 1960s and 1970s as well, particularly in California, including the Afro-American School of Culture, founded in 1967 in Los Angeles; Omowale Ujamaa of Pasadena, founded in 1973; Winnie Mandela Children's Learning Village, founded in 1973 in Compton; the Marcus Garvey School, founded in 1975 in Los Angeles; Uhuru Shule, founded in 1978 in Los Angeles; and Ile Omode, founded in 1986 in Oakland (Kifano, 1996, p. 210). These schools, similar to Nairobi, were community-led initiatives aimed at more appropriately educating African American students. Many of these schools were destabilized through shifts in administration and leadership, and subsequently closed. As a result, there is limited research on these schools. Nairobi, however, provides a general depiction of the early formations of Afrocentric education (Hoover, 1992).

Between the 1960s and 1980s, many Afrocentric schools were renamed in order to appeal to wider audiences (Rickford, 2016), such as Weusi Shule in Brooklyn, New York, which was renamed the Johnson Preparatory School. The Kubu Learning Center in Philadelphia, Pennsylvania, was renamed The Lotus Academy (Rickford, 2016). Afrocentric schools consequently saw an increase in enrollment across the United States (Bush, 2004). By the 1980s, there were over 400 independent Black schools nationwide (Ratteray, 1990). In 1986, parents of Newark's Chad School were surveyed regarding their choice of Afrocentric education for their children. Parents reported that small class sizes, personalized education, cultural awareness, and knowledge of Black heritage were important factors (Rickford, 2016). Additionally, with growing demands for student achievement and standardization, Afrocentric schools in the 1990s witnessed growth and widespread change. Researchers thus began to document the academic success of Afrocentric education, as discussed in the next section.

AFROCENTRIC SCHOOLS IN THE 1990s

Molefi Kete Asante began the initial formations of "Afrocentric" research (under that name) in the 1970s. He eventually published *Afrocentricity:*

The Theory of Social Change in 1980, which iconized Afrocentricity into a social theory. In 1991, Asante merged the Afrocentric theoretical framework with education, and explored the implications of Afrocentric schools and education. Asante's (1991) main assertion distinguished the difference between Afrocentricity and multiculturalism. He contended that when multicultural education is implemented incorrectly, it could easily propagate racist Eurocentric research. Multiculturalism, too, required proper realignment with right knowledge and historical fact (Asante, 1991). According to Asante, multiculturalism must stem from Afrocentricity, not the other way around. The aforementioned *Portland Baseline Essays* (Portland Public Schools, 1987) provide an Afrocentric lens of multiculturalism, as Asante advocates. The *Portland Baseline Essays* include the contributions of all racial groups, but acknowledge Africa as the starting place of humanity. For African American students specifically, this is important for self-healing.

While many of these schools were appealing to parents and families, other early formations of public Afrocentric schools came in the form of African American "immersion programs" (Gill, 1991). Milwaukee was a pilot city for an immersion program in public schools (Leake & Leake, 1992a). The district's progressive response to African American student underachievement, in the form of immersion programs, coalesced the support of community advocates desperate for school turnaround. The initial tenets of the immersion programs included:

> (a) substantial reform of curricular content and instructional strategies . . .
> (b) involvement of the entire faculty in an a 15-credit program of coursework related to African and African American life experiences . . . (c) transformation of the school's physical environment through pervasive displays of textile prints, sculptures, banners, proverbs, quotations, and student work reflective of African and African American heritages . . . (d) commitments from each immersion school teacher to make a minimum of 18 home visits per semester . . . (e) establishment of an intermediate grades mentoring program which provides immersion school fifth graders with an adult from the local community who will serve as his or her mentor throughout the school experience. (Leake & Leake, 1992a, p. 29)

Two of the first schools, Martin Luther King Jr. Elementary School and Fulton Middle School, galvanized support from African American administrators and parents who resisted the miseducation of traditional public schools (Holt, 1991). Teachers were encouraged to utilize the *Portland Baseline Essays* (Portland Public Schools, 1987) in order to diversify their lesson planning and curriculum design (Leake & Leake, 1992b). These schools formed in direct opposition to racist research, such as *The Bell Curve* and intelligence (IQ) testing, which suggested that African American students somehow best performed alongside White students (Leake & Leake, 1992a).

The results from initial immersion schools displayed the exact opposite. Murrell (1993) case-studied Martin Luther King Jr. Elementary School, one of the inaugural immersion sites, and found that students attending immersion schools were more developed and fared better cognitively, socially, and emotionally. Sanders and Reed (1995) also comparatively examined Milwaukee African American student performance at immersion and traditional schools. In their study, 5th-grade students attending immersion schools demonstrated a higher level of intellectual achievement in comparison to students attending traditional public schools (Sanders & Reed, 1995).

Since Sanders and Reed's (1995) research was conclusive only for 5th-grade students, it is important to explore studies with more comprehensive research across grade levels. It is imperative to also present research conducted in other cities besides Milwaukee, in order to assess Afrocentric educational experience more holistically. Alongside Milwaukee's initial formulation of immersion schools, other public school districts including Detroit, Los Angeles, Minneapolis, Oakland, Atlanta, and Washington, DC, concurrently introduced forms of Afrocentric education in the 1990s (Kifano, 1996; Murrell, 1993; Span, 2002). By the late 1990s, the term "Afrocentric" was more widely used in place of immersion. These school models spread beyond the Midwest toward the coasts and abroad (Dei, 1994; Hopson et al., 2010). Afrocentric supplementary schools were also emerging in the United Kingdom in the 1990s (Dove, 1993). Afrocentric schools often were established in large urban cities because they typically were home to higher numbers of African American students. As these new schools spread, so did surrounding research. Studies in the late 1990s and early 21st century placed a concerted effort on better understanding Afrocentric schools.

In the 1990s, the Afrocentric Marcus Garvey School in Los Angeles was a place of distinction (Hammer, 1994). Economist Walter Williams (1999) described the school as an extraordinary environment, with teachers, students, and families who expressed unabashed pride in their African heritage. This school was founded in 1975 and remains in operation today. According to the school's website, over 90% of its students have graduated and then matriculated into notable universities, including the University of California, Berkeley; the University of Southern California; UCLA; Stanford University; Howard University; and New York University (Marcus Garvey School, 2019). In the 1990s, Hammer (1994) reported that Marcus Garvey students outperformed state schools, while using only 60% of the state's per-student expenditures. Today the school operates entirely on student tuition and alumni donations.

Other Afrocentric schools received notable attention in the 1990s and early 21st century as well. Delpit (2006b) described the experiences of students at Sankofa Shule, an Afrocentric school in Lansing, Michigan. Delpit (2006b) notes that the Sankofa Shule:

has produced low-income African American students who are reading from two to four levels above grade level, who are doing algebra and calculus in grade school, and who outscored Lansing School District and the state of Michigan on the state accountability test (MEAP) in 2000 in mathematics and writing. (p. 221)

In fact, in their April 1998 issue, the *U.S. News and World Report* called this school "an educational powerhouse" (Toch, 1998). While the school has since closed due to administrator turnover, it is important to acknowledge the long historic legacy of high-performing Afrocentric schools such as Sankofa Shule. Many of these schools witnessed heightened success in the late 20th century.

In regard to student achievement, Anselmi and Peters (1995) comparatively examined African American middle school students attending Afrocentric and traditional schools. They performed character assessments on participating students and found noticeable differences between Afrocentric education and traditional schooling, specifically in regard to positive self-outlook. Initial findings from Anselmi and Peters (1995) reveal that:

[when] expectations are institutionalized (as in the Afrocentric school), students internalize a positive valuation of self and thus anticipate more events in the life course, more career-related achievement, and are more optimistic about the likelihood of achieving their goals. (p. 7)

Results from this study further indicated that students attending the Afrocentric school demonstrated increased expressiveness, instrumentality, affirmation and belonging, narrative density, future optimism, and career density (Anselmi & Peters, 1995). Of all the results, the measurable gains were found in students' increased optimism regarding their future career goals. This means students attending Afrocentric schools had a more optimistic outlook on their futures and possessed internal confidence to succeed.

Hopkins (1997) also examined the impact of Afrocentric schools on students' character development, conducting several case studies to assess Afrocentric school designs in Detroit, Baltimore, New York, and Milwaukee. During the formative years of African American immersion schools, Hopkins (1997) researched male academies specifically. He conducted case studies at Malcolm X African Centered Academy, Paul Robeson African Centered Academy, The Center for Educating African American Males, Malcolm X African American Immersion School, and the Martin Luther King Jr. Immersion School. Hopkins's (1997) research, focused on in-school and after-school Afrocentric programs, concluded that the best strategies for African American males were early intervention, single-sex classrooms, and the infusion of African and African American history into the curriculum (Hopkins, 1997). Students in Hopkins's study experienced increased self-esteem and improved achievement. While Hopkins's research is compelling, it is limited in that it applies only to African American males.

Similar to Hopkins, Webb (1996) researched students at Afrocentric schools in the Midwest. Webb's research examined the experiences of both male and female students. Webb (1996) studied 6th-, 7th-, and 8th-grade student achievement at an Afrocentric academy located in Minneapolis. Students in this school spent half of the academic school day at their traditional public school, and half at an Afrocentric academy. The philosophy of the Afrocentric academy was to emphasize collectivity and community over individualism. Webb's study investigated the impact of the half-day Afrocentric educational experiences on the students' achievement, self-concept, and behaviors. The study examined both White and Black students in the program, and had a control and experimental group. The students in the control group stayed at the traditional school for the entire school day, while the experimental group spent half of their day at the Afrocentric academy. The pre- and post-test results demonstrated that the experimental group experienced gains in mathematics. The initial results from Hopkins (1997), Sanders and Reed (1995), and Webb (1996) confirmed the benefits of Afrocentric schools for African American students. However, the aforementioned studies focused on the benefits of Afrocentric schools in comparison to traditional public schooling. Research, up to this point, failed to explore student and teacher experiences in depth at Afrocentric schools. As the 1990s experienced a resurgence of Afrocentric education (Dragnea & Erling, 2008; Hopkins, 1997), research began to look more deeply at student, teacher, and parent experiences at these schools.

Kifano (1996) researched parent satisfaction at Mary McLeod Bethune Institute (MMBI), an Afrocentric supplementary Saturday school in the Crenshaw neighborhood in Los Angeles. The study revealed that both students and parents benefited from Afrocentric schools. Parents at MMBI were important to the learning process within the school community (Kifano, 1996). Parents in the study exhibited satisfaction with the school's enrichment practices and family engagement opportunities. They reported appreciation for the school's role in instilling a renewed interest and enthusiasm in students. Kifano's study also found that students benefited from Afrocentric education. MMBI's instructional practices contributed to students' political, moral, and cultural development (Kifano, 1996)—tangible evidence of education as self-healing power.

Whereas Kifano's (1996) study focused primarily on parent satisfaction, Manley (1997) researched teacher satisfaction and teacher training. Manley (1997) examined teacher feedback on the *Portland Baseline Essays* (Portland Public Schools, 1987) from Atlanta Public School educators. As mentioned, the *Portland Baseline Essays* were the first comprehensive attempt at formulating an implementable Afrocentric curriculum. These essays were used in several urban districts in the 1990s, including Portland, Milwaukee,

New York, and Atlanta. Teachers in Manley's (1997) study were asked to rate how effective the essays were as a basis for curriculum development, lesson planning, and classroom instruction. Manley surveyed Atlanta teachers ranging from 1 to 45 years of experience. The study revealed no relationship between teachers' preparation and their perspectives on the essays; however, teachers noticed behavioral changes in students after implementing the *Portland Baseline Essays*. Teachers related that students were more engaged and involved in the Afrocentric lessons. Teachers also explained that the most noticeable difference in student behavior came from low-performing students, who exhibited a newfound interest in the curriculum. The self-healing power of education in Manley's (1997) study thus helped to motivate students and stimulate their academic interests.

As demonstrated in Manley's (1997) study, curriculum design and pedagogy are important in Afrocentric schools. Archie (1997) examined social studies curriculum methods at three Afrocentric schools in Philadelphia, Detroit, and New Jersey. The purpose of this study was to determine the level of uniformity within Afrocentric curricula. The results demonstrated the importance of teacher knowledge about African history. Archie concluded that Afrocentric education must consistently recenter Africa as the starting point of history (Archie, 1997; Asante, 1991, 2009a). Archie found that the greatest deterrence to Afrocentric curriculum implementation was teachers who approached Afrocentricity as an additive means to incorporate student culture. Across the three Afrocentric schools in Archie's study, there was philosophical disharmony on whether all teachers could adapt to the Afrocentric pedagogical model. Archie noted that teachers disagreed on whether all teachers could learn and apply Afrocentric pedagogy in their classrooms. Meanwhile, the students in Archie's study had a much more agreeable perspective on Afrocentricity. Students considered the Afrocentric curricula as valuable for "career and academic opportunities" (Archie, 1997, p. 139). The overall findings from Archie's study suggested that Afrocentricity must be embedded in, not simply added to, school culture. The rejection of additive history is what Asante (1991) formerly found as a distinguishing factor between Afrocentricity and multiculturalism. As Afrocentric education continued to flourish in the 1990s, so did academic research surrounding the differences among Afrocentricity, mainstream, and even multicultural learning environments.

The 1990s saw a proliferation of Afrocentric schools (Bush, 2004; Murrell, 1993; Span, 2002), again providing impetus for further studies. Murrell (1993), Sanders and Reed (1995), Hopkins (1997), Webb (1996), Kifano (1996), and Manley (1997) all cited benefits of Afrocentric education for students and families. While their research approaches were different, they each provided insight on exploring alternative forms of education. These initial studies on Afrocentric education opened new epistemological avenues in academic research.

21st-CENTURY AFROCENTRIC SCHOOLS

The 21st century offers a newly evolved milieu for Afrocentric education. As the educational climate changes, so do schools. The introduction of high-stakes assessments such as *No Child Left Behind* and *Common Core State Standards*, along with the reappearance of private and charter vouchers, have impacted current Afrocentric schools (Hopson et al., 2010). Charter schools (i.e., independently governed public schools) typically allow for additional curricular flexibility. This is often advantageous for emerging Afrocentric schools (Hopson et al., 2010; Murrell, 1999; Piert, 2006; Townsend, 2005). However, charter schools also typically require less district accountability, and many are found to underperform (Piert, 2006). This change in the landscape brings to question the effectiveness of Afrocentric school designs today. Today, fewer than 100 Afrocentric schools across the United States are open and in operation. These schools include public, charter, private, and independent schools. As of our writing in 2021, we should note that many of these schools have recently closed due to changes in district guidelines and the revocation of school charters. Still, the existence of present-day Afrocentric schools indicates a continued demand for alternative forms of education for students.

In a 2001 study, Reese examined the charter school issue, investigating student, teacher, administrator, and parent perspectives on Afrocentric education at Benjamin Banneker Charter School (BBCS) in Massachusetts. Participants were asked to discuss the advantages and disadvantages of Afrocentric education for teaching underserved Black students in impoverished urban communities. The 2001 case study at BBCS revealed that the Afrocentric program was under much scrutiny from local residents who were fearful of having an Afrocentric program nearby. Contrary to studies in the 1990s, Reese's study displayed community apprehension about Afrocentric programs. Nevertheless, the BBCS staff and parents advocated for Afrocentric education. In Reese's study, teachers and parents considered Afrocentric education an important curricular approach, for both Black and White students, in the 21st century. Reese notes:

> [Teachers] asserted that it was good for [Black students] to see themselves as major contributors in a historical context and it was good for [Whites] to see that [Blacks] had played a major role in the building of America and major civilizations in general. (2001, p. 286)

The recasting of curricula helped to positively restore and shape student learning. This is a key tenet in *education as self-healing power*. In addition to students, parents considered it important for their children to see positive Black role models and leaders within their curriculum and at their school (Reese, 2001).

Similar to Reese (2001), Mitchell (2003) researched parent and teacher experiences at an Afrocentric school in Southern California. MAAT Academy, an Afrocentric after-school program designed for African American students, aimed to help struggling students. Many students at MAAT were "at risk" of academic failure and needed additional instructional support. Mitchell conducted an ethnographic case study that examined the parent and teacher perceptions of students attending Afrocentric schools. Teachers in the study felt an internal connection to MAAT and chose to work in an Afrocentric environment as a means of giving back to the community. Teachers believed that the education at MAAT was more holistic than that at traditional public schools, and as a result they experienced greater job satisfaction. Parents in the study noticed observable changes in their students, including increased self-esteem, improved self-respect, and heightened academic focus (Mitchell, 2003).

Similarly, Rayford (2012) examined student, teacher, and parent experiences at Columbus, Ohio's Africentric Early College in a study that looked at 7th-grade male students' self-concept, self-esteem, and racial identity. Aiming to assess students' perceptions of Afrocentric education, Rayford interviewed two principals, eight teachers, nine students, and three parents, and found that each stakeholder was influential in the educational outcomes of students. Data findings revealed that students at Columbus Africentric Early College demonstrated increased awareness of positive self-history through manifestations of Nguzo Saba. Additionally, students did not view their "Blackness" negatively (Rayford, 2012), suggesting that the school fostered a nurturing learning environment (again illustrating the self-healing power of right knowledge and education). Teachers and principals were viewed as vital to the Afrocentric learning process. Rayford also found that it was imperative for teachers to support Afrocentric education in their pedagogical styles in order to educate students holistically.

Similarly, Shockley (2003, 2011) found that Afrocentric teachers were important in the development of African American students. Shockley's (2011) single case study observed an Afrocentric teacher for 3 years. In this study, Shockley observed a teacher's dedication to Afrocentricity both inside and outside the classroom, noting that:

> Afrocentric teachers are impassioned and desperate, and they mix those emotions together with their deep passion for African history and their knowledge of the reality of the global situation in which Africans now find themselves. What results from emotions and knowledge is an investment in the well-being and development of students, which in turn attracts the students to these teachers and creates a family atmosphere within schools wherein personal relationships are formed. Afrocentric teachers find creative ways to learn things about students' families so they can tether those things in when they need to remind a student of the school-home connection. (p. 1031)

Shockley (2011) found that Afrocentric teachers engaged students both in pedagogical style and curriculum development, and constantly recentered all knowledge back to the ancestors. Teachers and parents in Shockley's (2011) study confirmed that the re-centering of ancestral knowledge was important for students' educational success.

When determining Afrocentric schools' effectiveness, it is important to examine longitudinal data. Piert (2006) explored the long-term impact of Afrocentric education, looking at how students' educational experiences influenced their lives retrospectively. Piert (2006) case-studied seven adult participants who were graduates of the same Afrocentric charter school. Participants reflected on their experiences in Afrocentric education, describing a sense of family and community that extended past graduation. Participants also described a greater self-concept from the nurturing, loving, and energetic learning environment. Teachers expected "greatness from them," and these high expectations were among the most formative memories of their Afrocentric education (p. 169). The participants also described how the principles of Kemet, as taught in Afrocentric schools, helped them in adulthood. In fact, Piert notes that participants:

> relied on [Kemetic] values as they interacted with their fellow peers while away in the pursuit of higher education; also that they passed these values on to their children and utilized these values and principles in contemplating decisions of daily living. (2006, p. 170)

Here, the transmission of Kemetic knowledge shows the self-healing power of education. In comparison to the majority of U.S. students, participants in Piert's (2006) study acknowledged the importance of ancient Kemetian history. The only points of regret from the participants came from feeling "different" from their peers who attended traditional public schools (p. 160). Piert's (2006) longitudinal study provides a unique perspective of Afrocentric education often neglected in the research.

AFROCENTRIC CURRICULUM IN THE 21st CENTURY

In 2002, Murrell's *African-Centered Pedagogy* presented a comprehensive epistemological overview of Afrocentric pedagogical techniques. Murrell's research also thoroughly formulated Afrocentric curriculum design theories. Murrell asserted that Afrocentric pedagogy was much more than lesson planning; rather, it was an embedded philosophy that guided behavior. In addition, Murrell concluded that when Afrocentric pedagogy was implemented correctly, students were equipped to become "cultural learners" who were able to critically examine and confront hegemony (2002, p. 169). Murrell contended that Afrocentric pedagogy was important for *all* learners because it created a community of care and respect. Murrell's (2002) research also provided a theoretical overview of Afrocentric pedagogy.

More recently, King and Swartz (2018) have suggested the importance of Afrocentric curricula for the sake of justice. In their book *Heritage Knowledge in the Curriculum*, they suggest that school curricula should promote *heritage* relevancy, in contrast to the popular notion of cultural relevancy (2018). This is to ensure that African-descent people are "historical agents whose ideas and actions remain connected to their heritage" (p. xii). In this research, King and Swartz refer to "heritage" as a group's cultural memory, which should eventually enable *all* students to have shared, collective continuity with their culture (2018). Here, ancestral knowledge is paramount. Through this systemic redevelopment of school curricula, educational reformation and transformation are possible. In fact, King and Swartz promote the idea of educational freedom through Afrocentric praxis. In many respects, ancestral and heritage knowledge are central for education's role in healing and restoration.

Several studies have explored Afrocentric curriculum and pedagogy in K–12 schools, including Gbaba's (2009) research on Afrocentric curricula, specifically language arts and literacy. Gbaba researched the Chiandeh project, created to counter the monolithic and Eurocentric curriculum standards, noting that the project:

> center[ed] African American children in their own ancestry to enhance their cultural esteem and learning, and specifically highlight[ed] the term cultural esteem and the lack thereof by many Blacks as an important issue affecting Black children's learning. (2009, p. iii)

Gbaba's study interviewed students, conducted classroom observations, and used discourse analysis for students' written reflections through a K–12 school and after-school program in Pennsylvania. The study revealed that when African American children were centered as *contributors* in their own history and culture, they demonstrated more interest in literacy, displayed awareness for Afrocentric values, and showed increased respect for their ancestry. The study also found that culturally relevant instructional materials enhanced learning outcomes for students of color and increased student self-awareness.

Shockley and Frederick (2011) also acknowledged the importance of cultural relevancy within Afrocentric curricula. Shockley and Frederick's study disaggregated Afrocentric educational research based on six distinct categories. These categories included identity and Pan-Africanism, African culture and values, reattachment, Black Nationalism, community control and institution-building, and education. Shockley and Frederick found that within Afrocentric education one of the most important aspects was the incorporation of Black cultural practices. This stems from the belief that Eurocentric education inadequately services Black students. Thus, the Afrocentric school model fostered more cultural continuity and restoration toward self-healing. Shockley and Frederick (2011) found that establishing Afrocentricity within schools requires "re-Africanization," "redefinition," and "rediscovery" of lost historical knowledge (p. 1224). This process of regaining cultural centeredness is imperative for Afrocentric educators. They found that Afrocentric education must serve as counterhegemony, and should also present information in a manner relevant to 21st-century learners. Shockley and Frederick (2011) claim that:

> Afrocentric educationists advance our understanding of culture and how it works by presenting the notion of culture as steadfast and traditional yet able to protect African people from European, American, or any other universalism, supremacism, and hegemony. These cultural assertions undergird what Afrocentric educationists wish to transmit to students in Afrocentric schools. (p. 1225)

They found that multiculturalism does not adequately address African American students' needs. Most diversity and multicultural initiatives superficially include modest additions to the curriculum, without properly realigning history (Shockley & Frederick, 2011). As a result, they suggest that the benefits of Afrocentricity extend to all racial groups, not just African Americans.

Cultural relevance, as mentioned in Gbaba's (2009) and Shockley and Frederick's (2011) studies, is important for all curriculum types (Ladson-Billings, 1994). Even the most earnest attempts of Afrocentricity are not always received well among students. Traoré (2002, 2007) and Ginwright (2004) found that much of Afrocentric curricula, although meaningful and important, is irrelevant to today's students. This is due to the students' need for more contemporary instructional styles. Ginwright asserts, "many Afrocentric reform efforts, particularly for middle and high school students, are simply out of touch with urban black youth culture and, as a result, experience limited success" (p. 132). Traoré's (2007) study came to the same conclusions. Traoré examined the misconceptions of Africa among high school students and revealed that African history was propagated and distorted. As a result, students in the study were initially uninterested. This again underscores a need for right knowledge and restorative education. After the researcher engaged participants in critical discussions to correct falsified African history, students addressed key issues that were relevant to them, including film, Africans in America, stereotypes, and personal values. Traoré (2007) found that:

> in just five activities, the African American students changed their interest level in Africa from disinterest to very interested, from ignoring Africa to wanting to

know more, from stereotypes of all things African to an awareness of the ways in which school, home, and the media have not contributed to their knowing their history and culture as people of African descent. (p. 673)

Just as Ladson-Billings (1994) argued for the implementation of culturally relevant pedagogy in public schools, Afrocentric schools must reflect contemporary relevancy for students (Murrell, 2002; Robinson & Jeremiah, 2011). This suggests contemporizing instructional activities that engage students.

Ginwright (2004) found that incorporating hip-hop in Afrocentric education connected African American history with newfound agency. Ginwright (2004) notes:

Expanding and strengthening Afrocentric reform through hip-hop culture . . . requires a bold and courageous paradigm shift on the part of educators and reformers to conceptualize [Black] youth culture as an asset rather than a liability in educational change efforts. (p. 135)

To that end, Afrocentric schools should incorporate contemporary pedagogical strategies to provide engaging instructional activities for students. Hip-hop is one pedagogical avenue; yet there is room in academic research for other strategies.

In addition to imperative curricular needs, academic consistency across grade levels is also important for Afrocentric schools. Giddings's (2001) study found that effective Afrocentric schools must encompass the entire 13-year educational tenure for students. Yet one challenge many Afrocentric teachers face is the absence of a comprehensive kindergarten through 12th-grade curriculum framework (Durden, 2007; Giddings, 2001). Aside from the aforementioned *Portland Baseline Essays* (Portland Public Schools, 1987) and Asante and Karenga's *Handbook of Black Studies* (2006), there lacks a concise attempt to streamline Afrocentric curricula. To date, there is a myriad of knowledge accessible for teachers and educators at Afrocentric academies, but no 21st-century instruction model (Giddings, 2001). This leaves curricula amorphous and inconsistent across Afrocentric schools.

Squire's case study examined the journey of an Afrocentric school in the initial stages of development. Findings indicated that Afrocentric schools offer spaces for nationalism and communalism, which "affirms the African spirit and identity" (Squire, 2012, p. 18). This is beneficial for both students and teachers. In addition, Squire's study found that Afrocentric education typically considers multiple perspectives, in comparison to more traditional school settings that promote rigid hegemonic binaries. However, Afrocentric schools are not without limitations. Squires's findings also indicated that teacher recruitment is a strenuous task in Afrocentric schools, because deciphering teaching philosophies and commitment is difficult. Similar to what was found in Giddings's 2001 study, creating or acquiring resources and materials was difficult for the Afrocentric schools in Squire's study. Ginwright (2004) presents a compelling case regarding curriculum's role in students' educational experiences. Additional curriculum development is important for the sustainability of Afrocentric schools in the 21st century. In addition, more research that explores student perceptions, daily educational experiences, and the healing power of education is important to better understand Afrocentric education in the 21st century.

AFROCENTRIC SCHOOLS: WHERE ARE WE NOW?

How are Afrocentric schools performing in the 21st century? In many cases, Black excellence in education is confined to fit within Western metrics of success. Thus, it is important to note that Afrocentric schools today also promote the importance of character education, holistic learning, and cultural life skills crucial for African American children's development (Murrell, 2002; Wiggan & Watson, 2016). Whereas research overwhelmingly supports that student cultural identity is stronger at Afrocentric schools (Gbaba, 2009; Hopkins, 1997; Mitchell, 2003), little information is available on current student achievement.

Students at Afrocentric schools take classes across subject disciplines, and subsequently complete corresponding summative assessments to display mastery. At Asa G. Hilliard Academy, the site of this research study, student achievement is among the highest in the nation, with 77% proficiency in reading and 70% in mathematics. Although student achievement at Afrocentric schools is higher than the national average, we should acknowledge that many Afrocentric schools have low standardized test scores. As noted, each Afrocentric school is different based on leadership, teacher quality, and instructional effectiveness (Piert, 2013).

As mentioned earlier, there are some exemplary Afrocentric schools, such as the nationally recognized Columbus Africentric Early College in Ohio, where 65% of students are at or above proficiency in mathematics and 77% are at or above proficiency in reading, both of which are above the state average (Rayford, 2012). Rayford reveals that in 2011, Columbus Africentric Early College:

> had a graduation rate that was higher than their school district and the State of Ohio. The teaching philosophies of teachers, although varied in ideologies, were similar with a commitment to assist students in excelling academically. This commitment was complementary with the mission statement of developing well-rounded students. (p. 376)

As indicated, Asa G. Hilliard Academy also performs above state achieve-ment levels, which is why it was selected as the site for this study. As other studies suggest, the effectiveness of Afrocentric schools largely depends on several key factors, which include leadership, community support, and teacher commitment to Afrocentric pedagogy.

Today, dozens of Afrocentric schools exist across the country, with a concentration in Northern urban cities such as Washington, DC and Phila-delphia, and in areas where there are organized educated Black communi-ties. There are also African-centered schools in other regions of the world, including Nsawam, Ghana; North Preston, Nova Scotia; Toronto, Canada; London, United Kingdom; Port of Spain, Trinidad and Tobago; and others. Similar to Afrocentric schools in the United States, many of these schools focus on the importance of heritage, community, culture, and student men-torship. Within the United States, many Afrocentric schools are either pri-vate schools or charter schools. Due to recent shifts in federal legislation, there has been an influx of school charters and public school privatization. While this is advantageous for many Afrocentric schools, as it allows for more curricular flexibility, there are numerous flaws within the charter system.

STATUS OF AFROCENTRIC EDUCATION TODAY

Research has at least looked at most areas of Afrocentric education, includ-ing pedagogy (Ginwright, 2004; Murrell, 2002), curriculum design (Gbaba, 2009; Ginwright, 2004; Traoré, 2002), teacher effectiveness (Shockley, 2003, 2011), parent satisfaction (Kifano, 1996; Mitchell, 2003), student performance (Sanders & Reed, 2005), and student experiences (Piert, 2006; Rayford, 2012). This book makes a new contribution to the field, as it is primarily an introspective framework and approach to education as healing for the oppressed.

As mentioned in the previous section, there is limited research on Afrocentric schools in 21st-century contexts. In 2010, Sharma helped to expand the scope of research exploration on Afrocentric schools by incor-porating student perceptions and perspectives. Sharma's study focused on understanding the reasons why high school students would attend Afrocen-tric education, and asked participants to identify curricula foci that were appealing. In this way, Sharma's study is most closely aligned with this book's research focus.

Sharma's 2010 study examined two primary questions: (1) What is the youth perspective of Africentric schooling? and (2) Would students volun-tarily attend an Africentric school? Sharma interviewed 10 high school stu-dents regarding their perspectives on Afrocentric education and reported the findings using grounded theory. Until Sharma's study, research was lacking student voices regarding Afrocentric education. Sharma's study focused on these missing perspectives and presents a compelling case for inclusion within Afrocentric education. Sharma's findings reveal that youth desired inclusive schooling, but generally had mixed feelings about Afrocentric curricula due to stereotypes and racial stigmas. Students in the study who were apprehensive revealed that Afrocentric curriculum would be more desirable if it represented *multiple* cultures. It is important to note that Sharma's participants were high school students who did not attend Afrocentric schools. So they were not talking from experience but simply giving their *perceptions* of Afrocentric education.

The work done by Sharma helped to shape the focus of this book. However, the discussion of education as self-healing power is still missing from research. Existing research currently has less treatment on the usefulness of corrective history, as found in Afrocentric schools, in the reshaping of positive identity formation in students. This book seeks to build on Sharma's study by providing multiple perspectives of *various* stakeholders within an Afrocentric school, including teachers, students, and administration. In addition, the data collection procedures proposed for this study examine more than just student interviews. The current study gathers three forms of data, including interviews, classroom observations, and student essays. All of the data procedures center on the topic of education as self-healing power, a focus largely absent in the current research.

SUMMARY

The current state of the literature reflects two major waves in empirical Afrocentric educational research. The first wave encompasses the initial studies of the 1980s and '90s. To start, the *Portland Baseline Essays* (Portland Public Schools, 1987) provided tangible examples of nonhegemonic curricula. These *Baseline Essays* were implemented into many Afrocentric schools in the 1990s (Binder, 2000; Leake & Leake, 1992b). As Afrocentric schools saw an emergence in the 1990s, often through immersion programs, many empirical studies aimed to quantitatively compare Afrocentric and traditional schools' student achievement data (Kifano, 1996; Manley, 1997; Murrell, 1993; Webb, 1996). Other studies conducted in the 1990s, including work done by Archie (1997), Hopkins (1997), and Webb (1996), qualitatively explored the benefits of Afrocentric schools for Black students.

Meanwhile, the second wave of Afrocentric educational research is found in 21st-century studies. These studies reflect contemporary issues, including charter school designs, curriculum relevancy, parent satisfaction, and modern modes of implementation such as hip-hop (Gbaba, 2009; Ginwright, 2004; Mitchell, 2003; Murrell, 2002; Piert, 2006; Rayford, 2012; Sanders & Reed, 2005; Shockley, 2003, 2011; Traoré, 2002). These studies provide a comprehensive overview of Afrocentric schools, specifically within qualitative research methods. Yet, since our research is positioned over 2 decades into the 21st century, there are additional educational issues that many students face today that must be considered—such as high-stakes assessments and zero-tolerance discipline policies. Also missing in educational research are varying perceptions of Afrocentric education, specifically among students and teachers (Sharma, 2010). In addition, there is a void in current research regarding Afrocentricity's role as education as self-healing power. Since traditional public schools racially neglect students of color, it is important to actively seek educational models more inclusive of non-White cultures and perspectives.

Overall, the literature conveys that Afrocentric schools are created in direct response to the ineffectiveness of traditional school models in serving African American students. These schools, however, are not limited solely to African American students. Afrocentricity, both in theory and in school design, is the preeminent form of humanistic inclusion. Yet there is little research that has shown how these schools can benefit diverse student populations. Therefore, more research must be conducted in this area in order to better understand Afrocentricity's role in mediating self-healing and restoration. Appendix M explains the process of creating a qualitative research design and discusses sampling, data collection, and data analysis procedures in order to understand how Afrocentric schools can be used to systemically address hegemony and miseducation.

CHAPTER 4

Asa G. Hilliard Academy

In order for us as poor and oppressed people to become part of a society that is meaningful, the system under which we now exist has to be radically changed. This means that we are going to have to learn to think in radical terms. I use the term radical in its original meaning—getting down to and understanding the root cause. It means facing a system that does not lend itself to your needs and devising means by which you change that system.

—Ella Baker, "The Black Woman in the Civil Rights Struggle," 1969

One cannot expect positive results from an educational or political action program, which fails to respect the particular view of the world held by the people. Such a program constitutes cultural invasion, good intentions notwithstanding.

—Paulo Freire, *Pedagogy of the Oppressed,* 1970

The previous chapter explained the current status of Afrocentric education today and the ways in which this book offers new understandings of education's role in promoting healing and restoration. This chapter is divided into three parts. The first part provides narrative information about the study's case: Asa G. Hilliard Academy (pseudonym), or AGHA. The nature of this research study requires a thorough description of Afrocentric learning environments. This section thus relies on field notes and observations to descriptively depict the atmosphere of AGHA. The second part of the chapter provides demographic and background information on the 20 individuals who participated in the study. As noted, four teachers, one administrator, and 15 middle school students were involved. We felt it important to present descriptions of the research participants, specifically their educational experiences and tenure at AGHA, in order to properly frame their responses.

The third part of the chapter presents an overview of the six major themes and subthemes that emerged from the data. Afrocentricity is the theoretical framework used to guide data analysis. This perspective allowed for more in-depth understanding of nontraditional educational paradigms and frameworks. An Afrocentric theoretical framework also allowed cultural identity and race to be at the forefront of discussion. These student and teacher interviews demonstrate the distinctive differences that AGHA exhibits at the pedagogical level, in comparison to other school models. Data were organized based on the two research questions and categorized into major themes. The themes represented reflect the lived experiences of teachers, students, and one administrator attending an urban private Afrocentric school. The six themes that emerged helped to encapsulate the larger theme of the book: education as self-healing power. These themes include:

1. Unique Environment: "This School Is Just Different"
2. Support System: "A Close-Knit Community"
3. Morning Devotion: "Spiritual Encouragement in an African Worldview"
4. Black Education: "Every Day of the Year"
5. Reframing Afrocentricity: "Centering the African Child"
6. Restorative Education: "Promoting Positive Black Identity"

ASA G. HILLIARD ACADEMY

As noted earlier, AGHA is a self-described pre-K through 8th-grade Afrocentric private school located in a large metropolitan city in Georgia. The 2014 student achievement scores reflect the most recent school data. Figure 4.1 presents the results from the Stanford Achievement Test and the Otis-Lennon School Ability Tests. Students' scores were compiled by grade and averaged.

Overall, the average achievement percentages for AGHA were 77% in reading and 70% in mathematics in 2014. The noticeable decline in the 8th-grade mathematics score was reportedly due to high turnover ratings for advanced-level mathematics teachers for older grades.

To provide additional contextual information, Figures 4.2 and 4.3 provide past achievement data from AGHA in 2007 and 2012, respectively.

These graphs help to illustrate student achievement at AGHA, which is the primary focus for this book. In 2007, student achievement was 93% in reading and 89% in mathematics. In 2012, student achievement was 73% in reading and 63% in mathematics. AGHA experienced an observable decline in the 2012, most notably due to changes in school leadership and administration. In 2014, the increase in student scores can be explained by improvements in the retention of teachers and the administrator. Although AGHA's scores have fluctuated from 2007 to 2014, due to teacher and administrator transience related to salary, these numbers still significantly outperform the surrounding school district.

The above figures demonstrate AGHA's achievement ratings and academic caliber. It is important to also capture the uniqueness of AGHA's

Figure 4.1. 2014 Asa G. Hilliard Academy Student Achievement Scores (K–8th grade)

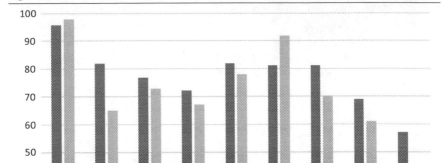

Figure 4.2. 2007 Asa G. Hilliard Academy Student Achievement Scores (3rd–8th grade)

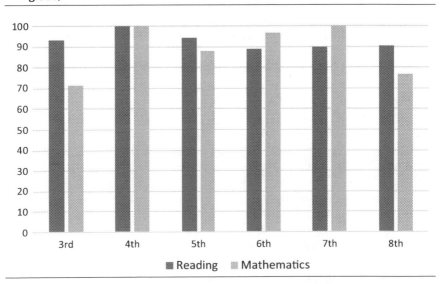

Figure 4.3. 2012 Asa G. Hilliard Academy Student Achievement Scores (K–8th grade)

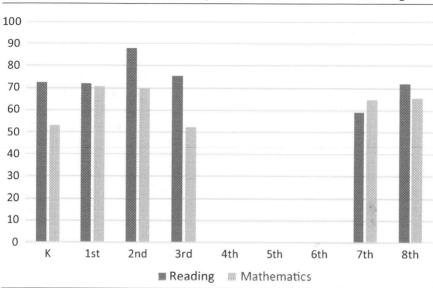

learning environment in order to better understand Afrocentric education. The distinction of Afrocentric schools is evident in the learning environment. Although the exterior of AGHA looks like a traditional school, its interior and décor illustrates the uniqueness of Afrocentric schools.

On first glance, Asa G. Hilliard appears to be a traditional school. Students wear navy and white uniforms, teachers are dressed in "regular" business casual clothes, and a yellow school bus is parked out front for student pick-up and drop-off. Students are clustered into grade groupings—K–1st, 2nd–3rd, and so on—and every Monday the school meets in the cafeteria for an assembly with the principal. Middle school students go to homeroom in the mornings and rotate classes for the rest of the day. Students have daily homework. Every Friday is "dress down" day, on which students are not required to wear their school uniforms. Like traditional schools, the Student Government Association (SGA) hosts "Spirit Weeks," where students participate in Hat Day, Pajama Day, Wacky Tacky Day, and the like, and classes go on local field trips if time and scheduling permit.

Yet despite the normalities that mirror traditional schools, AGHA has various distinctions that make it a unique learning environment for students and teachers. When a person walks through the front doors of Asa G. Hilliard, they will find a Pan-African flag and pictures of prominent Black role models displayed near the entrance. Pictures of Maulana Karenga, Carter G. Woodson, Martin Luther King Jr., W.E.B. Du Bois, George Washington Carver, and Harriet Tubman are framed and displayed in a lighted showcase accompanied by student work and projects on display for visitors to see. Immediately adjacent are the front office and receptionist desk, where various parent sign-ups, PTA notices, and field trip announcements are posted. Down the hall a bit further, a Nguzo Saba poster (see Appendix G) and other positive affirmation posters (see Appendixes H–K) hang side by side under a banner that reads "Student Expectations." The rooms on the main floor include Pre–K3 and Pre–K4, health, literature, and grammar classrooms, as well as a cafeteria. Down the hallway, a large multicultural "Freedom Quilt" hangs above the office, signifying the unity of all people, including African-descent people. Before entering the stairwell downstairs, a large display entitled "They Came Before Columbus" highlights Native American history and provides information on various Indigenous American tribes. The majority of the classrooms are housed downstairs, including K–1st, 2nd–3rd, science, mathematics, and a computer lab. Lockers run along the downstairs hallway, and more artwork, including a "Women in History" poster, lines the hallway. In an adjacent building, a large gymnasium, history classroom, counselor's office, and band room are held for 4th- through 8th-grade students. Overall AGHA's campus is relatively small, serving approximately 100 students. Yet it is evident that the culture of the school and its learning environment differ from traditional school settings. Through the school's Afrocentric focus, AGHA promotes right knowledge and corrective history—key features of an institution that stresses education as self-healing power.

PARTICIPANTS

Snapshots of the study's participants are presented in Table 4.1 (teachers/administrators) and Table 4.2 (students). We also provide brief capsules on each of the 20 participants, as well as some of their own words to capture them as individuals. This section presents teacher and administrator introductions first, followed by students.

Ms. Humphries

Ms. Humphries is a veteran teacher who has worked at AGHA for over 20 years. For 7 of those years she has been a lead classroom teacher. Before teaching at AGHA, she taught in the public school system. She currently teaches K–1st students. When asked to describe her typical day, she explains the multitude of activities and lessons she prepares for her students:

> My typical day consists of going over calendar skills with the children, discussing current events, the weather. Um, we're working on our language skills, which consist of phonics, writing, dictation, reading,

Table 4.1. Teacher/Administrator Participant Snapshot

Pseudonym	Role	Gender	Age Range	Grade(s)/ subject(s) taught	Years at AGHA	Taught in public schools?
Ms. Humphries	Teacher	Female	50s	K–1st	20	Yes
Ms. Saleem	Teacher	Female	40s	2nd–3rd	6	Yes
Mr. Griffin	Teacher	Male	30s	4th–8th history	5	Yes
Mr. Lacey	Teacher	Male	30s	2nd–8th technology and drama	7	No
Ms. Jeffrey	Administrator	Female	30s	N/A	2	Yes

math, science and social studies. We have lots of hands-on activities as well as written seatwork and then they have an opportunity to go to different centers, and have activities as well.

Ms. Humphries is well known around the school and somewhat of a legend within the AGHA family. She was one of the first teachers hired, and began teaching during the school's 2nd year of operation.

Ms. Saleem

Ms. Saleem has been teaching at AGHA for 6 years. Her child also attends Hilliard. Ms. Saleem teaches 2nd and 3rd grade across all subjects, and also serves as the French teacher for interested middle school students. When asked to describe her typical day, she provided a detailed overview of her daily and weekly schedule:

Ok, I arrive by 8 o'clock for most days. I come down to my classroom and prepare for today's lessons. I put work on the board, work in the centers, make sure that the area is clean and ready for the children. I pick my students up at 8:15 in the morning. We do devotion, which is wonderful . . . I pick the students up at 8:15; we come downstairs and start devotion, which is student-led. I have a leader, a reader, and a motivator. And then we do Black history, which is very integral to our day . . . Then after Black history, we have our bathroom breaks and come back into the classroom and we start with language arts on a typical day. We have reading/language arts, then we move into social studies, math, and science. I usually have my students all day . . .

except on Tuesdays. I do have an hour break when they go and sing in chorus. We have lunch at 11:30, and I sit in lunch with the students. After lunch we come back down for a little more language arts and or social studies, and I usually give them 30 minutes outside every day, because this age group really needs to get outside. And we go outside for 30 minutes, come back in, and then go back into our studies. And we work, well, until about 2:30, and then we get ready for our dismissal at 2:30, get their homework down, get their book bags, and then finally we dismiss.

Ms. Saleem reflects on how teaching at AGHA compares to other teaching positions she's held. Before teaching at Asa G. Hilliard, she worked for the local public school district. She shares that the school's curriculum flexibility allows for innovative lessons, meaningful learning, and nontraditional pedagogical methods:

> What I love about this school is I can be an "out the box" thinker. That's what actually took me out of public schools . . . The thing that's good about working here is that you can teach their core skills in many different ways, you can be out the box. You know, we did ordinal numbers the other day so I bought a scale and then we weighed all the children and then we put them in order by their weight. It was just out-of-the-box thinking where instead of just some random numbers, we used numbers that really meant something to them. That's what I like about AGHA.

Mr. Griffin

Mr. Griffin is a 4th- through 8th-grade history teacher who has been at AGHA for 5 years. He is one of the younger teachers, so many of the middle school male students look up to him in a very evident way. Aside from teaching, he is also the school's assistant basketball coach. When asked to describe his typical day, he talks about academics and extracurricular activities:

> Hmm, typical day. This year I just teach social studies, but I've taught social studies and I've taught math. I'm usually on cafeteria duty and I watch the kids in the mornings, greet them when they come in, and watch them until their teachers come and get them, which is usually between 8:15 and 8:30. Then at 8:30, I get my first class, which is usually one of the 7th- or 8th-grade classes. They're split up into two groups. So I usually get the 7th- and 8th-grade class. After school on Wednesdays, sometimes the kids have basketball practice. I'm also an assistant coach for the basketball team.

In comparison to his teaching positions at other schools, Mr. Griffin likes the added autonomy he has in his classes. Like Ms. Saleem, he enjoys the flexibility and independence gained from a private atmosphere:

> I like the autonomy that I have. When I first got here, it was my first full-time teaching position, and I didn't expect for my principal to have so much faith in what I was doing . . . I had worked in other schools and other programs where the administration would want to know exactly what you're going to say . . . I like the fact that they trust me to teach the way that I want to teach. And teach in a way that feels comfortable for me . . . And it's been like that ever since I've been here, and I haven't had any problems in that way, so I like that.

Mr. Lacey

Mr. Lacey is a "jack of all trades" teacher who is integral to the learning environment at AGHA. Outside of work, Mr. Lacey is a devout community performer and storyteller, which is evident in his teaching style and extroverted methods. He has been teaching at AGHA for 7 years and has taught only in Afrocentric school settings. When asked about his typical day, he shared:

> [Laughter] I am everywhere, but for the most part: Monday, I'll have 7th- and 8th-graders and we'll do health . . . And then after that, I will have the 5th- and 6th-graders and I'll work with either health or drama, depending on the schedule. From there, I'll have 2nd and 3rd grade. And I'll have them for computer [technology class] and I work with them on different basic computer fundamental skills. We've actually been participating in the stock market game this year, which is exciting. Then I have the 4th-, 5th-, and 6th-graders again for computer [technology class]. So if I have a class twice, I have them once for health, and if I have them again, I'll have them for computer technology.

Mr. Lacey explains that he was drawn to Afrocentric schools because of the flexibility and the ability to use nontraditional teaching methods. He believes drama and the arts are important for student learning.

Ms. Jeffrey

Ms. Jeffrey is the school's administrator, and currently serves as principal. She has been at Asa G. Hilliard for 2 years, and was hired by the school's founder to help run day-to-day logistics and to meet the school's growing needs. Since she is the study's administrative participant, her day-to-day schedule is unique to her role within the school community. She shares:

Well, I come in . . . and make sure that I greet all of my students and staff. And then the day begins. I talk to [the office receptionist], she runs down the day. We may [have] a special event or need to arrange correspondence with parents. I usually observe classes and evaluate teachers. That's a typical school day, I guess. I don't have many discipline problems, so that's something I don't have to deal with too much. But if I do, then of course, I just kind of deal with the students as they come in the office.

Before serving AGHA as principal, Ms. Jeffrey was a former teacher and instructional coach in the surrounding public school district. Although she is one of the newer faculty members on staff at Hilliard, she has over 10 years of prior experience in the public school system.

Table 4.2. Student Participant Snapshot

Pseudonym	Gender	Age	Grade	Years at AGHA	Attended another school?
Aaron	Male	12	7th	7	Yes
Bryson	Male	13	8th	9	No
Cameron	Male	12	7th	7	Yes
Daphne	Female	12	7th	9	No
Enoch	Male	13	8th	1	Yes
FeFe	Female	12	7th	7	No
Garrett	Male	14	8th	8	No
Hannah	Female	12	7th	9	No
Ian	Male	14	8th	5	Yes
Jacob	Male	13	7th	1	Yes
Kelsi	Female	13	8th	3	Yes
Lily	Female	12	7th	1	Yes
Madeline	Female	13	7th	1	Yes
NaShawn	Male	14	8th	2	Yes
Oakleigh	Female	12	7th	2	Yes

Aaron

Aaron is a 7th-grade student who has been attending AGHA since preschool. He describes a moment when he left for 2 years—3rd and 4th grade—in attempts to "[try] a new experience" at a larger public school, "but eventually came back." His personal interests include soccer and marine biology, in which he hopes to pursue both of his dreams. When asked to reflect on his daily school routine, Aaron describes the following events in a "typical day at Asa G. Hilliard:"

> I talk to people, socialize, and I do work, then um, we'll have P.E. on Tuesdays and Thursdays and on Fridays, um, we have art classes. And yeah, Monday through Thursday have our core classes, so we'll have like drama, health, P.E., literature, grammar, math, science, and history. And on Fridays, we have French, art, and we have a class with our counselor.

Bryson

Bryson is an 8th-grade student who has been attending AGHA his entire academic career. He started attending Asa G. Hilliard in preschool. Bryson has ambitious dreams of becoming an entrepreneur because of the apparent need within the Black community. Bryson's expressed interest in the Black community comes from an interest in helping people. He demonstrated, more than once, his desire to change the world. When asked to describe a typical day at Asa G. Hilliard, he describes the following events:

> Ok, well a typical day, first we would go to [literature], um, I would probably, I would get somewhat frustrated if we would have to write a paper that day, only because I'm not that good at writing. Um, next would be either have um, [drama] or [history]. Mr. [Griffin] is Wednesday through Friday and Mr. [Lacey] is Tuesday.

Cameron

Cameron is an energetic 7th-grade student who has been at AGHA for 7 years. For preschool, he lived in another city and attended Catholic school. Cameron is a self-described class clown who loves to make his peers laugh. Cameron appreciates the social aspects of school, and describes "hanging out with friends." He notes:

> So it's like a twenty-minute drive so . . . I wake up around 5:30, get dressed and wake up my mom around 6:45. We leave and we get here around 7:20. Then I wait for the rest of my friends to get here. So, um, a typical day for me is hanging out with my friends and that's pretty much it. And just learn . . .

Although his peers describe him as silly, many teachers consider Cameron a leader throughout the school. Cameron is also a known vegetarian who enjoys explaining to his classmates why certain foods are "unhealthy" for them and/or the environment.

Daphne

Daphne is a 7th-grade student who has attended AGHA for 9 years. When asked about her long tenure, and being only in the 7th grade, she explains that she started in Pre–K3 and Pre–K4 before kindergarten. Daphne is an outspoken, poised young lady who has dreams of becoming a zoologist because of her interest in biology. She describes loving to watch Animal Planet at home, and thoroughly enjoys biology and life science. When asked to describe her typical day, she states:

> Um, well usually our first class will be literature and on Monday. We'll
> have it for an hour and a half, and on maybe Tuesday will have it
> for just an hour and then we go to either history or math, and we go
> homeroom later and then we go straight to lunch. And after lunch, we
> go to health, and then history again. Or we'll go to . . . health, or then
> we go to science and or band.

Daphne is a proud big sister whose siblings attend AGHA as well.

Enoch

Enoch is a quiet 8th-grade student who recently transferred to AGHA from a nearby private Christian school. When asked about transferring schools, he asserts that "the academics were better [at AGHA]." When asked about his typical day, he gave a brief description: "I come in here, I probably go to homeroom, Devotion, we sing and state poems. Every day they give us a speech on Africa. Then, I go to my first class and get started on work." After college, Enoch has plans of becoming a chef because he "loves to cook."

FeFe

FeFe is an energetic, bubbly 7th-grade student who has attended AGHA her entire academic career. FeFe's favorite class is literature because of her interests in reading and writing, with her favorite author being Maya Angelou. She describes her typical day as consisting of "rotating" schedules:

> Um, mostly um, we go to our lockers and then after that we go to
> homeroom. So then we do Devotion and [my teacher] tells us what
> announcements we have. And then, we go to our couple classes um . . .
> We'll have something different on like Mondays and Wednesdays. On
> Monday and Wednesday we'll either have Mr. [Lacey] or Mr. [Griffin],
> then we'll have literature then science, then lunch. And then, math,
> then music, then science again.

FeFe has dreams of becoming a physical trainer after she graduates.

Garrett

Garrett is an 8th-grade student who has attended AGHA since kindergarten. His best friends are Cameron and Ian, and they typically are seen together at lunch and throughout the day. Garrett provided commentary on his typical day at AGHA: "My typical day, um, usually I stay in the cafeteria and we start Devotion. Where we um, we first state *The Seven Principles of Nguzo Saba*, and then we, um, say a list of poems." Garrett's favorite class is history. This is evident throughout classroom observations and in his interview. Garrett beams with excitement whenever his classmates talk about history, or when they want to engage in historical debates with him. He describes his interest in history and Mr. Griffin's class:

> Um, history's never been a challenge for me because um, I've always had a love for history, like when I had a chance to read, I'd read about like, people, Mahatma Gandhi, Malcolm X, people like that. But um, there's not really a challenge for history so my teacher, um, gives me extra assignments . . . When we go to history class, I feel it's on a way higher pedestal because like, um, our teacher is very free. Like, if we're talking about another topic, he can talk about a topic that relates. Maybe we're talking about the Civil Rights Movement, he can talk about a personal story in his life that probably affected him and made him like, appreciate what we did, what happened in the Civil Rights Movement. Um, and basically the reason why we're here today, like why he appreciates that and how it applies to that story he just told.

Garrett has an interest in working in Congress when he grows up because he wants to better "run this country."

Hannah

Hannah is a 7th-grade student who has attended AGHA "since I was able to go here." She has attended Asa G. Hilliard for a total of 9 years, which includes starting in Pre-K3 and Pre-K4. She describes a typical day:

> Well, a typical at [Asa G. Hilliard] Academy would probably consist of a series of classes. My favorite of course would be um, literature and math. We stay in two buildings, on Mondays we stay in this building most of the time and for second to last period we go to the other building. And, it's a pretty good day.

Hannah has interests in becoming a veterinarian when she grows up because of her love for both dogs and cats.

Ian

Ian is an 8th-grade student who has been attending AGHA for 5 years. Before that, he went to a small private school in the city. When asked about his typical day, he shares:

> Oh, so when I first arrive at school, um, what I do is I go down to my lockers and I switch out the books I need for next class or put away my books or anything I don't need for any of the classes. Then we go to our first class, which is on Monday um, sex ed [education], and then after, after that we go to language arts and literature. Then we head from there to science, and then from science to math class, and then from math, uh, to music class.

Ian's favorite classes are mathematics and science; he hopes to become a mechanical engineer after graduation.

Jacob

Jacob is a 7th-grade student who transferred to AGHA this school year. Prior to Hilliard, he attended a well-known prestigious private school in the city. When asked about his recent transfer to AGHA, he shares that diversity at his former school was an issue. Jacob shares that a typical day at Hilliard consists of:

> Um, let's see, so morning either health, history or [literature] class, which is really fun. And all those classes, they have usually good discussions and stuff, stuff like that. And uh, after that is either science or math and those are my two favorite subjects, other than literature, because I love to write. And, I like math because, I'm just pretty good at it.

Jacob loves mathematics and has accelerated to one of the top math classes at the school. He has an interest in becoming an international marine geologist after graduation. He shares:

> I like languages and I like different cultures. At the same time, I'm really into geology and the study of rocks and uh, just under water because I feel like it can tell us the past, and some stuff in the past is just not as clear as it could be so, certain things could tell us the past, in, among rocks and certain things. Yeah, like that.

Jacob is also a devout vegan who, like Cameron, likes to share the importance of sustainable eating with his peers.

Kelsi

Kelsi is an 8th-grade student who has attended AGHA for 3 years. She
is the Student Government Association (SGA) president, and many of the
younger students look up to her. Before coming to Hilliard, she attended a
local charter school in the area. When asked about transferring to AGHA,
Kelsi admits that her former school "focused on behavior and disciplining
the children." When asked about her typical day, she shares:

> Um, so I usually go to all my classes, then I work on SGA, cheer
> practice and I do homework after school and then I help with the little
> children, then I usually go home or to soccer practice with my best
> friend [Daphne], who also goes here.

After graduating high school, Kelsi plans on becoming a marine biologist or
journalist.

Lily

Lily is a new 7th-grade student who transferred to AGHA this year from a
local public school. She expresses that transferring was a "big change," and
likes Hilliard, "because it is more hands-on and I understand [things] better.
But at [my old school], it was just you would either got it or you don't."
When asked about her typical say, she shares: "Um, my typical day is I go
to all my classes, then I have cheer practice, sometimes I have dance practice, sometimes I'll have SGA meetings, different stuff of that nature." Like
Kelsi, Lily is also an SGA representative and likes helping people. After high
school, she plans on becoming a dental hygienist or orthodontist.

Madeline

Madeline is a new 8th-grade student who recently transferred from a public
school in Florida. She admits that AGHA is the smallest learning environment she has been in, but she enjoys it because of the teachers. When asked
about her typical day, she provides great detail about how the school is
organized each day:

> Well, um, we go a lot of classes. We have after-school programs that
> are also provided . . . So when I first walk in, we usually go sit in the
> cafeteria 'cause that's where we usually go. Sometimes I might go
> downstairs to get my books for the first period class. The first period

we have homeroom, it was like, we say our Devotion and then that's when we split up to go to classes. We have 7A and 7B. Um 7A is with 8A. Then they split all the 8th-graders up so we're with 7A, 8A they're with 7B, 8B. Um, Monday through Tuesday, we have health and then the rest of the week, for the first period we got history. So on Monday, we go to health then we spend like 30 minutes in there, then we go to [literature], we go to science, and then we eat lunch and have homeroom. And we go to math, and then we go to band and on Monday, we have five classes. On Tuesday, we have six classes, so it changes up. And then, that's when we also have to bring our band materials to school for band practice.

Madeline's favorite class is literature because she really enjoys books. Her favorite so far is Maya Angelou's *I Know Why the Caged Bird Sings*.

NaShawn

NaShawn is an 8th-grade student who transferred to AGHA last year from St. Louis, Missouri. He describes transferring to Hilliard as "different" because it is much smaller than his previous school. When asked to describe his typical day, he shares: "When I get to school um, we first get together, we do Devotion in the morning to uh, lift our spirit up each day, even if we're going through something at home. Then we, uh, go to class." NaShawn is an avid break dancer often seen dancing in the cafeteria with his friends gathered around. When asked about his dreams after high school, he said he desires to be an entertainer.

Oakleigh

Oakleigh is a 7th-grade student who transferred to AGHA last year. She moved from the suburbs into the city, and described the transition from public schools to a small private school. She enjoys the smaller environment, and likes how the curriculum focuses on topics that interest her. She compares the curriculum to her previous schools, and admits that in the public setting, "[Students] talk about what they had to do to pass or whatever." Instead, she describes that at Hilliard, "[teachers] go into lots of detail about other things and here, it's more of a free environment. Like you can talk about what you want to, or have a group discussion on something that you feel is very important." When asked about her typical day, she describes:

Well I usually, I just walk through the door and if I'm early enough, on Mondays we go in the cafeteria and then we have Devotion with everyone. And then if it's like a Tuesday or other days, when we go in the cafeteria and then we go downstairs and then we go to our lockers and go do Devotion in our class.

Oakleigh has plans to become an entrepreneur when she grows up: "I want to open up a business to help my community out."

THEMES

This third part of the chapter presents the study's findings that emerged from the participants' interviews, student essays, and field notes. Based on the interview questions (see Appendixes A–C), participants provided their perceptions and experiences of attending an Afrocentric school, and also elaborated on education as self-healing power. The collected narratives provided enriched descriptions that served as the primary source from which themes emerged. In order to be identified as a theme, at least half of the participants had to share that common experience. Themes were arranged and organized into categories during the data analysis process, and grouped according to their association with the two research questions. Teacher, student, and administrator data were analyzed using the same emerging themes, in order to capture each unique component's role within one cohesive study. After themes were analyzed, subthemes were also identified for more in-depth perspectives within the data. In order to be identified as a subtheme, at least three to four participants had to share an experience (see Table 4.3). The process of constant-comparative analysis allowed for continuous review throughout the data analysis process. All new themes that emerged were aligned with the corresponding research question (see Figures 4.4 and 4.5). The overall themes specifically highlight the participants' experiences at AGHA, which is an Afrocentric school. Six primary themes and subthemes emerged:

1. Unique Environment: "This School Is Just Different"
   Subthemes: Comparison to Other Schools; Engaging Classes;
       Difference in Curriculum; Diversity Issues
2. Support System: "A Close-Knit Community"
   Subthemes: Builds Character; Challenges Us to Do Our Best
3. Morning Devotion: "Spiritual Encouragement in an African
   Worldview"
   Subthemes: Affirmation; Motivation
4. Black Education: "Every Day of the Year"
   Subthemes: Precolonial History; Contemporary History
5. Reframing Afrocentricity: "Centering the African Child"
   Subthemes: Black Imaging and Representation; Depictions of Africa
6. Restorative Education: "Promoting Positive Black Identity"
   Subthemes: Student Outlook; Sense of Self

In order to better capture each of the six themes' alignment to research questions, graphic organizers have been provided in the form of flow charts.

Table 4.3. Major Themes and Subthemes

Research Question(s)	Main category	Themes	Subthemes
1. What are the experiences of students and teachers at a high-performing Afrocentric school?	Student and Teacher Perceptions of AGHA's Climate and Learning Environment	Unique Environment: "This School Is Just Different"	Comparison to Other Schools
			Engaging Classes
			Difference in Curriculum
			Diversity Issues
		Support System: "A Close-Knit Community"	Builds Character
			Challenges Us to Do Our Best
		Morning Devotion: "Spiritual Encouragement in an African Worldview"	Affirmation
			Motivation
2. What role does education or "right knowledge" play in helping oppressed groups to heal from trauma or social, cultural, and psychological domination?	Collective Reflections on Afrocentric Curriculum and Pedagogy	Black Education: "Every Day of the Year"	Precolonial History
			Contemporary History
		Reframing Afrocentricity: "Centering the African Child"	Black Imaging and Representation
			Depictions of Africa
		Restorative Education: "Promoting Positive Black Identity"	Student Outlook
			Sense of Self

Figure 4.4 provides a pictorial example of how three themes aligned with the first research question: *What are the experiences of students and teachers at a high-performing Afrocentric school?* Additionally, Figure 4.5 provides an organized snapshot of the remaining three themes' alignment with the second research question: *What role does education or "right knowledge" play in helping oppressed groups to heal from trauma or social, cultural, and psychological domination?* All of the participants, including teachers, students, and the administrator, provided data that support the six themes that are displayed in Figures 4.4 and 4.5. Each participant, however, contributed unique perspectives based on their own personal experiences.

During the interviews, participants were asked demographic questions. In addition to obtaining background information, teachers and students were asked to provide an overview of their tenure at AGHA. Each

Figure 4.4. Themes and Subthemes (Question 1)

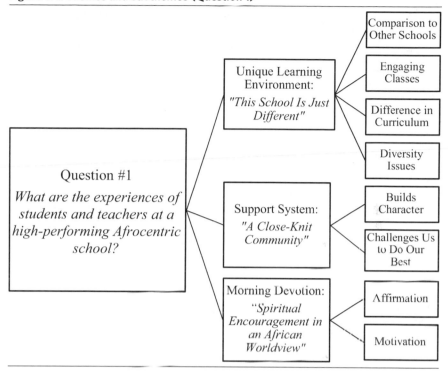

Figure 4.5. Themes and Subthemes (Question 2)

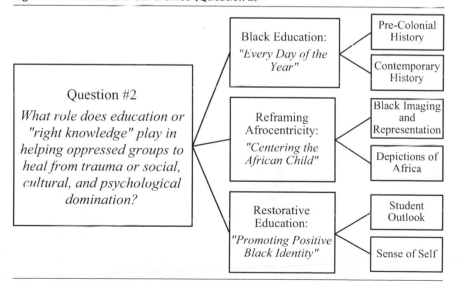

participant was also asked to elaborate on previous educational experiences in order to provide context for interviews and discussion. For example, students were encouraged to reflect on previous educational experiences. Additionally, teachers and the administrator were asked to provide information on prior teaching experiences. Gaining this demographic information allowed for constant comparison of AGHA's uniqueness with other learning environments. During the course of the interviews, participants began to offer a more critical, in-depth description of their Afrocentric education.

SUMMARY

The first part of this chapter captured a description of AGHA's learning environment. The second part provided demographic information about the participants, including students, teachers, and the administrator. In the third part of the chapter we have presented an overview of the six major themes and subthemes that emerged from the data. In a brief overview of participant snapshots, it is evident that AGHA offers a distinctive place for learning. In relation to the participants' specific perspectives and perceptions of AGHA, the next two chapters discuss this in greater detail. The first three themes, which are related to the first research question, are presented in the next chapter.

CHAPTER 5

Teachers' and Students' Perceptions of Afrocentric Schools

I believe unconditionally in the ability of people to respond when they are told the truth. We need to be taught to study, rather than believe, to inquire rather than to affirm.

—Septima P. Clark, 1975

As it is presently constructed for delivery in public schools from kindergarten through graduate school, the standard American school curriculum simply does not present the complete facts of history, literature, art, music, drama, science, or other aspects of America's diverse cultures. In particular, through omissions, distortions, and outright lies, Americans of African descent appear only negligibly in the history of national or global life.

—Barbara Sizemore, 1990

The previous chapter outlined the school site, Asa G. Hilliard, as well as students, teachers, and the administrator. Through their opening narratives, it is evident that AGHA is a unique place for learning. As discussed, AGHA teaches students using corrective history and nonhegemonic cultural information. In this regard, AGHA attempts to uncover education's self-healing power through positively venerating African and African American heritage. The following two chapters better outline the restorative role of education for AGHA students and teachers. More specifically, this chapter presents the major findings in relation to the first research question of the study: *What are the experiences of students and teachers at a high-performing Afrocentric school?* Themes emerged based on interview data, student essays, and field notes (see Figure 5.1). Figure 4.4 is re-presented here as Figure 5.1 in order to provide the organizations of themes related to this chapter.

The first emerging theme that emerged was the presence of a *Unique Environment*, which centered on statements from participants that described, "This School Is Just Different." In this regard, AGHA is different because it breaks the orthodoxy of White supremacy and cultural domination within

Figure 5.1. Themes and Subthemes (Research Question 1 Restated)

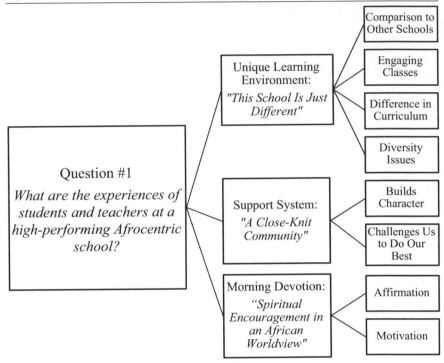

its curriculum and pedagogy. In relation to *education as self-healing power*, the overall school culture of AGHA incorporates African ontologies and epistemologies within its pedagogical design. To that end, the evidence of a unique communal atmosphere at AGHA is elaborated on through the participants' voices. Additional subthemes including *Comparison to Other Schools*, *Difference in Curriculum*, *Engaging Classes*, and *Diversity Issues* also provide context for participant's perspectives on Asa G. Hilliard's noticeably unique learning environment.

THEME 1: UNIQUE ENVIRONMENT:
"THIS SCHOOL IS JUST DIFFERENT"

When asked, "What is the most enjoyable aspect about this school?," the theme of AGHA's *unique environment* emerged from the data from all 20 participants. One student, Jacob, notes in his student essay that he enjoys how AGHA "is different." His rationale for the "unique environment" at AGHA stems from the school's sense of unity. He notes, AGHA "allows you to be yourself with self-knowledge and they encourage you to be better than your counterparts, but at the same time to be unified and to be together." The feeling of learning in a unique environment was not only important to Jacob; it was also evident in Hannah's response as well. Hannah describes in her one-on-one interview:

> Well, a lot of my friends say that their schools, there's a lot of um, like, fighting, and the teachers, they don't really care and they'll just be like "Get out," "I don't want you here," or they'll say stuff like that. But at this school, things of that nature don't happen here because of the environment. And the people at [AGHA] encourage you to be happy and ecstatic about learning.

In addition to student comments, teachers also provided descriptions of AGHA's unique school climate and learning environment. Mr. Griffin, the school's history teacher, provided comparative comments of AGHA with other schools. In regard to curricular and pedagogical flexibility, he notes:

> I have a lot more freedom here, um, my personal beliefs and ideas and principles are more in line with the mission of the school than with schools that I've taught in the past . . . I have more of a connection with many of the students and their parents and the faculty and staff here.

While Jacob, Hannah, and Mr. Griffin's narratives provide an introduction to the theme of AGHA's unique environment, additional students described detailed accounts of how the school differs from other learning settings. The theme of "This School Is Just Different" is divided into four subthemes: *Comparison to Other Schools*, *Difference in Curriculum*, *Engaging Classes*, and *Diversity Issues*.

Comparison to Other Schools

The participants were able to articulate how they viewed the learning environment at AGHA, and many mentioned specific comparisons to other learning environments, including both public and private schools. To start this discussion, it is appropriate to begin with Aaron, a student who transferred to Hilliard from another private school. He states that, "People are friendlier here . . . and um, the education to me is better." Aaron continues to describe the learning component of AGHA in comparison to his former school:

> 'Cause when I went [to another school], like I was ahead of everybody. And sometimes, people there were probably like a grade older than me but um, education here is better. I get more help. Um, I know that I actually have people who trust me, who have my back.

Aaron's observations comparing Hilliard to another private school yield noticeable differences in learning environment and teacher compassion. He continues by describing the academic rigor of AGHA, which is another observable difference:

> When I transferred from [AGHA] to the other school, um, I was pretty much ahead of my class. So like, they put me, since it was elementary school, they didn't have advanced classes so I went to a grade ahead for class sometimes.

Another transfer student, Cameron, also comments on the accelerated learning found at AGHA:

> I know a lot of kids who went here and then once they leave they went to a public school, they would be top of their class, honor roll. It's an accelerated school I feel like. Some kids in here feel that [they] are just not intelligent, but once you go out into the "real deal," you see that actually compared to the rest, you're really, really smart. So I feel like it really is accelerated and it really helped me with academics and stuff like that.

In addition to Cameron's description of the accelerated learning environment, which is discussed in another theme within the study, students also describe their academic growth. Ian, an 8th-grade student, describes how his writing abilities have transformed since attending AGHA:

> Um, oh yeah, when I first came here, I had extreme struggles with writing . . . Yeah and they really helped me with that. And now, my writing is, well my teachers say and my parents say it's phenomenal, the way I write now compared to the way I did [before]. So I feel that it's really helped me especially also with math. I was having some extreme struggles with math and they've really, they've really helped with that as well.

Like Ian, Jacob, a new student who has attended Hilliard for only a year, extends the conversation on the unique environment found at AGHA to include cultural aspects as well. He recently transferred from a prestigious private school in the local area and mentions:

> I transferred here mainly for the like, I thought it was a like a better place for Black people to learn than [my previous school], because [my previous school] wasn't really set up to teach us. It was kinda, they just kind of just dealt with us and that wasn't really the best

way to learn to because you were kind of like an afterthought all the time.

In addition to Jacob, two additional transfer students, Lily and Kelsi, provide descriptions of AGHA's learning environment. Lily, a 1st-year transfer student, notes that AGHA "is more hands on, and I understand the material better but at [my previous school], it was just you would either got it or you don't." Another student, Kelsi, shares her unique academic journey in her written essay. She notes how she transferred to AGHA, as well as to another school:

> I went here for 3 years, left for 3 years, and came back this year. Well at my last school, they literally got rid of every 8th-grade teacher they had. They completely replaced the 8th-grade staff. And often the new teachers at the school would come in and be so focused [on] behavior and disciplining the children that they didn't get much education across. My mom thought [AGHA] was a very good place for education so she brought me back.

In addition to student narratives, teachers also commented on how AGHA compares to other schools. Whereas students provided reflections on their past school experiences, Mr. Griffin describes how AGHA students excel after they graduate and matriculate into high school. He most notably attributes this to the rigorous learning environment at AGHA. He notes:

> Seeing [students] go to another school and applying it to a different environment. When I hear parents tell me you know, my child is in their history class and they're able to explain this better than the teachers or better than some of the students, you know and that sort of thing. It makes me feel good to know.

This sense of "uniqueness" within AGHA's learning environment was evident throughout student narratives, especially when comparing previous schooling experiences. However, the subtheme of *Comparison to Other Schools* led to other related, but distinct, subthemes pertaining to AGHA's learning environment, including *Engaging Classes*, *Difference in Curriculum*, and *Diversity Issues*.

Engaging Classes

Many participants describe the engaging pedagogy at AGHA. In relation to the overall theme of *Unique Learning Environment*, students specifically described how class lessons were "different" and "fun." One student, Lily, describes her classes as "fun and enjoying and instead of [teachers] like teaching and being all boring, they'll kind of make the subject fun and energetic with class, so I like that." Another student, Daphne, also describes the relevancy of classes and especially attributes this to her teachers:

> I mainly enjoy how the teachers interact with the students 'cause we don't exactly focus on one thing. Like we'll focus on, so let's say we'll do one thing Monday and it will branch out to multiple different subjects, and then later it will all relate to the next topic. So we just keep moving from where we start.

The school's administrator, Ms. Jeffrey, captures the importance of engaging classes from a school faculty perspective. She describes:

> I like to see the children talking and being involved in their learning . . . that's what I want to see. That's what I do see, what I don't want to see is um, the same thing over and over again. I want them immersed in new ideas, new thoughts and have the opportunity to create and make something, you know . . . more application.

To support Ms. Jeffrey's comments, one 7th-grade student, FeFe, describes an interactive technology class lesson with Mr. Lacey. As a veteran student, she notes how class lessons at AGHA are unconventional and "fun":

> Mr. [Lacey], he's the P.E. teacher, computer teacher, drama teacher, he is everywhere. He does this thing to where he tells stories . . . He comes, he dresses in full African clothing, put his hair [locs] up crazily and then he'll bring a drum. And he'll tell an African story like, um, about the river or something, like something about how they took us away from Africa. He'll sing a song, he'll have dancing. It's interactive and fun, basically. Because the stories are good. I mean, it's not like he just read a book and he's like, ok I'm going to tell you guys this. He actually does interactive stuff to actually get you into the story. He doesn't just say, bang a drum a couple times and then just read and sit there all relaxed sleeping and stuff. He's actually interacting with you.

Another student, Daphne, also describes AGHA's interactive pedagogy:

> I know last year we did a whole skit about how back in time, when they did everything. We talked about the Australians. We talked about Angela Davis [and] Maya Angelou. We talked about all those people,

and really um . . . they inform us about Black history through different skits. 'Cause I know we've done a skit where it was like, it was a child in a new environment and we had to teach him and they studied the subjects and how [AGHA] relates to people.

Similar to FeFe and Daphne, Jacob describes the engaging classes at AGHA. More specifically, he describes his history class with Mr. Griffin. He notes that class lessons expand beyond rudimentary textbook reading; rather, they are conversational and interactive. Jacob describes:

Um, I mean in history class, our teacher does a really good job of going out of the book and just talking to us about different things and how they correlate with us and how, the importance of what we're doing to what we're learning.

Overall, students and teachers described classroom learning as engaging, fun, and interactive. Some prevalent pedagogical strategies that surfaced throughout participants' descriptions included dramatic recreations, skits, and overall lessons that expanded beyond textbook memorization. To that end, participants described AGHA's engaging classroom pedagogy within the larger theme of *Unique Learning Environment*. In addition to classroom pedagogy, participants also described AGHA's unique curriculum. Thus, the following section discusses the study's next subtheme: *Difference in Curriculum*.

Difference in Curriculum

In addition to the difference in classroom pedagogy, many participants also described the school's distinct curriculum. In fact, within the theme *Unique Learning Environment*, over 75% of the students provided specific feedback on the difference in AHGA's curriculum. Interestingly, this theme is supported in the narratives of both veteran and transfer students. Additionally, teachers described Asa G. Hilliard's unique curricular focus. It is appropriate to begin the discussion of the subtheme *Difference in Curriculum* with Mr. Griffin, who explicitly described the unique pedagogical focus of AGHA. He comments:

We definitely [use] a culturally centered curriculum, uh, a curriculum that allows students to explore themselves, explore who they are, and truth. Teach kids the truth. All of this watered-down way of, of speaking to kids because the media and the news and reality gives them the unadulterated truth, you know what I mean? And so we do the exact same [thing], but with culturally centered truth.

Mr. Griffin's sentiments are evidenced in the following field observation in Ms. Humphries's class. The kindergarten and 1st-grade class discussed Native American tribes in relation to European settlement. Similar to Mr. Griffin's comments, this lesson explicated forms of culturally centered curricula and "unadulterated truth" in a primary school lesson.

November 20, 10:20 am

Ms. Humphries led K–1st grade students in a discussion about the Wampanoag Native American Tribe. One of the students said that the English settlers helped the Native Americans—but before Ms. Humphries could say anything—children interrupted and said "NO! The Native Americans helped the settlers! They were there first!" Later in the lesson, Ms. Humphries asked, "What kinds of foods do you think the Native Americans ate who lived along the coast?" One of the students said corn. Another said fish. Ms. Humphries said, "Very good . . . why do you think they ate fish?" After about three tries, one of the students said, "Because they were near water and rivers and that means they were fishermen!" Ms. Humphries then proceeded to a lesson on how the Native Americans were resourceful and kind.

It is important to mention that the school's culturally centered curriculum, as Mr. Griffin describes, is not relegated solely to history classes. Rather, teachers at AGHA embed lessons on cultural diversity within various subjects. To that end, below is another field note from a foreign language classroom. The school's Mandarin teacher provided a cultural lesson on popular Eastern celebrations, in comparison to the students' knowledge of Western holidays.

November 13, 1:15 pm

The school's Mandarin foreign language teacher led the class through basic vocabulary drills. At the end of the oral lesson, students learned how to say popular holiday words in Mandarin (in observation of the upcoming U.S. Thanksgiving holiday). The students then had a discussion about various holidays celebrated in different countries. The teacher shared from personal experience and discussed with students popular Chinese holidays and celebrations. At the end of the lesson, the teacher led students in a brief lesson on ancient Chinese history and explained why certain holidays are still important in China. Students briefly debated why they thought various Western holidays were important to American culture. Students discussed the historical inaccuracies of Thanksgiving and the religious influences of Valentine's Day and Christmas.

The above vignettes capture ways AGHA's curricula attempts to provide comprehensive and culturally centered lessons. One student, FeFe, mentions how the curriculum at AGHA is useful and distinct. She notes, "When you get to another school they're not always going to give you the same information that I got here . . . So, it's different curriculum, different time period basically, and that's just the way it goes." Similar to FeFe, Garrett mentions:

> Definitely Black history and a different way of learning, different styles of education. Like, I believe like just the way we are taught here is way different from public school based on how the teachers teach.

Another student, Kelsi, also mentions Black history in her description of AGHA's curriculum. She notes, "Um, we do focus more on Black history than the average school." NaShawn, a transfer student, also mentions, "Well, what I like about this school is the history. This is the first school that I've been to that actually talks mostly talks about African Americans." It is important to note that Kelsi and NaShawn's description of AGHA's unique curricula is discussed in a later theme. Notwithstanding, their comments echo sentiments about the unique learning environment at Asa G. Hilliard. One closing comment from NaShawn also highlights how AGHA's curriculum is not only distinctive in relation to history and culture, but also in relation to social justice issues and current events:

> The school is very different . . . Let's say on the news, we see like Trayvon Martin, Michael Brown, Tamir Rice. It's really different 'cause we get to learn ok, we know he got shot and the police did this. And, if I'm at my other school, we talk about it and just believe what we hear. This school is like a detective. Like we see like, we should look up the facts when you know about what happened and try to piece it together.

NaShawn's depiction of AGHA's curricula, both in relation to African American history and current events, encompasses the school's unique approach to learning. Collectively, many participants note the central tenet of AGHA's unique environment is the focus on cultural issues and curricular diversity. In fact, general matters of diversity emerged throughout the participants' narratives. Thus, *Diversity Issues* is another subtheme that emerged, primarily from students. This is connected to the larger theme of *Unique Learning Environment*, as discussed in the following section.

Diversity Issues

Many students express that Asa G. Hilliard's unique learning environment is beneficial for them academically. However, in relation to social or extracurricular activities, some students provided a contrasting look into Asa G. Hilliard's small—or enclosed—school environment. Bryson, an 8th-grade student who has attended only AGHA, describes the school's uniqueness as a slight disparity. He notes this both in terms of the school's lack of sports and diversity:

> This school is different. One, we don't have a whole lot of sports . . . And then um, we don't have a lot of diversity. 'Cause we're all Black at this school. Or you're mixed, but if you're mixed you usually have, like, Black and something else.

Bryson's comments stem from the fact that 100% of AGHA's students and teachers are African American or multiracial. Cameron and Ian mirror Bryson's comments and describe some potential social disadvantages to a small environment. When asked what they disliked about AGHA, they each mentioned the school's small size. Ian, a multiracial student, comments that he would like to see more diversity at AGHA. He admits, "One challenge is that it's a really small school so there's not a lot of diversity here . . . And that's kind of a turn-off for me, you know, 'cause it's just the same thing all the time." Another student, Cameron, provides greater detail on the disadvantages of having minimal diversity:

> I would want it to be more diverse. Because I know a lot of kids here, and our parents love [AGHA] and I love [AGHA] too, but I feel like, it's, we've been kind of shadowed from the rest of the world, so we haven't been prepared. Like, for me, I've never heard somebody outside of my actual race call me the "N word" or something racist. I don't want that to happen to me but I feel like it's a part of the experience. Like . . . we've been sheltered. I feel like we've been sheltered from the real world and how we're actually going to be treated and I feel like that's what [AGHA] is supposed to be preparing us for.

Cameron's critique of Hilliard's lack of diversity comes with a fear of the long-lasting repercussions of isolation. He continues that there is a lack of racial diversity as well, which is a point of contention for him. In this regard, Cameron considers the lack of racial diversity as an unrealistic snapshot of the real world. Whereas he advocates for the sense of cultural pride within AGHA, he wishes that the student population would diversify to provide him with opportunities to position himself in various multicultural contexts.

In contradistinction to the above comments, some participants liked the school's demographics, especially in relation to the academic benefits. Mr. Griffin notes:

Some people may feel like, yeah, their child needs diversity. They want their child to be around more people and there are some parents . . . who've allowed their kids to go to various diverse middle schools and high schools and they said, "You know, that it was good for them." But the reason why they came here first was to have a sense of self first. So I believe in, you know, integrating and being one and being in a diverse environment, but only after you have an understanding of who you are. And so, I think some, some parents may not understand it in that order and so because of that they may feel like this, like this school may not be the best place.

Mr. Griffin's defense of the school's homogeneous population stems from research on self-knowledge and collective communal understanding (Akbar, 1998). Similarly, another student, Jacob, also defends AGHA's demographics. As a recent transfer student, he notes:

At [my previous school], the Black people kind of had to scrape for everything that we got and I started a group there called A.A.L., African American Leaders, because there was just a general void of African American knowledge that me and that the Black kids needed. [We] needed to have self-knowledge that the school wasn't providing themselves. So that's something that [AGHA] does. We don't have to stress or worry about ever getting.

As demonstrated in the teacher and student narratives, Asa G. Hilliard's community is observably unique. Whereas many students and teachers appreciate the school for its diverse focus, some students would rather have more diversity within the student body. To that end, the overall theme of *Unique Learning Environment* highlighted some strengths and limitations of AGHA for students. One strength found throughout participants' description of AGHA is the school's close-knit *Support System*.

THEME 2: SUPPORT SYSTEM: "A CLOSE-KNIT COMMUNITY"

When asked, "What do you like about this school?" and "What do you dislike about this school?" over 60% of participants described the school's close-knit community. Thus, the theme of *Support System* emerged, with the following two subthemes: *Builds Character* and *Challenges Us to Do Our Best*. The supportive close-knit community at AGHA is communal, which is a part of African cosmology (Asante, 1991, 2010; Karenga, 1984). Whereas Western education typically promotes individualism and competition, AGHA disrupts traditional models of education by valuing the role of communalism and collaboration for students. In this sense, the communal atmosphere helps to promote stronger interpersonal bonds and unity. This, in turn, disrupts negative stereotypes regarding Black disunity and competition (Akbar, 1998). Instead, AGHA promotes self-healing through the promotion of "umoja," or unity (Karenga, 1965).

It is important to note that this theme emerges more profoundly in student narratives. Cameron, a 7th-grade student, introduces this theme perfectly by describing the overall familial atmosphere at AGHA. He notes that AGHA "is actually a very family-like environment, so my classmates, most of them have been with me since Pre-K, so it feels like you're family. You're brothers and sisters." Although Cameron has attended AGHA for the majority of his educational career, even recent transfer students like Jacob and Enoch describe the supportive and communal environment at AGHA. A 1st-year transfer student, Jacob, describes:

> All right, for students, I feel like they're my siblings, um, older and younger. And, I feel like I can basically say anything to anyone . . . like, just tell them whatever I need to and yeah, I pretty much love everyone here. Everyone's really awesome. And the teachers, they're . . . like aunts, grandma, grandparents, and that.

Similarly, another 1st-year student, Enoch, notes in his written essay:

> All the teachers are accepting and friendly and help you cooperate and do the right things. They'll always be there for you, even if you don't understand something. You can call them and then they'll help you through. It's more than family. Because family is sometimes you're just blood relatives, but I would say [AGHA] is like a God family.

In addition to the transfer students' comments, the school principal also describes the supportive environment at AGHA. Ms. Jeffrey mentions, "We're a family, definitely . . . I think the elders being here and a lot of men are here helps. We do have a lot of boys here." Additionally, Ms. Saleem notes:

> I like that it's a family and that I know the children. I've known most of these kids since they were like three, four, five. You know, I've known them for a while. And, I know which kids have allergies, I know which kid, you know, responds best to a teacher being right there with them. I know which kid responds best if you give them space. So that's the good thing too and then the parents trust you, you know. And they know that you're not out to ever hurt their children . . . you want the best for the children.

Part of Hilliard's supportive environment is attributed to the shared responsibility among staff, teachers, and students. To that end, the following section highlights the subtheme *Builds Character*, which falls under the study's larger *Support System* theme.

Builds Character

November 21, 11 am

The cafeteria manager and head cook let a select group of middle school students help cook and serve the younger students for lunch. This was an embedded component of their Home Economics class. The younger students enjoyed seeing the "older kids." There was an evident sense of "community" between the younger students and older students. Some of the younger students clapped and cheered "YAY!!" when the older students served them their lunch.

This vignette describes an incident witnessed in the school cafeteria, which serves as an opening example of the *Builds Character* subtheme. Collectively, students and the cafeteria staff worked to prepare and serve the younger students during lunch. Whereas in traditional schools roles and responsibilities are compartmentalized based on job description, at AGHA, staff and faculty worked together. This became a routine almost every Friday in the cafeteria. Students fulfilled their Home Economics course requirements by cooking and serving the younger grade levels, demonstrating unity and collective responsibility (which are key themes in the Nguzo Saba).

Several students explicitly describe how the support system at Hilliard helps to build character. One of the ways is most vividly seen with the older students. Seventh- and 8th-grade students are the oldest in the school, and are required by administrators to "set an example" for younger children. Kelsi describes:

I like that the teachers are very family-oriented, the students are all nice, there's not bullying, everybody likes everybody. They're more like family than teachers 'cause I've known them for a while and when I go into class, it's more than just "Sit down and do some work." [Instead] it's "How was your weekend?" "What'd you do yesterday?" And we do that with the younger kids too, mostly in the mornings. We ask them how their weekend was and make sure they're okay. We are always taught to be an example for them 'cause they look up to us.

As mentioned, character-building is a subtheme of *Support System*. Like Kelsi, Daphne describes the importance of helping younger AGHA students, and connects it to the principles of Nguzo Saba:

Um, we learned kinship, and we learned how to be in touch with
the soul . . . It's like, um, the Kwanzaa word ujima, which means
collective work and responsibility. That's why they want us to be
helpful and to be leaders for the young kids. 'Cause we all have to
work to support each other.

Cameron also notices how the supportive environment at AGHA helps
to build character. He specifically describes how AGHA has helped his
growth and maturity. He notes, "I really appreciate [AGHA] for teaching
me and helping me become the man I am today." Kelsi shares how teachers
play a role in character development:

Teachers spend their time making sure that you get your education
and also that you build up your character the proper way because they
don't want you to turn out like being a crappy person just with good
grades.

On the other hand, even when students are not demonstrating positive
character, Daphne explains these moments are handled in a supportive way:

I think that [teachers] are strict for a reason. Because sometimes, if
we [tell] rumors and the teacher happens to hear about it, they'll sit
us down and they'll give us life lessons on how that can affect us in
the future. So they teach us things we can use later on down the line
as in life . . . they'll sit us down and we all come together and they'll
teach us that you have to be careful what you say and what you do
in life because that will cause you to later be affected you could lose
your job, lose friends, something could happen, you could really lose
something that's important to you.

In addition to Daphne's comments, Bryson shares that behavior and
character development are recognized among teachers and are rewarded
during school awards and superlatives:

If [teachers] want to give you a prize on a certain area like it doesn't
even have to be like a normal prize for like valedictorian or things
like that and grade wise, but like behavioral wise or effort wise or
um, anything really. They can choose things out of the blue which I
like because it shows that they actually do pay attention. They pay
attention to what you do and they're watching you and how you act.

Aaron also describes how this sort of character development is beneficial to his own personal development: "A lot of people here, they have my
back and stuff. Like, just in case I ever face any issues I know I have people

behind me and that are going to actually help me." In addition to emotional and social support, students talk about the academic benefits of AGHA's support system. Daphne describes how her close relationships with students and teachers has helped her excel academically:

> We always work together. I know sometimes after school, we used to have a study group, we used to all get together in one area of the room and we'd all work on one subject to make sure everyone understood. And that everyone knew what they were doing and I think that's also influencing and it helps enhance your education because you can learn from different points of view.

Daphne's comments on AGHA's supportive students and teachers help to highlight some of the academic benefits of school community. It is important to note that researchers posit the social and emotional importance of promoting holistic education for Black students (Evans-Winters, 2011; Hopkins, 1997). This promotes education as self-healing power. The next subtheme, *Challenges Us to Do Our Best*, explains the academic benefits in more detail.

Challenges Us to Do Our Best

In addition to character-building, the school's academic requirements are evidenced within the subtheme *Challenges Us to Do Our Best*. This is another subtheme that emerged from students' comments about AGHA's supportive school community, which helps to nurture education as self-healing power. One way that students felt AGHA was supportive was by providing accelerated and rigorous learning. Teachers are described as "challenging," and students are generally accepting of the school's academic rigor. Oakleigh, a 2nd-year transfer student, begins by mentioning the "higher standard" AGHA teachers hold their students to. She notes, "Well, because they have like higher standards, they push you to do more, because they know that you're capable of doing it. They just want you to let yourself know that you can do it. So that you can reach your highest points." Cameron adds that the teachers' high expectations help students excel. He notes, "The teachers are very intelligent and people I look up to . . . They challenge us to do our best. We have teachers that push us and that will force you to try." Cameron continues by describing the accelerated learning environment at AGHA:

> I know a lot of kids who went here and then once they leave then they went to a public school they would be top of their class, honor roll . . . I feel like it really is accelerated and um, it really helped me with academics and stuff like that . . . I know [the literature teacher], she gives us books and some of us assignments that 12th- and 10th- and

11th-graders would do so we will be ready for high school and
even college. I feel like the thing about it being accelerated is that it
prepares us for something bigger than where we are right now. So, if
we're in kindergarten then maybe we will learn some 2nd-grade things
and some 1st-grade things. If you are in 8th grade we would learn
some 9th-grade things, some 10th-grade things. I feel like that's very
important. There's one 8th-grader who's learning calculus.

One way that participants explain AGHA's supportive and rigorous environment is through the incorporation of critical thinking within class lessons.
Daphne notes:

[AGHA] is one of those schools that they require that you critically
think all the time. Because if you have a complicated question and you
just put down a one word answer and you need to explain it, there is
no way to explain it so you're constantly critically thinking here. And
I think that's very helpful in multiple areas.

Similarly, a transfer student, Kelsi, notes that AGHA is comparatively
more rigorous than her previous school. She describes, "This school's a lot
more challenging than [my previous school] and they put a lot more hard
work into the lessons than just finding them online and giving them to you."
Kelsi's description of AGHA's rigorous environment is directly related to
teacher care and effort. To summarize this subtheme, Mr. Lacey describes
why AGHA chooses to promote academic rigor for students:

You know what, the learning environment is very challenging, but I
like it because it's, it's preparing them for, you know, high school or
for, just for whatever environment they get put into. I think at the end
of the day, we'll, know that they will be prepared, because we are so
challenging here. And even it being an accelerated learning school, the
kindergartners they're doing work on the 2nd-grade level, 2nd grade
on 3rd-grade level, and so forth. And, at the same time, we still meet
the student wherever they are. You see what I'm saying?

Similarly, Mr. Griffin notes how AGHA encourages students to do their
best through instilling confidence:

I've seen students come in with low confidence and they're soaring
and they're doing amazing things and that's because being here makes
them feel like they belong to something. You know what I mean? So,
I think that's probably the biggest thing, is just confidence. Instilling
confidence in a lot of these students. Um, I think that's probably the
best way to, to ensure they have a stable future.

Students and teachers comment on Hilliard's supportive school environment. Students positively describe character-building and rigorous learning, which are important aspects of AGHA's school culture. Teachers describe how AGHA encourages students to do their best, which ultimately increases their confidence. Thus, the theme *Support System* captures the academic, social, and emotional benefits of AGHA's school environment. In many regards, the self-healing power of education necessitates a supportive school environment. As demonstrated in the participants' narratives, there are academic, social, and emotional benefits of a supportive school community. The next subtheme demonstrates a particularly unique component of AGHA's school day: morning devotion.

THEME 3: MORNING DEVOTION: "SPIRITUAL ENCOURAGEMENT IN AN AFRICAN WORLDVIEW"

The previous subtheme captured the supportive environment at Asa G. Hilliard. An observable evidence of AGHA's unique environment is found in Morning Devotion, which is our next theme. Devotion is a daily routine in which teachers and students gather together to recite positive affirmations and poems (see Appendixes G–L for examples). Devotion is not described as a religious practice, but rather one that connects to African spirituality and holistic education (Akbar, 1998). It is important to note that while spirituality embraces notions of the divine, it is not oppositional to other belief systems or worldviews. Ani (1998) asserts that spirit and matter have a symbiotic relationship. Spirituality, in this sense, is a cyclical process of being, remembering, and becoming. Even within ancient Kemetian spirituality, precolonial philosophy laid a foundation for future religions (Hilliard et al., 1987). Whereas organized religion has been a source of historical tension within African American history, as demonstrated in the transatlantic slave trade (Frazier, 1974), the Devotional session at AGHA allows for cultural continuity across different religions and philosophies. Here, education as self-healing power manifests in Devotion through a holistic appreciation for character development, positive affirmation, and motivation.

At Asa G. Hilliard, Devotion is held at the beginning of the day for 30 minutes. On Mondays, students participate in Devotion together as a collective school body in the cafeteria. During the rest of the week, Devotion is generally held in students' individual homerooms, although some days the school unites collectively. In more than half of the interviews, Devotion surfaced as an integral part of school culture at Asa G. Hilliard. Additionally, half of the new 1st-year students mentioned Devotion as an important part of their day. The following vignette provides a descriptive picture of Morning Devotion:

December 16, 9:15 am

Students, staff, and teachers gather in the cafeteria for a morning pep-rally. Students used rhythm and music to start chants and cheers. One of the poems was called "Power," which was led by an 8th-grade student. The rest of the staff and students joined in with the words:

> I have the power to choose, and that makes me a powerful person.
> I have the power to make the right choices.
> I have the power to choose to be honest.
> I have the power to choose to be kind.
> I have the power to ask my parents, caregivers, or teachers when I'm not sure what choice to make.
> I have the power!

The morning pep-rally ended with the Black National Anthem: "Lift Every Voice and Sing." This song was written by James Weldon Johnson.

Bryson provides an appropriate overview of what Devotion entails. He shares in his written essay, "We normally say: The Nguzo Saba, *The Seven Principles, The Ultimate Student, Can't, I Have the Power*, and *Nobility*. We also sing *Lift Every Voice and Sing* by James Weldon Johnson. Then we say our grateful moments or things that we're thankful for and that's usually it." Ms. Jeffrey, the school's administrator, also mentions that Devotion includes the acknowledgment of Black history: "Well, during Devotion, the children are able to read a Black history moment and then we tell what we're thankful for." Although it might appear trivial and ritualistic to outsiders, students and teachers recognize its importance. In fact, it is an embedded part of the school's daily routine. To that end, Madeline, a recent transfer student, notes, "Devotion is like the Pledge of Allegiance for us." Additionally, since devotion is often understood to have religious undertones, Mr. Griffin distinctively describes it as the school's "morning pep-rally." He adds:

> I know a lot of times people think about Devotion, they think of um, something that is of a religious nature. You know what I mean? This isn't a religious school or affiliated with any particular denomination. Students recite um, affirmations, so certain affirmations that are important to the school.

Several students highlight how Devotion shapes the rest of their school day. Aaron explains:

Saying Devotion makes me feel like I'm going to have a good day if, I'm not already in a bad mood. I try not to be in a bad mood, 'cause I don't like it. It puts like a bad flow energy into the air so I, it kind of helps me if I'm in a bad mood. I'll get into a good mood and, um, it says to me that I have something to stand for and live for. And I am something and I can be what I want.

Cameron also mentions the power of Devotion for saying daily affirmations. He speaks to the power that words have in fostering positivity: "Uh, Devotion's a very powerful thing for me." Likewise, Jacob, Hannah, NaShawn, and Garrett mention the benefits that Devotion brings, including providing daily affirmations. Jacob said: "I use it as a time for like, gathering my thoughts and internalizing the different affirmations that we do." Another student, Garrett, mentions that Devotion improves his self-esteem. He also adds that the poems and affirmations remind him that he is a "scholar." He explains that Devotion "informs you that you are a scholar and we have potential to be great and it basically says if we apply ourselves, we can like be future presidents." Student narratives such as these provide the long-term benefits of Devotion at AGHA.

Like the students, teachers and the administrator also believe Devotion is important. Their comments suggest that Devotion is significant not only for daily affirmation, but for shaping student identity as well. Ms. Jeffrey explains:

It's the most important part of the day. It's time for them to reflect, it's time for them to be thankful, it's time for them to get their minds, body and soul ready to receive any knowledge, or whatever they're going to receive for the day. We're clear about the expectation, you're trying to be an "ultimate student," and we say that so that you remember that you are the ultimate student, that you solve your problems, you don't cry over them. It's the "internalization" of positivity, you know?

Like Ms. Jeffrey, Ms. Saleem believes in the power of Devotion and its important role in the student experience at Asa G. Hilliard:

Devotion is key . . . Devotion is the opportunity for them to empower themselves and to say, you know, how important they are. Devotion, as I say to my students, is sacred, and it sets the tone of the day. If you're playing in Devotion, nine times out of ten you're going to play all day. You're going to be off task all day. But if you take Devotion seriously and you listen to what it, what you're saying and you digest that and you allow it to really become a part of you, then some of things that you see, the behaviors that you see will change.

Ms. Saleem speaks to the transformative power of Devotion for students and its long-lasting influence on student behavior. Ms. Humphries, a veteran teacher, is known throughout the school for her famous words, "Devotion is the most important part of the day." She asserts that Devotions serves as a daily reminder for students to become agents of change within their own lives and communities.

Throughout the participants' narratives, Devotion appears to be an important time to recognize and recite Black history, affirm positive identity, and cultivate positive behavior. Within this theme, the subthemes *Affirmation* and *Motivation* emerge to help capture the overall theme of Devotion.

Affirmation

Within the larger theme of Devotion, several students describe the affirming nature of the various poems and chants the students recite each morning. This promotes healing. Kelsi explains that her favorite part of the day is when she gets a chance to recite the poem *Nobility* (see Appendix H), which is said in Devotion. She states, "I like saying *Nobility* because it takes time to learn and by the time you learn it you've got the meaning of it." Another student, Jacob, also describes the role of affirmations in Morning Devotion:

> Uh, Devotion is a time set aside every day to kind of reflect . . . My favorite for me it's probably the Black National Anthem: *Lift Every Voice and Sing*, because it's just so much different from my, uh, from my last school and it's pretty cool too that our heritage is celebrated so much and so well here.

Teachers also acknowledge the positive affirmations within Morning Devotion. Ms. Saleem describes how various poems and affirmations from the morning devotion are restated throughout the day in her classroom:

> So, I can say that in the middle of the day . . . "I have the right to fail but I do not have the right to take other people with me." Think about it. And, I'm getting chills just saying that, but just to be able to say it throughout the day, you know, we could stop in the middle of doing a math project and I could say, "Who was the most important person?" "I am. This is my time and my place and I accept the challenge" [they respond]. Just to empower them. Sometimes it may be slipping and just to say that gets [students] back on task. Or if I tell my class "Excellence breeds, excellence, breeds, excellence, breeds, excellence." And you'll see those kids that really may not be on task, say [to themselves] "Let me get it together, my whole class is getting it together, let me get it together."

Similarly, Mr. Griffin also recognizes the importance of daily affirmations for students, especially within African American communities:

> I think maybe only one, two of the affirmations are what some might consider Afrocentric or was designed for particularly children of African descent. I think the other two are just positive in general. And so, what we hope that it does for the kids is number one, make them proud of who they are, make them proud of what they see when they look in the mirror, make them proud to be Black.

Similar to *Affirmation*, the Devotional time at the beginning of the AGHA school day is also seen as motivational for students. Thus, the following section details the next subtheme within the larger theme: *Motivation*.

Motivation

As mentioned, Devotion is an integral part of the school day at AGHA, so much so that this morning ritual connects to education as self-healing power, and emerged as its own theme within the study. In addition to being a source of affirmation, students and teachers find devotion to be motivational. One student, Bryson, describes his favorite poem, *The Ultimate Student* (see Appendix I), "because it always encourages me to be better at my schoolwork and what I'm trying to do and try to be the best at it." Similarly, FeFe describes her favorite song during Devotion, especially for its uplifting message in light of the tumultuous political and social climate. She states:

> Um, *Lift Every Voice and Sing* . . . I think it was [written] around segregation and basically what they were doing is he was saying lift every voice and sing as basically a song of hope for African Americans. So yeah, I think people need hope today, especially with Ferguson and stuff right now.

While Enoch could not identify a favorite poem or song, he describes how the entire Devotional routine is a source of motivation for him:

> In [Devotion], we sing and state poems. Every day they give us a speech on Africa. I guess what I like most is when we say what we're thankful for. . . . This helps and motivates me in my education because it encourages me to think "bigger" about myself.

Similar to FeFe, Mr. Griffin explains the importance of the collective devotion experience, especially in relation to motivating students:

[Students] say a couple of the affirmations, just kind of remind the students that they can be successful if they put their minds to it. Just to give them a sense of inspiration in the beginning of the day. Our hope is that what it does it just kind of puts them on the right foot. And they kind of remember these things as they're being examined, as they're being tested, as they have to ask and answer questions and you know, go through the whole academic process and they can kind of just reflect on these affirmations and hopefully that will give 'em, just kind of an edge.

Like Mr. Griffin, Ms. Saleem provides a detailed account of the effects of Morning Devotion, relating its positive influence on student behavior:

I had two young men that came in. They were new and at first they really weren't feeling Devotion. "I don't wanna do that, that's silly." But I started seeing them digest it. And it showed, it's showing up in their work. It's showing up in, when they're behaviors were corrected. They don't take all day to get it together, they're not melting down. They get in line because now it means something.

Students along with teachers describe the importance and influence of Morning Devotion. The participants' descriptions of devotion emerged continuously throughout the interviews. This important part of AGHA's school day helps to describe the uniqueness of the school's learning community. Each of the above three themes support the first research question: *What are the experiences of students and teachers at a high-performing Afrocentric school?* The remaining three themes are a response to the study's second research question, as demonstrated in the following chapter.

SUMMARY

This chapter presented the major themes and subthemes that emerged from the data in response to the following research question: *What are the experiences of students and teachers at a high-performing Afrocentric school?* The following chapter presents the major findings in relation to a second research question: *What role does education or "right knowledge" play in helping oppressed groups to heal from trauma or social, cultural, and psychological domination?*

CHAPTER 6

Benefits of Afrocentric Schools in Addressing Historical and Contemporary Trauma

To handicap a student by teaching him that his Black face is a curse and that his struggle to change his condition is hopeless is the worst sort of lynching.

—Carter G. Woodson, 1933/1977

Because you can't hate the roots of a tree and not hate the tree. You can't hate Africa and not hate yourself . . . You can't have a positive attitude toward yourself and a negative attitude toward Africa at the same time. To the same degree your understanding of and your attitude toward Africa becomes positive, you'll find that your understanding of and your attitude toward yourself will also become positive.

—Malcolm X, 1959

Chapter 5 outlined the educational perspectives of students, teachers, and the school's administrator at AGHA. As mentioned, the first three themes— *Unique Learning Environment, Support System,* and *Morning Devotion*— are integral components of teachers' and students' daily experiences at AGHA. These themes directly align with our first research question: *What are the experiences of students and teachers at a high-performing Afrocentric school?* The next three themes connect to our second research question: *What role does education or "right knowledge" play in helping oppressed groups to heal from trauma or social, cultural, and psychological domination?* These themes capture the participants' specific views on Afrocentricity and *education as self-healing power.* These themes include *Black Education, Reframing Afrocentricity,* and *Restorative Education and Black Identity.* Students, teachers, and the administrator provide collective insight into how Afrocentric schools foster healing and redirection for African American students (see Figure 6.1). Similar to the previous chapter, the themes in this chapter emerged based on interview data, student essays, and field

Figure 6.1. Themes and Subthemes (Research Question 2 Restated)

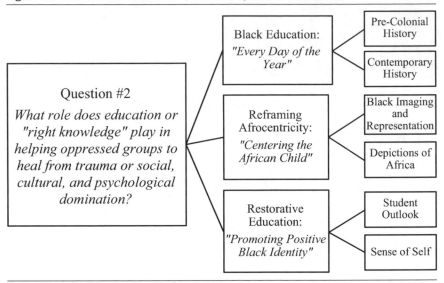

notes. Figure 4.5 is restated here as Figure 6.1 to help conceptualize the three themes related to this chapter.

THEME 4: BLACK EDUCATION: "EVERY DAY OF THE YEAR"

The first appropriate theme is *Black Education*, since it serves as the school pedagogical framework at AGHA. Students and teachers describe the presence of Black education "every day" at AGHA. This is an important point to distinguish. Considering that traditional U.S. curricula only marginally incorporate non-White history and achievements (Asante, 1991; Dei, 2012; Woodson, 1933/1977), students at AGHA receive corrective history every day. In this regard, students are exposed to the self-healing power of education within daily pedagogical practice. According to AGHA's teachers and students, the school promotes positive self- and group concepts, and promotes daily self-healing. Here to begin this discussion a more comprehensive understanding of Black Education is needed. To start, Ms. Humphries notes the incorporation of Black history and multicultural perspectives into lesson planning:

> Oh goodness, yes, every day. There's a book that we have, it's 365 days of our African American history and we read facts and they hear new things about something that happened. For example, today, [we] talked about the lady who um, was the first African American lecturer.

So they talked about how it was important for her to talk about education. Um, you know, she didn't necessarily agree with, you know, the "Back to Africa" movement; however, she thought that education was important. Um, so every single day.

As an instructor, Ms. Humphries describes methods of incorporating Black history into class lessons. But we again emphasize that Afrocentric education involves much more than history classes. The school's administrator, Ms. Jeffrey, comments on some misconceptions of Black education:

I think there's a misconception that we're actually not learning anything. That we're, you know, doing a lot of dance, maybe. You know African drumming. I hear a lot of that, "Do you do African drumming?" Like we do, but you know, that's not a class.

In addition to the stereotypical assumptions of drumming and "not learning anything," as noted by Ms. Jeffrey, another misconception is that students learn solely Black history. One student, Daphne, lists the classes that she takes at AGHA, each of which has a focus on Black and multicultural education. She describes in her written essay, "We take all the basics and we take extracurricular [classes] like art, drama, health, history, math, science, literature, grammar, media, computer, and foreign language." Note that within an Afrocentric curricular framework, students take traditional classes while antiracist and multicultural contributions are infused within the curriculum and pedagogy. One way to visualize the incorporation of Black contributions within history is in the following vignette of an art lesson:

October 27, 1:20 pm

A local artist from the community led middle school students in a discussion about 20th-Century Panel Art and took inspiration from Jacob Lawrence, a famous Black painter. (They studied Lawrence's paintings the previous Friday). The artist discussed the widespread impact of the Great Depression in the U.S. by examining Lawrence's "cubism" art style. Students engaged in a discussion about what they learned in U.S. history class about the Great Depression. Students raised their hands and shouted: "low wages," "The Dust Bowl," "famine," and "unemployment." The art teacher probed them further by asking students to consider how Lawrence's identity as a minority in the 1930s and '40s might have influenced his artwork. Students were left with an important takeaway: art reflects the historical movements of the time period.

This vignette details an art lesson that incorporates historical knowledge within the class lesson. To that end, Ms. Saleem continues the conversation on Black education and describes the pitfalls of many U.S. schools in relation to curricular content. Specifically in relation to Black heroes, she notes:

> [Students] should know so many more Blacks than, um, Martin Luther King . . . Which he is phenomenal, you know. Has been a forefront runner for all of us but, that light dusting of African American history that we're getting in public schools, if they went a little bit more in-depth. I believe if, if everybody knew what everybody has contributed to um, the world then we might be able to respect each other a little bit more, you know?

Like Ms. Saleem, Madeline also mentions how her perspective of Black education relates to content being factual and historically accurate. She too sees the advantage of all students learning the invaluable accomplishments of Black historical figures, who are often marginalized in mainstream curricula. She mentions, "In normal schools, I mean, they tell you but they 'sugarcoat' and they don't give you everything. So, um, [AGHA] has shaped my mind about African culture period because it's given you that outlet." Similarly, another student, Hannah, describes how AGHA's curriculum style has expanded her world outlook:

> [AGHA] makes me take a more broad look of a society and how I look at things so like um, it's, I think it's good to know that when you watch the news and you find out what's going on around the world . . . I know more about history, my own history, after coming to this school.

As mentioned in the participants' responses above, the Afrocentric educational framework of AGHA is unique to the school's culture. Within the scope of Black education, two subthemes emerged: *Precolonial History* and *Contemporary History*.

Precolonial History

Within the larger theme of *Black Education*, participants described specific historical time periods that were influential in their educational experience. The most evident topic that emerged in 100% of the participants' responses was *Precolonial History*. However, since it is situated under the larger scope of *Black Education*, it serves as a subtheme, not a theme. Here, "precolonial" most accurately describes the history of native and Diasporic Africans prior to colonialism. Whereas in most traditional schools African history is told solely through the lens of slavery or the Civil Rights Movement, AGHA is distinctive in that it recasts historical knowledge. Thus, since AGHA has an Afrocentric focus, students are exposed to knowledge and history prior to the cultural invasion of slavery and colonialism, which helps to promote healing. One student, Cameron, provides an opening argument to demonstrate AGHA's distinctive education. He notes, when reflecting on other schools, "They don't put in the important things about our people. They only have like one section that talks about slavery, when there's way more to slavery than just, you know." To that end, the importance of ancient precolonial history to participants was paramount. Participants continuously referenced the Nile Valley, Kemet (Egypt), and the ancient multi-genius Imhotep, especially when mentioning important aspects of Black Education. Aaron asserts, "At [AGHA] we've learned a lot about Egyptology. Um, our main thing that we learn about is Black history, or yeah, or the things from Africa." He continues to describe the systemic removal of Egyptian history from mainstream education, which is another distinctive trait of AGHA. He continues:

> You have the Nile River and how it developed into civilization, [the books] talked about some doctors, such as Imhotep, and other people and um, I learned about some Black history here today . . . Some of the movies only show like the bad part of Black people and things like that. My parents and [AGHA] teach me some of the great things and all these great historical figures, too.

Cameron mirrors Aaron's comments about the strategic removal of Egypt's history by acclaiming, "[The] Greeks and Romans, they copied our religion. Everybody based their religion, based their civilization, based everything off the Egyptians, we started it all."

Note that Cameron's use of the pronoun "we" within the description of ancient African history shows an acknowledgment and reverence regarding the importance of the ancestors to his own identity. Overall, the students' appreciation for the precolonial content at AGHA is evidenced throughout their narratives. However, there were additional historical movements that were equally influential in participants' responses. The next section provides a look into the second subtheme: *Contemporary History*.

Contemporary History

In addition to precolonial history, participants also mentioned the importance of contemporary information and world events. Thus, *Contemporary History* emerged as another subtheme within the larger realm of Black Education. When participants mentioned *Black Education*, many of them expressed a deep connection to course content and classroom lessons. Many students specifically reflected on class lessons that were culturally engaging and relevant to their identity as Black students. Many of the reflections on contemporary history include current events, social justice issues, and connections to the Civil Rights Movement. The following vignette depicts a middle school lesson that encompasses contemporary history.

December 5, 10 am

The teacher engages middle school students in a discussion about the Eric Garner case. He opens class with a loud announcement. "CLASS! WE HAVE A PROBLEM! A man was choked to death for illegally selling cigarettes!" Students offer their opinions about the case, either for or against the decision. Everyone engages in dialogue about the criminal justice system and how each of them is impacted. Without prompting, they begin to locate themselves within their own education and experiences and also reflected on Tamir Rice, who was killed more recently. The teacher provided arguments and counterarguments from many different perspectives to make the students think deeply and critically about the topic, while the students analyze the circumstances surrounding Garner's and Rice's deaths. The class was observably outraged and students responded by creating social action signs for anti-police violence demonstrations.

The above field note captures the students' passion and interest in social justice issues, especially when they are relevant to their lives. The relevance of police brutality to the Asa G. Hilliard school community emerges from the data as a case of social justice, more so than simply a "Black issue." During data collection (2014–2015), the shooting death of an unarmed Black man, 18-year-old Michael "Mike" Brown, captivated the nation. Students and teachers at AGHA discussed this current event issue along with the shooting deaths of Eric Garner and Tamir Rice, both in Morning Devotion and throughout class lessons. One student, Lily, describes how staying abreast of current events has helped her worldview:

My mother just, she doesn't really talk about Black history until it gets to Black History Month. She loves Coretta Scott King for some reason. . . . But because I'm Black, and I need to know where I came from and yeah, [AGHA] shows me that like . . . how to be informed and more aware of what's going on around me. We talk about stuff happening now, not just the past . . . like the real stuff with protests today.

Student narratives explained that teachers allowed the class to formulate their own opinions about justice, protests, and democracy. Students specifically described connections to the Civil Rights Movement. One student, Garrett, explains:

> [AGHA] is an Afrocentric school so when we go to history class I feel it's on a way higher pedestal because like, um, our teacher [is] very free, like, if we're talking about another topic, he can talk about a topic that relates. Maybe we're talking about the Civil Rights Movement, he can talk about a personal story in his life that probably affected him and made him like, appreciate what we did, what happened in the Civil Rights Movement. Um, and basically the reason why we're here today, like why he appreciates that and how it applies to [today].

In addition to U.S. history, students are also exposed to global stories of the African Diaspora. In a reflection of a literature class, Daphne details an extended class discussion:

> We talked about how the Australians they traded off all their land for jewels, we talked about how Angela Davis was determined to change the world because she thought it was wrong. We talk about Malcolm X and MLK, the Civil Rights Movement and how they feel that they should have changed more and that they could've done better to decrease racism and segregation in our communities.

Cameron notes additional moments in contemporary history that are often inaccurately told in traditional schools. In relation to transatlantic slavery, Cameron critiques the way curriculum is often diluted and inaccurately portrayed:

> I learned about how they took the ships over to Africa and how they just had people sitting in there, they were shackled and it was just crazy, inside the ship . . . Like, a lot of times, what you hear on T.V., what you hear on the radio is not necessarily true, they just "PG-13 it," you know? And, what I like about [AGHA] is that they real it up for you.

Similarly, NaShawn describes his learning experiences at AGHA in comparison to other schools, especially in relation to the school's Afrocentric focus:

> I learned that, I learned that not just slavery but African American inventors and entrepreneurs who became very successful. It helped me by knowing myself more and helped me realize like, the products, the most products are like, are made by Black inventors.

As noted above, *Black Education* and the acknowledgment of African American historical contributions is something that proves meaningful for students. Students assert that learning about the history often untold in traditional schools provides feelings of *self-knowledge* and *influence*, especially when recognizing the accomplishments of African Americans. This helps to promote education as self-healing power, especially considering the falsified and dehumanizing curricula in mainstream schools. The next theme highlights the importance of AGHA's Afrocentric framework and delves into Afrocentricity as a pedagogical philosophy.

THEME 5: REFRAMING AFROCENTRICITY: "CENTERING THE AFRICAN CHILD"

Students, teachers, and the administrator described in the previous theme the power of Black Education for motivating students and adding personal confidence. The next theme, *Reframing Afrocentricity*, provides a more detailed depiction of AGHA's philosophical underpinnings. We should mention that participants use the terms "Afrocentricity" and "African-centered" interchangeably. Here, participants describe how AGHA reframes the Afrocentric framework by intentionally centering students within their own learning. This is a key tenet of Afrocentric educational frameworks (Asante, 1991). In this regard, the centering of Black students helps to reinforce intergenerational knowledge and heritage pedagogy (King & Swartz, 2018). Since Afrocentricity is a lifelong and transcendent paradigm (Asante, 2003), the self-healing power of education is enforced and extended across generations.

Within this theme, it is important to note that teachers and the school administrator provided most of the evidence for this theme. This is most notably due to the specific questions on Afrocentricity in the interview protocol (see Appendixes A & B). More specifically, teacher and administrator participants were asked to provide thoughts on the following interview questions: What does the word "Afrocentricity" mean to you? How would you describe an African-centered education? What are the benefits of African-centered curriculum models for students of color? To begin this discussion, Mr. Griffin offers a definition of "Afrocentricity":

So [Afrocentricity] is the standard, that is in the canon in which you understand cosmology, in which you understand psychology, in which you understand sociology, in which you might understand religion, in which you understand all these things from the, from the central being of the African person.

He continues to explain his definition of how this framework could possibly assist historically marginalized groups, even in regard to educational disparities today:

> We at [AGHA] feel like that is extremely important, when we talk about the success of Black children, and we see just the disproportionate number who end up dropping out of school or um, who don't do well in education. So many different people have all these different solutions or things that they think are solutions to the problem in education. We at [AGHA] believe knowledge is important to the educational reform problem.

Other teachers also commented on the role of Afrocentricity in helping students and correcting historical trauma. Ms. Humphries provides her opening definition of Afrocentricity, especially in relation to being an African American woman. Note that Ms. Humphries's definition of Afrocentricity complements Asante's (1991) and Akbar's (1998) theories on education. According to Asante, Afrocentricity serves as an evolving continuum of learning and becoming. Ms. Humphries notes:

> As African Americans, embracing who you are um, really studying what makes you who you are. Understanding the struggle that went on before you and not just studying that but also honoring that, as well as contributing, to make who you are as an African American, um, better. Not just to say this is what was done before me and "[now] we've arrived," but now it's acknowledging that it's your responsibility to continue the success, the progress.

In relation to the Afrocentric education, Ms. Humphries continues by describing the distinctions of AGHA's framework:

> An education um, that's set up to talk about nurturing. Afro-centered, or African-centered values, one that will talk about ancestors and contributions. Um, also, applying them to your daily lives and knowing how to do that . . . I think that's mainly the problem with people thinking that talking about Africa and Afrocentric things is just about wearing certain clothing or a certain hairstyle. It's deeper than that.

Ms. Saleem mirrors Mr. Griffin and Ms. Humphries's comments and also describes the philosophy behind Afrocentricity or Afrocentric education. She notes:

I believe an African-centered education is one where you do uplift the values of your African heritage. You focus on those values and make sure that you have a strong ground with those values but also, not excluding the other histories that are, you know, that are important to know so that you can know what the truths are and what they're not . . . You have to pull in everything that's part of us, you know, our language, um how we communicate in our bodies, how we communicate with our voices. Um, how we look, the styles that we wear, um, appreciating who we are and, you know, and the things that we've done and just not, not excluding other parts history but just knowing where our history, our story really is.

Similarly, Mr. Lacey describes his interpretations of Afrocentric philosophy in relation to educating children:

When I think of Afrocentricity, I think of a philosophy, or a mentality that eschews the values, the lifestyles, the soul of African people . . . You can't measure our experience you know, uh, tangibly. So it's like, you know what our shared experience here is why we can call ourselves Black folk, you know . . . I said, the word Afrocentricity it's a mindset, it's a way, it's a belief system, it's a way of, of doing things that we can call on, our roots, our African roots, but at the same time, it more focuses on our experience here in America. You know what I'm saying?

Despite the common misconceptions about Afrocentricity and Afrocentric education, as aforementioned, the school's administrator, Ms. Jeffrey, provides an excellent concluding explanation of Afrocentric education:

We take your child, which is the African, right in the center and use everything that we can to make sure that child is successful and learns and does exactly what it is he or she is supposed to do, in life or for that day or you know. And be there for them when they go through challenges, when they have successes, and so. Just keeping them in the center . . . . [And] we're not sitting a child in the center because he or she is African, we're sitting the child in the center because he or she is the focus.

The teachers' and administrator's narratives provide evidence for the theme of *Reframing Afrocentricity*, which emerged throughout the interviews. Students additionally had comments in relation to the subthemes. Thus, this theme contains the following two subthemes: *Black Imaging and Representation* and *Positive Descriptions of Africa*. Both of these subthemes emerged from the overarching importance of *Reframing Afrocentricity*.

Black Imaging and Representation

One step in aligning with Afrocentricity is correcting and redefining historical facts. One of the greatest atrocities within U.S. contexts is the negative typecasting and imaging of African Americans through the news media. Under the larger theme of *Reframing Afrocentricity*, one subtheme that consistently surfaced is AGHA's positive recasting of Black representation and imaging. Many teachers and students commented on how attending Asa G. Hilliard exposed them to positive representations of Black culture that reshaped their identities. This is evidence of education as self-healing power, especially considering the negative portrayals of African Americans in mainstream media. AGHA allowed students to better see themselves and, in turn, definitively correct their perspective of what it means to be Black.

One student, Bryson, mentions the importance of positive Black imaging and representation. He explains his appreciation to AGHA for instilling a counternarrative within students:

> I guess that's what it teaches me about me. About how I should be proud that I'm Black. I shouldn't take it for, um, for granted and I shouldn't like, uh, I shouldn't think any less of myself. I should be always thinking that I am number one. I am better, I am the smartest, or I am the most athletic, or I am just the greatest of everyone I am around. Because [AGHA] really teaches you that you should be thankful for what you have and what you are and the color of your skin.

Similarly, Enoch highlights in his written essay the importance of positive imaging. He notes:

> [AGHA] teaches you that Black culture is important even though it's not usually seen around the world. Like in the United States, you don't always see Black culture everywhere. But in this school, it teaches you that Black culture is important.

Jacob also describes how AGHA's Afrocentric focus has helped him. He notes in his written essay, "The education here has helped me. The biggest part is probably self-knowledge, [and] knowing your history and background to succeed in the world right now."

Aside from the students, teachers also described the utility of Afrocentric education in positively recasting positive Black images. As both a parent and teacher, Ms. Saleem describes the importance of AGHA in correcting historical misinformation:

> They know their history, they know who are and say for instance, we were talking about the slave trade and how one of the little girls said,

"It was just a shame how they ripped out kings and queens for that," so she knew that we are kingly and queenly people, royal people. So, to me, the fact that we instill that in them *early*, when they leave here, wherever they go they're gonna know who they are and they could be surrounded by White America, Hispanic, Latino . . . they could appreciate everybody's culture because we teach everybody's culture here, but, we're solidly based on African American principles. It's made *my* child a better person.

Note that while Ms. Saleem celebrates a "royal" or "priestly" lineage, some African people were farmers, workers, or merchants. In the same way that social status and meritocracy are celebrated in Western society today, it is important to acknowledge class diversity within precolonial African history. To that end, Mr. Griffin also provided insight into AGHA's positive recasting of Black representation in the school's curriculum:

This [is] probably the most effective way to really um, educate our young people in our community . . . When this information is established and then everything that they learn, they're able to say whether it's true or false, whether it applies to them or not. Whether they take it, they learn it for a test and then they leave it, because they're understanding things from their own Black perspective, their own Black centeredness.

In conclusion, Ms. Saleem provides a personal narrative about her son, a 4th-grader at AGHA, in relation to the transformative power of AGHA in recasting Black history and accomplishments in a positive light:

I've never seen anything like it. I've never seen students as young as pre-K that are so in tune with their Black heritage. Um, I have a son in school here and he knows so much about his heritage and he's known it since he was three being here . . . This school is, it's not radical, it's, it upholds our principles.

In addition to positive *Black Imaging and Representation*, participants also were asked to describe their perceptions of Africa. Thus, *Depictions of Africa* became the second subtheme.

Depictions of Africa

November 14, 2:15 pm

After reading an excerpt of "Anansi and the Spider," the 3rd-grade teacher [Ms. Saleem] engaged the class in a discussion about fables.

The class briefly discussed how fables were different from poems and had to identify the moral of the story. Next, the teacher mentioned that the Anansi tales came from the Ashanti Nation in Ghana. She asked students if any of them had heard of the Ashanti Nation, specifically. One student asked if they were like the Zulu Nation. Ms. Scott informed the student that it was a different tribal Nation. She then assured the class that "a long time ago," there were many Nations in Africa and there are thousands that exist today.

The above narrative in Ms. Saleem's classroom describes a 2nd- and 3rd-grade literature lesson where students read a Ghanaian fable and made appropriate connections to moments in history. Within this classroom observation, students had positive perceptions of Africa and viewed this story within the larger scope of African world literature. As mentioned in the previous subtheme, the positive recasting of Black images is important. At AGHA, students and teachers at Asa G. Hilliard explain how positive Black imaging at AGHA often contrasts with negative portrayals of African Americans on television and throughout the media. However, in addition to African American imaging, participants were also asked to provide descriptive words to describe Africa. This question was asked in relation to a recent study that suggested most students have negative perceptions of Africa (Traoré, 2007). Since AGHA purposefully confronts negative hegemonic narratives, it was important to capture how participants differed from the Traoré (2007) study. The discussion section discusses these findings in more detail, especially in relation to the role of right knowledge and corrective history in healing oppressed groups.

Student and teacher participants were asked the descriptive question, "How would you describe Africa?" Participants provided a myriad of responses. We want to note that 100% of the participants' responses were generally positive, which is distinctive to prior studies on African perceptions (Traoré, 2002, 2007). Participants were allowed to list descriptive words, in no particular order, to capture their immediate perceptions of Africa. To start, Aaron describes Africa as, "Nice, historical, beautiful. It's warm. Um, amazing, big, huge. I'd probably want to go to Ghana or the Ivory Coast . . . I think those are like my favorite two countries there and also, um, those are favorite two soccer teams." Similarly, Enoch describes, "Well some parts are, um, desert-ish, like they're dry and vast. Um, it can be hypnotizing, it's a wonder when you see the pyramids. Um, also other parts can be very rich and contained." Garrett continues:

> Africa, I would say Muslim. I would say hard working, I would think of people of color, I would think of Pharaohs, kings, I would . . . think of land. I would think of the Nile River. I would think of pyramids.

Hannah adds:

> I would say the motherland, beautiful, I would think very um, warm,
> beautiful, green grass. I would think of the Black people of course.
> I would think of developing, developing businesses and doctors,
> architects, all these phenomenal people.

Jacob contributes: "I would say Ghana. Nigeria. Um, beautiful, wealthy.
Uh, some parts are rural. Kind of a fast lifestyle, it's pretty cool, it's fun.
Uh, people are friendly." Similarly, Kelsi describes Africa as, "Very multicultural. Very accepting of other people, um, varied place rich in like culture
and education, where they value what they have a lot more than we do."
While most students had not traveled to Africa, they shared positive perceptions of what they imagined Africa to be.

In addition to student responses, teachers also provided descriptions of
Africa. This from Mr. Griffin:

> I think that is the motherland. I think of it as home. Um, I think of it
> as a place of rest, solitude, um, growth. I think of Africa as a place.
> I guess sometimes I have a very, um, idolized view of Africa, you
> know . . . what it was prior to you know, colonialism and, and prior
> to the European invasion. Um, I know it wasn't all great. There were
> wars and things like that that were happening and, of course, women
> in various parts of Africa, were not treated um, as equal and things
> like that. But I don't know, it just seemed like it was just much more
> conducive to the way in which we exist, in which Black people exist.

Ms. Humphries also talks about some of Africa's history:

> Black people, struggle, apartheid, slavery, Nelson Mandela, Ebola,
> Sierra Leone. Oh my goodness, things are just going through my mind.
> The Ivory Coast, Serengeti, beautiful culture, history, slavery. Mmm,
> oh my goodness. Blood, the ocean, the ships, um Darfur.

Mr. Lacey additionally notes how his original perceptions of Africa have
changed:

> Um, I think of city. I think of civilized. I think of greatness. I think I've
> reprogrammed myself to have these thoughts. Because previously, I
> would think uncivilized or, or hungry children and starving, you know
> what I'm saying? Because those are the images that were continuously
> bombarded, that were just thrown at us consistently, and at the same
> time, they still are unfortunately. Yet, we want to tear those images

down and recreate a new image of what Africa is. It's the motherland, you know, it's the home of, it's the birthplace of life.

Ms. Saleem uses the following words to describe Africa: "royalty, freedom, purity. And then it flips . . . struggle. Gold, need, peace. There's a lot of stuff flooding my mind right now . . . heritage, passion, children." Similarly, Ms. Jeffrey uses some of the same terminology as Ms. Saleem. Her description includes, "Black, gold, rich, mighty, powerful, misunderstood, mislabeled . . . home." As demonstrated in the narratives, students and teachers at AGHA expressed a positive outlook on Africa and African contributions. According to Afrocentric philosophy, the positive recasting of Blackness—both within the United States and internationally—is of paramount importance (Akbar, 1998). Thus, the next and final theme explores *Restorative Education* in relation to positive Black identity.

THEME 6: RESTORATIVE EDUCATION: "PROMOTING POSITIVE BLACK IDENTITY"

Throughout participant interviews, students and teachers expressed that knowledge about their history has a personal effect on their personal identity. In this regard, this theme explores evidence of *Restorative Education* at AGHA. This theme helps to disrupt the Black pathological reframing of deviance, which include media imaging and symbolisms of Black as villain. To begin this discussion, Akbar (1998) notes that non-White historical figures are often negatively typecast in discourse as deviant. Additionally, Adams and Stevenson (2012) and Jan (2017) also contend that contemporary forms of Black media are often pervasively filled with toxic and distorted images of African Americans. These vitriolic messages are perpetuated through the commercialization of fallacious stereotypes. In contradistinction to this, AGHA purposively confronts and disrupts negative images of Blackness, Africa, and African American thought by showcasing positive figures in history. Research on the importance of accurate cultural representation is widely evident (The Opportunity Agenda, 2011). Thus, *education as self-healing power* addresses the psyche of students, and helps to reshape their pathos and ethos. From an educator's perspective, Ms. Jeffrey provides opening thoughts on the recasting of Black identity with oppressed groups:

> Our identities have been blurred so I think it's deeply important, we have to go back to appreciating one another, appreciating who we are, where we come from, what our ancestors and things did before us and move toward growth . . . Some of us, have lost the way, or have conformed to ideas that don't match our people, or what we stand for,

or good things, you know, so, um, yeah we definitely have to bring that back to our morals and values and things.

Similarly, Mr. Griffin explains:

> Just a higher sense of self-esteem. I always believe that if you can see yourself inside of what you're learning, then it's more applicable to you. . . . If you're looking in a book and you don't see nobody that looks like you and none of it traces back to you, it doesn't really stick with you. . . . All I have to do is just go inside myself and pull it out, but I can do this because all the people that came before me did this.

In addition to confidence and acknowledging ancestral contributions, as mentioned by Ms. Jeffrey and Mr. Griffin, students provide firsthand accounts of AGHA's restorative role in student identity. FeFe explains specific examples of how AGHA negates colorism and prejudice within the school community:

> At [AGHA], it's not like since you're different, light-skinned, dark-skinned, nobody's going to talk to you. We're all African American in some kind of way . . . [AGHA] gives students a curriculum and close family for African Americans, 'cause that's not really out there as much as it could be.

In relation to the intangible principles that AGHA instills in students, Jacob notes, "That's something that they give you at [AGHA] and that they don't really give you at other places." Similarly, NaShawn describes how the positive imaging at AGHA promotes student confidence:

> It will help us in life because like, this school teaches us that um, 'cause some kids here, I know they have like low self-esteem, like, you have power, you just have find the powers within. And you just have to try to find it and you can use that in life, who you really want to be.

In addition to providing student confidence, Ms. Saleem notes how AGHA is a rehabilitative place for students. She relates a story where a parent sought AGHA as a sort of intervention for her child:

> One parent told me [AGHA] was a place of survival for her. It was necessary for her child's progress. It's necessary. It's like survival. And to hear that, I was like wow . . . It helps a child, especially that child that some people say, "Ah no, we're just gonna write him off." No, when you get them in this, uh, this environment you find out, my goodness, they have a wealth of things to say, they know a lot of things but they just were not afforded the opportunity.

As shown in the narratives, AGHA provides restorative education for students, especially in relation to Black identity and educational outlook. To that end, the following subthemes emerged within the larger theme of *Restorative Education*: *Student Outlook* and *Sense of Self*.

Student Outlook

In relation to AGHA providing restorative education, many participants provide reflections on student transformation and improved student outlook. *Student Outlook* thus serves as a subtheme within the larger theme of *Restorative Education*. To start, Hannah provides opening comments on the utility of AGHA's education in her life:

> This school has really taught me to work for what I want and to be determined and not give up . . . I know [AGHA] is going to help me later in life, because this is going to give me the mindset that not everything is given to you. You have to fight for some things and you have to have the drive and dedication for some things . . . Things aren't just handed to you. You have to do something for them. You have to earn them.

Another student, Bryson, comments on the relevance of "real-life" situations at AGHA, especially in relation to being a Black man. He explains that AGHA "teaches you that a Black male is being a struggle nowadays and . . . they also teach you like, like how to do different ways to solve problems, other than violence and crime and things like that." In addition to the practical knowledge that Bryson and Hannah appreciate, Oakleigh finds restoration in the knowledge of ancestors and their contributions:

> [AGHA] teaches me that even if someone tells me just because I'm Black, I can do anything. It lets me know that my ancestors had it worse and they still made it far. This school teaches students that they are better than what people tell them, they can do whatever they want to as long as they work hard.

The positive reframing of student outlook is essential, especially in today's contexts where many students fail to have "self-knowledge" (Akbar, 1998; Woodson, 1933/1977).

Mr. Griffin describes the importance of AGHA's restorative practices for students:

> We hope that it shapes their identity that way and they are proud of what they see when they look in the mirror, and they're proud of their classmates and they're proud of their community and things of that

nature. Even though sometimes the media or what they see outside doesn't, doesn't portray that, you know what I mean?

Mr. Griffin continues by providing firsthand accounts of student transformation:

> I've seen students who come in and just their disposition is just very low, and um, and then you know after being here for maybe a semester or two, they just, you know sit a little higher you know they speak out more, um, and they feel little bit more comfortable in their skin.

Ms. Jeffrey, the school's administrator, also notes improved student outlook:

> We send [students] off with a sense of confidence, with knowledge of self, or some type of way to get it. We send them away with a level of respect that they know they deserve, a level of respect that they know they give, and they know why they give it . . . I think the best thing is with independence and confidence, so they're able to run the world, you know, come back and tell us about it. And they do. So many students come back and tell us about how they've changed. Their whole world outlook has changed.

In addition to restoring students' outlooks, the final subtheme captures how students have gained a greater *Sense of Self* by attending AGHA.

Sense of Self

Within the theme of *Restorative Education*, the subtheme *Sense of Self* consistently emerged in participant interviews. To begin this discussion, Mr. Griffin provides a cursory overview of why having a greater "sense of self" is important:

> Kids understand who they are, because for me personally, I just feel like that's extremely important. And that's what I want to do for my future children as well. That's something that I'd want to instill in them, is to have a sense of self, to know who they are.

Mr. Griffin continues by attributing AGHA's restorative education to the incorporation of Black history. This is discussed in an earlier theme. However, according to Mr. Griffin, one tangible result of Afrocentric education is instilling in students a greater awareness of self in relation to culture:

I like the fact that they put an emphasis on Black history . . . But the education that the students receive here isn't just a good Black education it's just a good education period. And in addition to that, what makes it a good education is, is being culturally centered and having that, having that knowledge of who they are

Similarly, students describe how AGHA's curriculum has helped to instill greater personal awareness. Cameron speaks of how AGHA has helped to counter negative stereotypes within the Black community:

Not only how the White people portray us, or the other races portray us, but how we portray ourselves. The ghetto Black man, the ghetto Black woman, um, [AGHA] has taught me that's not who we are but that's how we portray ourselves. But it taught me that's not who I am, that's not who I feel I'm supposed to be. I know 'cause, and also I feel like, [AGHA] taught me that anything's possible.

Similarly, Bryson describes his own greater awareness of self in relation to negative stereotypes. Like Cameron, Bryson explains that "Being a thug really isn't being Black. It's just what now has come into this current time . . . [AGHA] helps me view myself as like, well one that you should be proud that you're Black." Aaron also mentions the role of culture and history in having a greater sense of self: "[AGHA] teaches us about our history . . . That means that as you get older, you should have a sense of self and know who you are, so you should do better in life. 'Cause you actually know who you are." As depicted in the participants' narratives, many students attribute AGHA's curricula to their positive self-development. Teachers and the school's administrator also attest to the visible transformation of many students once they are exposed to cultural truths and right knowledge. In relation to the second research question, *What role does education or "right knowledge" play in helping oppressed groups to heal from trauma or social, cultural, and psychological domination?*, many participants describe the active role that schools play in reshaping social, cultural, and psychological (identity) information. These issues are discussed in greater detail in Chapter 7.

SUMMARY

This chapter has provided participants' perspectives on education as self-healing power. Students and teachers at AGHA describe how right knowledge and restorative learning help to positively reshape Black student identity. This is imperative for students, especially considering the inaccurate depictions of African-descent people in school curricula. The following three themes were discussed in the chapter: *Black Education, Reframing Afrocentricity*, and *Restorative Education and Black Identity*. Students, teachers, and the administrator provide collective insight on how Afrocentric schools foster healing and redirection for African American students. Chapter 7 provides an in-depth analysis of the themes presented; merges the study's findings with the Afrocentric theoretical framework and existing research; and presents implications and recommendations for future research.

Education as Healing Power
Findings and Policy Recommendations

> Knowledge could empower marginalized groups in ways that formal legal equality couldn't.
>
> —Septima P. Clark, 1954

> Racists will always call you racist when you identify their racism. To love yourself now is a form of racism. We are the only people who are criticized for loving ourselves.
>
> —John Henrik Clarke, 1992

In summary, the six themes that emerged from the data were (1) Unique Environment: "This School is Just Different"; (2) Support System: "A Close-Knit Community"; (3) Morning Devotion: "Spiritual Encouragement in an African Worldview"; (4) Black Education: "Every Day of the Year"; (5) Reframing Afrocentricity: "Centering the African Child"; and (6) Restorative Education: "Promoting Positive Black Identity." Each of these themes connects to the larger focus of the book: *education as self-healing power.* In this chapter, the findings are discussed and analyzed using an Afrocentric theoretical lens. Additionally, this chapter provides suggestions for future research studies, as well as policy recommendations.

This book has investigated the perceptions and experiences of teachers and students at a high-performing Afrocentric school. As mentioned in Chapter 2, while the early foundations of Afrocentric schools are laudable, we acknowledge today that education for Black students must extend beyond mere standardized testing metrics, which are normed for Whites. While we recognize that early pioneers in Pan-Africanism laid the foundation for Afrocentric schools today, contemporary Black excellence is not tied simply to academic success, but to social, communal, and cultural awareness as well.

Thus, this book has explored the role of Afrocentricity as a framework for academic, social, and cultural inclusion in schools. To accomplish this task, the theoretical framework of Afrocentricity helped the analysis of the participants' responses. Afrocentricity strategically places the African experience at the center of analysis (Asante, 1991). It responds to miseducation by recentering the curriculum toward a restorative and historically accurate place. This helps to promote self-healing. Based on the findings of this case study at AGHA, this chapter is organized around the six prevailing themes listed at the start of the chapter.

Each of the themes' headings provides a discussion of the findings and their connection to the theoretical framework and existing research. The second part of this chapter explains the implications of the study and provides directions for future research. The first three themes, *Unique Environment*, *Support System*, and *Devotion*, are examined in connection to the first research question, while the remaining themes, *Black Education*, *Reframing Afrocentricity*, and *Restorative Education and Black Identity*, are discussed in relation to the second research question. In relation to education as self-healing power, the first themes help to conceptualize the learning environment at AGHA. In order to promote restorative education that nurtures self-healing, it is valuable to detail the learning environment and classroom pedagogy. To this end, the remaining three themes showcase participants' perceptions of Afrocentric education and its usefulness within their lives. This, in essence, better explains the effects of self-healing on students and teachers.

THEME 1: UNIQUE ENVIRONMENT:
"THIS SCHOOL IS JUST DIFFERENT"

When teachers and students were asked what makes AGHA unique, all 20 participants mentioned the school's learning environment. Many students compared AGHA to former schools they attended. One student, Cameron, relates that he had previously attended a parochial school and a different Afrocentric school, both noticeably different from AGHA:

> The first school I ever went to was [a Catholic school] in Georgia . . .
> I remember me going there and then I never exposed to learning about myself. I've never heard the, the word "Afrocentric" there. . . . Then I also went to [a different Afrocentric school] it was very, very deep and Afrocentric, but the thing that wasn't there was academics. All they focused on was, um, our culture. When I came to [AGHA] I had to catch up to the rest of my class because, well, when I came from [a different Afrocentric school], they just weren't teaching me what I actually needed.

Note that Cameron's prior experience in an Afrocentric school was not necessarily transformative. Myths about all Afrocentric schools being monolithic must be dispelled. Just as in traditional schools, rigorous class-room learning must be promoted. Cameron views his experience at AGHA as one that encourages academics, not just cultural activities. As mentioned earlier, AGHA does not teach only Black history; the school teaches all sub-ject areas, and is high-performing, as evidenced by scores that surpass the state average. Thus, education as self-healing power is a framework that promotes restoration and right knowledge, which is a necessity for learning to take place.

Hopkins (1997) and Mitchell (2003) found that distinctive learning environments are beneficial for African American students. Hopkins (1997) examined several Afrocentric schools across the Midwest and found that more intimate educational environments were favorable for Black male students. Hopkins studied various Afrocentric school designs, including inclusion programs and after-school programs. Like Hopkins, Mitchell (2003) found that small learning groups were helpful for struggling students attending MAAT Academy, an Afrocentric school in California. Most of our study's participants similarly cited AGHA's small size as a positive.

Although the more intimate and personable learning environment at Hilliard would appear advantageous for prospective families, many parents choose not to enroll their children for financial reasons or lack of resources. AGHA's administrator, Ms. Jeffrey, highlights reasons for Asa G. Hilliard's small size. As the administrator, Ms. Jeffrey has experience with student enrollment that extends beyond the teachers' and students' narratives. When asked, "What do you think are people's misconceptions about this school? Why do you think more families don't explore [AGHA] as a via-ble option for their children?," Ms. Jeffrey provides several reasons. First, she notes that Asa G. Hilliard has limited special education services. Sec-ond, she states that the school lacks citywide exposure and self-promotion. She explains: "Our downfall is business and marketing—a lot of people don't know about us." She also claims that the school's tuition is often an obstacle and that many prospective parents want extracurricular activities that AGHA does not offer, such as an athletic program. These issues help to explain Hilliard's small size. While parents' perceptions are beyond the scope of this study, their feedback needs to be noted.

Many students found AGHA's learning environment to be a positive characteristic. In relation to the school's size, Garrett comments on the aca-demic benefits of the smaller classrooms: "There's fewer children in our classes, so it gives us more time to learn the topics that we're not so strong on." Similarly, Aaron said that teachers at AGHA "really care about my education and are willing to push me . . . my friends and classmates are very close to me here. They will help me when I am in need and are just like my brothers and sisters.

" However, while many students saw AGHA's small family environment as beneficial, this feature was not without criticism.

As mentioned, three veteran students cited AGHA's lack of racial diversity. Bryson, Cameron, and Ian's desire for non-Black students to attend their school demonstrates room for growth and expansion at AGHA. Several students mentioned the benefits of having non-Black students attend their school. In relation to the interview question that asked participants to consider the benefits of AGHA's curriculum for all students, not just African Americans, Ms. Humphries notes:

> I think it will allow other students to be able to respect and
> understand the struggle of Africans, African Americans, being able
> to understand their struggle and respect it. I think that's what I hear
> when I look at the news, when I listen to comments, that people, they
> don't, it's kind of like a disrespect for our contributions to this world
> and the importance that we, the value that we've made to America.

Similarly, Ms. Saleem mentioned the importance of AGHA's curriculum for *all* students:

> From the construction of it, to the benefits that they have to enjoy in
> this country. Being able to hear that and understand that, that our
> contributions were made and that we are American just like someone
> that does not look like us. That's important for all students to learn.

Note that students and teachers did not view their education as separatist or unwelcoming; instead, they wished for increased racial diversity. All of the teachers and the administrator expressed that any child is welcome at Asa G. Hilliard. Of course, we agree that the self-healing power of education at AGHA would be valuable for every student, not only African Americans.

THEME 2: SUPPORT SYSTEM: "A CLOSE-KNIT COMMUNITY"

From an Afrocentric perspective, having a supportive learning environment is central to delivering high-quality education (Ani, 1994; Gbaba, 2009; Piert, 2006). In fact, communal relationships help to foster education as self-healing power. The participants' narratives regarding the supportive environment at AGHA connects to Rodney's (2011) research. Rodney (2011) states, "In Africa, before the fifteenth century, the predominant principal of social relations was that of family and kinship associated with communalism" (p. 36). Whereas the European ethos often promotes individualism and competitiveness within schools and society, Afrocentricity does not (Akbar, 1998; Dei, 2012; Murrell, 2002; Obenga, 2004; Rodney, 2011). Dei et al. (2006) asserts that Afrocentric education embraces community and unity. Piert (2006) and

Shockley (2011) found that teacher relationships are important in Afrocentric schools. Shockley (2011) explains that home and school relationships are strengthened when schools have caring teachers who create a family environment. Similarly, Piert (2006) describes the positive role that teachers and positive adult mentors have in Afrocentric schools.

Hopkins (1997) and Evans-Winters (2011) investigated effective strategies for teaching Black boys and girls, and found that students are better engaged in learning when they are supported in schools. Both Hopkins (1997) and Evans-Winters (2011) found that for Black boys and girls, having additional support at the school level increased the students' sense of belonging. A culture of learning and support is essential for effective education, and is a key attribute of AGHA (Akbar, 1998; Dei, 2012; Murrell, 2002; Obenga, 2004; Rodney, 2011). AGHA teachers described the impact of the school's supportive environment, especially in regard to student success. Mr. Lacey explains:

> One of my students, I started teaching here in 2007. I had a real challenge with him in regards to discipline. His parents were definitely both a part of his life and they were very active in the school, but it was just something that, I think he was on this rebellious type of kick and trying to get through to him was kind of like, "Oh my God! I hope I'm getting through, I don't know if I'm getting through" . . . But seeing him 4 years later, after he went off to high school, he graduated from high school, [and] he came up to me and he said "Mr. [Lacey], thank you, I'm going to Morehouse!" That touched my heart because it was kind of like "Wow, I was a part of his growth and development." And the craziest thing about it is, I knew his potential and it's kind of like, they sometimes don't even know their [own] potential.

Similarly, students describe how the supportive environment at AGHA helps them with character development and maturity. Bryson notes:

> They teach you more than just school stuff. They teach you on like world situations and like, street-wise. Like how to be safe on the street, how to take care of yourself, or the things you should look at, the things you should be around. The positive influences you should look into.

Students and teachers describe the importance of AGHA's supportive school community, which is consistent with the research on Black education. Connecting to the theme of support, the third major theme addresses a school practice that provides an additional layer of emotional support: Morning Devotion.

THEME 3: MORNING DEVOTION:
"SPIRITUAL ENCOURAGEMENT IN AN AFRICAN WORLDVIEW"

Students and teachers at Asa G. Hilliard consistently describe the impor-tance of Morning Devotion, which is the study's third theme. This morning ritual is another example of how the school is African-centered. As men-tioned, Devotion in this case is a nonreligious daily ritual that more closely aligns with African spiritual worldviews. Here, teachers and students gather together and recite affirmations, encourage each other through motivation, and venerate ancestors through reflection and meditation. As discussed in Chapters 2 and 3, countless ancestors have made important contributions to world history, demonstrating the holistic effects of education as self-healing power.

As mentioned, we must make distinctions between formal, Western religions and spirituality. Within the contexts of Afrocentric schools, devo-tional practice is described as "spiritual," due to the promotion of holistic affirmations and meditations. It should be noted that precolonial African spirituality is not oppositional to religion (Hilliard et al., 1987); rather, it is an access point for holistic thinking and consciousness. To that end, many students positively reference Devotion when describing their daily routine. Bryson also adds that his favorite moments in the school day include singing *Lift Every Voice and Sing* and reciting *The Ultimate Student* (see Appen-dixes L and I). He says, "I like *Lift Every Voice and Sing* and *The Ultimate Student* because it's more saying how you should look at your past because you should know where you came from and be thankful for what you have today."

Additionally, Aaron explains the importance of these affirmations. Throughout his interview, he explains how Morning Devotion serves as a moment of affirmation for him. When asked about his favorite poem, he responded:

> My favorite is "I Have the Power." [It goes], "I have the power to choose what makes me a powerful person, I have the power to make the right choices, I have the power to choose to be honest, I have the power to choose to be kind, I have the power to ask my parents, caregivers or the teachers when I'm not sure what choice to make, I have the power."

The school's devotional practices are directly aligned with African "centeredness." The MAAFA, or damages caused by the transatlantic slave trade, created an abrupt disconnect between Africa and African Americans (Ani, 1994; Hilliard, 2002). An opportunity for students at Afrocentric schools to rediscover knowledge lost from the MAAFA is provided during daily Devotion. The school's Morning Devotion reconnects students with ancestral history and "centeredness," as it provides time for positive affirmation and unity among students and teachers. Although participants explain that Devotion is not religious, the spirit of affirmation and daily meditation is beneficial. Asa G. Hilliard (1998) explains that the "spirit" of Africa is found in the people of the Diaspora. Additionally, students learn about lesser-known Black history facts in Devotion. This connects students to information lost in the MAAFA.

Gbaba's (2009) study focused on Black history in Afrocentric schools. This study found that Black history systemically confronts hegemony and dominant ideology. Additionally, Afrocentric curriculum models "produce equity pedagogy for children of color" (Gbaba, 2009, p. 33). This distinguishes Afrocentric schools from traditional schools. Rodney (2011) describes the colonial framework found in traditional schools:

> The [colonial school system] was not an educational system that grew out of the African environment or one that was designed to promote the most rational use of material and social resources. It was not an educational system designed to give young people confidence and pride as members of African societies, but one which sought to instill a sense of deference toward all that was European . . . Colonial schooling was education for subordination, exploitation, the creation of mental confusion, and the development of underdevelopment. (pp. 240–241)

Throughout morning devotion, students describe feelings of "affirmation" and "motivation." This counters mainstream Western education, as described by Rodney (2011), and is another demonstration of education as self-healing power.

THEME 4: BLACK EDUCATION: "EVERY DAY OF THE YEAR"

The fourth theme describes the presence of Black history and Black education at AGHA. Williams's (1961) *Rebirth of African Civilization* extensively explored African schools and the role of education in the rebirth and development of Africa. According to Williams, education refers to the "development of understanding that leads to effective action related to the improvement of life" (p. 291). To fully recover from the psychological, emotional, and physical trauma from slavery, Williams postulates, there must be a reawakening of African education. Afrocentric schools help to address these traumas through right knowledge and corrective history, again promoting education as self-healing power.

According to Williams (1961) and others (Akbar, 1998; Asante, 1990, 1991; Dei, 2012; King, 2005), education plays a pivotal role in the universal transformation of African-descent people. Many of these scholars contend that Black history and the systemic incorporation of right knowledge is imperative (Dei, 2012; King & Swartz, 2016, 2018). To that end, students and teachers relate that Black history is taught every day at Asa G. Hilliard. While Mr. Lacey has taught only in Afrocentric schools, he compares AGHA to his former experiences as a public school student:

> Yeah [when I was in] school, we had Black History Month and that was in February, and that was it. That's the only time we talked about Black people, so unfortunately, there was no Chinese History Month. There was no Native History Month. You know what I'm saying? Like, yeah, so the public school system can be very um, non-inclusive. Because it does not really incorporate other people's, other cultures.

Additionally, teachers describe that Black history is interdisciplinary and applicable in various subjects. As mentioned earlier, the assumption that Afrocentric schools restrict their teaching to Black history is misguided and false. Still, it remains a common misconception regarding Afrocentric schools. Many teachers at AGHA expressed a desire to actively change this assumption. AGHA teachers and students describe their typical school days as including mathematics, art, science, social studies, language arts, foreign language, and drama. Each of these subjects is taught using an Afrocentric approach, which aims to remove hegemony from the curricula.

Teachers and students at Asa G. Hilliard describe the use of nonhegemonic curricula that positively display Black heroes and their contributions. Note that Black historical figures are not *specific* to Black history (Akbar, 1998; Dei et al., 2006). This was first demonstrated in the *Portland Baseline Essays* (Portland Public Schools, 1987), which provided Afrocentric curriculum guides for social studies, science, language arts, mathematics, art, and music (1987). Teachers and students describe how the curriculum at AGHA comprehensively covers world history, not just Black history, by offering multiple classes and subjects. These classes aim to expose students to nontraditional ways of thinking and learning. This again demonstrates AGHA's holistic and self-healing approach to education.

Additionally, Afrocentric curricula can be considered holistic because they are based on the seven virtues of MA'AT: truth, justice, harmony, balance, order, reciprocity, and propriety (Hilliard & Amankwatia, 1998; Hilliard et al., 1987; Murrell, 2002; Nobles, 1990). Karenga (1966) re-coined MA'AT into 20th- and 21st-century principles, known as the Nguzo Saba. Elements of the Nguzo Saba include unity, self-determination, collective work and responsibility, cooperative economics, purpose, creativity, and faith (Karenga, 1966). Teachers use the Nguzo Saba in their daily teaching practices (see Appendix E).

Dei et al. (2006) explain that students are disserved when schools use traditional curricula. They advocate for the implementation of nontraditional curriculum methods, which counter colonialism's negative and pervasive damages. In order to accomplish this task, Dei et al. (2006) suggest recentering the curriculum and using updated and more historically accurate approaches. Dei's curriculum suggestions align with the Afrocentric theoretical framework and advocates for greater inclusion of African contributions in the curriculum (Asante, 1991, 1998). This realignment is imperative for the promotion of education as self-healing power. These nontraditional curriculum practices are found daily at AGHA. The importance of Black education for students leads to the next theme, which is the reframing of Afrocentricity.

THEME 5: REFRAMING AFROCENTRICITY: "CENTERING THE AFRICAN CHILD"

Afrocentricity argues for the African perspective to be *centered* versus marginalized (Asante, 1998). While acknowledging the Greeks or Romans as influential contributors to their education, students at Asa G. Hilliard also see the value and significance of Ancient Kemetians (Egyptians). For example, Cameron notes, "I know who I am and I know what Black people did thousands of years ago, back in Egypt and stuff. We were powerful people who changed the world." Additionally, students uncover the historical truth about their ancestors, which is often ignored in most public and private school settings (Akbar, 1998; Dei et al., 2006). Traditional schools, teaching through Eurocentric normative lenses, often fail to teach corrective history. As demonstrated in the narratives of the participants in our study, the restorative power of Afrocentric education helps to create self-healing and awareness in students in a way that mainstream education cannot or will not do.

As we have emphasized, the importance of corrective history is imperative for all students, not just African Americans. In making our case for Afrocentricity's utility for *all* people, it is helpful to look again at Asante's (2003) definition:

> [Afrocentricity is] a mode of thought and action in which the centrality of African interest, values and perspectives predominate. In regards to theory, it is the placing of African people in the center of any analysis of African phenomena. Thus it is possible for anyone to master the discipline of seeking the location of Africans in a given phenomena [*sic*]. In terms of action and behavior, it is a devotion to the idea that what is in the best interest of African consciousness is at the heart of ethical behavior. Finally, Afrocentricity seeks to enshrine the idea that blackness itself is a trope of ethics. Thus to be [Black] is to be against all forms of oppression, racism, classism, homophobia, patriarchy, child abuse, pedophilia and white racial domination. (Asante, 2003, p. 2)

Asante's definition of Afrocentricity dismisses any form of exclusion or oppression, calling instead for inclusion and restoration. Additionally, it helps to demystify the misnomers about Afrocentricity's primary focus. As mentioned in Chapter 2, the primary focus of Black Nationalism and Pan-Africanism was the promotion of unity, upliftment, and a collective understanding of the value of Black people and accomplishments. In this same vein, Afrocentric schools were developed to promote these principles, providing further historical evidence of education as self-healing power. Asante (2000) continues:

> [The] mind of Africa is inclusive and can accommodate many different ideas at the same time. It is not an exclusive world that prevents other ideas from surfacing. In fact, Africans accept strangers, admit ideas, and absorb cognate cultures into their own canopy of values. The reason for this has a lot to do with the idea that everything is everything in the African view, that is, everything is related, connected, and nothing is discrete, isolated. (p. 5)

This distinguishes Afrocentricity from other educational perspectives. Based on Africa's rightful place in history, Afrocentricity helps to *include* all cultural perspectives. One student, Daphne, describes how AGHA incorporates an Afrocentric perspective:

> We're kind of centered around Black power and Black studies so what we'll do is, we'll study maybe an African American or someone who has set the standards for us, and we use them as an example of what we should be. We learn about all histories and races, but we will start with the Black person first.

Under this model, the Afrocentric curriculum framework challenges *hegemony*, not Europe. Afrocentricity removes the "lens" of colonization from self-perception and recenters Africa to a more historically accurate starting place. This is imperative when promoting *education as self-healing power*. Students and teachers suggest that all students should learn from an Afrocentric perspective in order to increase racial respect and understanding.

Corrective history and positive Black images affirm the students at Asa G. Hilliard. Additionally, as discussed later, AGHA students demonstrate a nonhegemonic, holistic depiction of Africa. Rayford's (2012) study revealed that students attending an Afrocentric school in Ohio demonstrated positive self-perceptions and descriptions of Blackness. In contrast to Traoré's (2002, 2007) research, students and teachers at AGHA overwhelmingly cast Africa in a positive light. Research strongly supports the notion that African contributions are negatively propagated or ignored. Traoré (2007) also suggests that students often consider Africa to be a primitive, subhuman place. In contrast, AGHA students repeatedly recognized Africa for its substantive role in world history, and also acknowledged social, economic, and political pitfalls that have decentered Africa from a more rightful place in global thought. AGHA students impressively demonstrated a recast view of Africa—further evidence of the healing power of education.

Considering the distinguished role of African accomplishments in world history, this type of reimaging is essential for restorative education. This leads to the sixth theme.

THEME 6: RESTORATIVE EDUCATION: "PROMOTING POSITIVE BLACK IDENTITY"

The participants in the study described overwhelming evidence of AGHA's promotion of positive Black identity. This is also defined as "knowing yourself," which is essential for Black students (Akbar, 1998). Arguably, this theme is one of the most tangible indications of education as self-healing power. Students and teachers explain that Asa G. Hilliard's learning environment fosters identity formation and reflection. This ultimately brings healing and historical realignment, known as "sankofa." As noted earlier, sankofa is an Akan word that means "go back and fetch," and is pictorially symbolized as a bird looking behind or to the past (King et al., 2014). The concepts of sankofa respond to the MAAFA, which are the traumatic effects left from the African Diaspora. The MAAFA has negatively influenced education, especially in regard to student learning and identity. This demonstrates even more why restorative education is necessary. As we have argued, today's public schools propagate the ideologies of slavery and colonialism. The psychological damages of hegemony are important for educators to address, especially at the curricular and pedagogical level (Akbar, 1998; Dei, 1996; Ighodaro & Wiggan, 2011). Onyeweuenyi (2005) states that:

> The Western educational system has extolled the achievements of Europeans and denied African contributions so that white students' knowledge of Africa and Africans is limited to the usual stereotypes of the primitive, the savage, the inferior. They have been taught that Africa was stagnant before the arrival of the Europeans, who brought civilization and education. (Onyeweuenyi, 2005, p. 33)

Onyeweuenyi's (2005) findings are troubling, and sadly the reality for most students. Students in traditional school settings who presumably do not have access to right knowledge run the risk of never *knowing* themselves.

Similar to Onyeweuenyi's research, over 80 years ago, Carter G. Woodson's (1933/1977) *Mis-Education of the Negro* explained the connection among schooling, miseducation, and identity development.

In contrast, AGHA students demonstrate the self-healing power of education when realigned with historical fact. Having a more positive sense of self, as described by the participants, reverses the pervasive damages left from the MAAFA and positively corrects student identity. Na'im Akbar in his work *Know Thy Self* (1998) asserts that Black identity, consciousness, and cultural awareness are all connected to education. In traditional schools, cultural hegemony undergirds curriculum practices (Dei et al., 2006; Ighodaro & Wiggan, 2011). This miseducates students and damages their self-concept (Akbar, 1998). Ighodaro and Wiggan (2011) coined the term *curriculum violence* to describe "the deliberate manipulation of academic programming in a manner that ignores or compromises the intellectual and psychological well-being of learners" (p. 2). These damages are most pervasive toward African Americans, who have been continuously typecast as *objects* rather than contributors in history (Asante, 1998). This results in today's African American students having toxic perceptions of themselves, their culture, and their ancestry (Akbar, 1998).

From an Afrocentric perspective, the participants' comments regarding their positive cultural identity and historical outlook are best understood as benefits of teaching truth, which does not equate to ethnic superiority or arrogance (Piert, 2006). Instead, it nurtures the self-healing power of education. To capture this sentiment, Ms. Saleem states, "When you feel like you are worthwhile you will do whatever it takes to be ultimate, when you know your worth." The process of realigning history with right knowledge allows students to "know" themselves. Additionally, Cameron states:

> This school has taught me about myself and my heritage and I
> appreciate it because I feel like I wouldn't be the same person I am.
> And, now that I feel like I know who I am, I know who I want to be, I
> feel like it's kind of preparing me for the world.

Ms. Saleem and Cameron's comments connect with Akbar's (1998) research, in which he explains that when students know themselves, they are able to make more meaningful contributions to society. Most importantly, students are able to experience education as a self-healing power as they begin to reverse the psychological, emotional, and historical damages from the MAAFA. As demonstrated in this theme, the positive recasting of Africa and African historical accomplishments showcases a greater awareness of accurate history. This sort of reframing helps students to more accurately grasp their cultural heritage and understand their role in human history, a pure implementation of education as self-healing power.

IMPLICATIONS OF THE STUDY

Based on the research findings, students, teachers, and the administrator overwhelmingly believe that Afrocentric education is positive and important. The participants noted increased self-awareness and academic success. The data directly support the participants' positive experiences at Asa G. Hilliard. Students particularly noted the benefits of learning about themselves and their ancestral history. Yet, the majority of students in the surrounding school district do not receive this same information. Dei and colleagues (2006) suggest that the traditional curriculum is still colonized and not necessarily historically accurate.

In the United States, negative stereotypes and misunderstandings undermine Africa (Traoré, 2007). This is because textbooks often reflect propaganda, not fact (Loewen, 1995). The avoidance of critical issues ignores the needs of all students, but especially students of color who have grappled with omitted and distorted histories in U.S. classrooms and textbooks. Considering the recent 2020 uprisings over the deaths of Walter Wallace (Chavez, 2020), George Floyd (Murphy, 2020), Ahmaud Arbery (McLaughlin, 2020), Breonna Taylor (Costello & Duvall, 2020), and Tony McDade (Deliso, 2020), these tragic events point to a tremendous need for critical and transformative conversations in the classroom (Baker, 2020). The fortunate case for AGHA students is that they are exposed to nontraditional curricula and anticolonial histories on a daily basis. Again, we want to emphasize that Afrocentric schools teach traditional subjects such as math, reading, science, history, and the arts, and typically adhere to state curriculum standards. No one should ever assume that Afrocentric schools teach *only* African American history—and yet it happens. Such misconception is important to address when considering Afrocentricity's utility as a method of healing for *all* students.

Overall, students and teachers describe the value of Asa G. Hilliard's educational model, especially when considering traditional public schools. In light of today's federal curriculum and assessment reform initiatives, such as *No Child Left Behind*, *Common Core State Standards*, and *Race to the Top*, the educational landscape is shifting toward quantitative measures of student achievement. With high-stakes state assessments and neoliberal curriculum policies that quantify student learning, traditional methods of public education are suffocating the natural genius within all children. African American students are suffering the most (King, 2005; Perry et al., 2003; Wilson, 1992). Qualitative research consistently demonstrates the importance of cultural relevancy for students (Gay, 2000; Ladson-Billings, 1994). According to student and teacher narratives, AGHA provides *relevancy* for students. Murrell (2002), a researcher on Afrocentric pedagogy, explains the importance of Afrocentric education:

> African-centered pedagogy is necessary to appropriately address the social, cultural, and historical context of the schooling experience of African American children and the disconnection between African American cultural heritage and contemporary educational practice. (p. xxix)

When reflecting on the students' narratives regarding police brutality and social justice, for example, it is evident that 21st-century education must continuously provide spaces for critical inquiry and discussion.

Students and teachers describe many benefits of Afrocentric schools. Since traditional public schools are underserving many students, the role of curriculum development in educational reform must be further investigated. There are insidious ways in which schools prohibit widespread liberation and change (Kelly, 2016; Freire, 2000). From standardized curricula to punitive discipline policies, many Black students are impeded from expressing their true genius (Wilson, 1992). Additionally, there have been recent federal legislative attacks on critical school curricula—as demonstrated in the Trump administration's criticism of *The 1619 Project* and, more broadly, critical race theories (Lang, 2020; Perez & Guadiano, 2020). As such, critical and antiracist theorists recommend some best practices to promote racial equity and inclusion in the classroom. The following is adapted in part from Roberts's (2010) research on Culturally Relevant Critical Teacher Care [CRCTC] and existing research on African American psychological and cultural epistemologies (Akbar, 1998; Evans-Winters, 2011; Hopkins, 1997):

1. Teaching the whole child: Promote social and cultural knowledge, life skills, and character development along with academics
2. High expectations: Ensure that academic excellence is expected for every student, not inaccurate achievement gap measures
3. Positive student identity: Reinforce images, texts, and resources that positively reflect the diverse student demographics in the classroom and the nation at large
4. Instructional relevancy: Ensure that pedagogy is pertinent and applicable to students outside of the classroom
5. Familial and community relationships: Establish partnerships among schools, community, and classroom, including investments in the local neighborhood

Kelly (2016) additionally suggests ways in which schools can promote love and respect for Blackness. According to the Black Liberation Collective, which recently created demands for Ivy League universities across the United States, some of these recommendations include, but are not limited to:

1. The numbers of Black students and faculty should reflect the national percentage of Black folks in the country.
2. Tuition should be free for Black and Indigenous students.
3. Schools should divest from prisons and invest in local communities.

According to Kelly (2016), this involves a resistance to disingenuous or inauthentic notions of "saving" a community or inauthentic gestures that minimally include non-White perspectives. Rather, this requires "relentless struggle, deep study, and critique" (Kelly, 2016, para. 32). As hooks (1994) suggests, transformative learning requires *authentic* pedagogical interactions that question and antagonize the realms of normalcy. Considering that race is still a delicate topic in U.S. classrooms, this requires a radical overhaul of discriminatory practices, starting with the curriculum. Additionally, this requires intense training for faculty, staff, administration, and students. As suggested by the findings of this study, these are just some of the ways in which schools can promote anti-racism and invoke the transformative and self-healing power of education.

There are also some direct implications for further research on Afrocentric school designs. It is recommended for future research to explore the role of curricular relevancy within 21st-century Afrocentric schools. It is also important for future research to investigate diverse student perspectives in Afrocentric schools and interrogate other demographic classifications such as gender, sexuality, and class. These additions to research on Afrocentric schools will extend the conversation of racial inclusion. It is recommended that parents and families explore Afrocentric education options for students. Although Asa G. Hilliard is a private school, there are several public Afrocentric schools across the United States in cities such as Philadelphia, Columbus, and Detroit. Alternatively, parents and teachers can advocate for the inclusion of antiracist or African-centered curriculum guidelines within their local school district. This was briefly witnessed in the 1990s with the introduction of Afrocentric curricula in public school systems (Binder, 2000; Leake & Leake, 1992b), and is equally needed today. The overwhelming positive feedback from teachers, students, and administrators confirms that Afrocentric schools and curricula could be beneficial for *all* students on the basis of academics, social skills, and cultural knowledge.

LIMITATIONS

This study's site was a small, private Afrocentric school, which is separate from the surrounding public school district. Asa G. Hilliard's small size and low student-teacher ratio could have solely contributed to the positive learning experiences of participants. Because the research intent was to explore

Afrocentric schools in general, the ability for this small private school to represent the surrounding population is limited. Additionally, all participants included in this research identified as Black. AGHA is comprised of 100% African American students and teachers. Therefore, participants responded to questions about AGHA based on their personal perceptions as African Americans. Notwithstanding, these narratives were important for determining AGHA's school culture and education as self-healing power.

Additionally, parent socioeconomic status is important to consider. Although AGHA is in a low-income neighborhood, it is a private school. Parents are assumed to be of working- or middle-class backgrounds, with at least some college education. This differs from the school's surrounding neighborhood. Additionally, as a private school, parents generally have a vested financial interest in the school's academic performance. Although this is beyond the scope of this study, this could possibly be a contributing factor to AGHA students' academic success.

Additionally, Afrocentric schools vary in their design and curriculum. There is no one generalizable Afrocentric school model; however, as we have noted throughout the book, there are some common tenets that most Afrocentric schools share. Additionally, it should be noted that school-level implementations are governed by individual school leaders and administrators. As with any case study, the findings cannot be generalized, as the contexts of each case likely differ (Creswell, 2013).

Last, we acknowledge that there are gender and class differences among Black students within Afrocentric schools. While the examination of class and gender were outside the study's scope, we want to acknowledge that students across various subgroups can benefit from the self-healing power of education. As for racial diversity, we emphasize again that all races will benefit from applying the principles of this book: the self-healing power of education works for all cultural groups. In the future, we welcome more nuanced explanations of education's self-healing power across gender and socioeconomic lines.

POLICY RECOMMENDATIONS

Today's student population is extremely diverse (U.S. Census Bureau, 2015). Population trajectories predict that by 2060, the U.S. student demographic will reach 64% minority students, with biracial and multiracial students increasing at rates of 226%. As such, today's public school students are vastly diverse in terms of language, religion, sexuality, national origin, immigrant status, and ethnicity. Meanwhile the teacher workforce is stagnant, with more than 80% White teachers, and is not diversifying at the same rate as the student population (NCES, 2017a). Although there are academic advantages regarding having diverse student and teacher populations

(Egalite & Kisida, 2016), educators must continue to explore critical alternatives in order to address pervasive legacies of omission, falsification, and historical and cultural distortions throughout school curricula. As our data have clearly shown, Afrocentric schools are a possible alternative model that could be beneficial for students.

Throughout this book, we argued that the implementation of Afrocentric education is a step in the right direction, especially for African American students, who are often left marginalized and decentered within their own educational experiences. Although the U.S. government and constitution delegates educational power to individual states, there is still a need to unify some multicultural policies in order to benefit the nation collectively. Research has consistently shown the benefits of ethnic studies programs (Donald, 2016; Romero, 2010), yet these initiatives are often faced with divisive political discourse. Thus, the federal government, along with individual states and local governments, should consider the following recommendations in order to better accommodate the needs of the nation's diverse learners. As such, these policies and recommendations include but extend beyond Afrocentric schools and are also intended for general public school reform, as public schools are the institutions that are intended to educate all children.

Federal/National

It is imperative that national educational reform become nonpartisan. Party politics should not usurp or undermine sound school reform. The transient nature of federal reform initiatives and policies are damaging for students and teachers, as the reforms generally follow the path and fate of the political party that introduced them (Hernen, 2016). To that end, although there are constitutional barriers, the Secretary of Education position should be restructured as a nonpartisan executive position, instead of a cabinet nomination. For sake of reference, this should be a national position with input from all stakeholders. Perhaps the Secretary of Education position should be revisited, and instead a Executive Education Officer position (with supporting employees) created that is a nonpartisan federal position. In this office, a team would be hired to help deliver effective reforms aimed at equity. Education is a public good and should work for all citizens. As an executive position, the Executive Education Officer should have national public performance reviews with stated objectives and target goals. Performance reviews can also justify the hiring or replacement of the person in this office. The job description should reflect that of a person who is highly trained, experienced, practitioner-focused, and knowledgeable about public schools, research design, and reforms. The performance review of the Officer should also be supported by program evaluation, which helps to ensure that effective school policies and recommendations are being implemented. Also, the disparities in school finance across states should be addressed nationally to create greater equity across states and districts. Within this role, it is imperative that at the national level the Officer provide consistent and cohesive guidelines for school reform and multicultural education. As mentioned, the pervasive dangers of traditional multiculturalism are ineffective and often reify European ethos; thus, it is important for multicultural curricula to be realigned to be more inclusive in public schools. This includes revising national standards and introducing multicultural assessments, textbook guidelines, and school reforms. Additionally, another national recommendation is to increase federal funding to better compensate teachers in general, and specifically qualified teachers in high-needs, low-performing schools (Beese & Liang, 2010; Children's Defense Fund, 2017). In the United States, the national average for new teacher salaries is less than $38,000 per year; it is not competitive with other fields. Also, although the effectiveness of Title I funds has been debated (Dynarski & Kainz, 2015), it is undeniable that teacher quality has a direct impact on student achievement (Darling-Hammond, 2000).

State

Considering that the current structure of education in the United States allows primary autonomy to individual state governments, it is imperative that teacher education programs adequately address cultural diversity. This includes restructuring preservice teacher education, professional developments, and curriculum method courses. While this book showcases a private Afrocentric school, there are even broader strategies that are useful in public school settings. Some of the strategies found in this research include extending the scope of multiculturalism, student-centered learning, current events and civic engagement pedagogy, and embedding student heritages within classroom curricula. At the preservice and in-service teacher levels, these are important avenues to explore in relation to training and professional development.

As mentioned, states must implement policies that deliver antiracist training at all levels. This is also a key for educational leaders. Recent research supports the importance of embedding heritage pedagogy, instead of solely focusing on cultural relevance (King & Swartz, 2018). Within individual states, the implementation of antiracist and critical multicultural education should always be considered. These curricula and pedagogical methods are beneficial for all students, not just those of African descent (Donald, 2016). Teachers should focus on teaching strategies that connect to students' respective cultures. Additionally, states need to revisit curriculum textbooks and pedagogical practices that reinforce hegemony. Ultimately, state governments have the primary responsibility to modify state standards and textbook curricula to be more inclusive and to reflect greater accuracy.

Local

Local schools can benefit from the teaching practices at AGHA in several ways. Regardless of school type, local schools should constantly be revising their means of providing professional development to teachers. To start, one key tenet for local schools to consider is the mindfulness of student heritage and culture in the classroom. While the state recommendations described above are a positive attempt at change, educators must be diligent in incorporating heritage knowledge that pertains specifically to individual student populations. Students should be encouraged to embrace, not deny, their cultures and their surrounding school communities. This helps to encourage positive student identity and heritage development (Agyepong, 2010). In this same vein, teachers should also be aware of their own heritage and embrace the importance of positive identity formation within classrooms. This is an important tool when communicating with students, parents, and community members.

Additionally, although Gay (2000) and Ladson-Billings (1994) contend that understanding student culture is important when implementing relevancy and relationship in classrooms, King and Swartz (2018) extend this argument by highlighting the need for heritage-based practices that rely on ancestral knowledge. In this regard, schools should create space for critical thinking and discussions, specifically surrounding topics of race, racial identity, history, and current events (Freire, 2000; Nieto & Bode, 2008). The benefits of these critical discussions for students are widely researched, and adaptable for students across geographic locales and school types.

SUMMARY

Inaccurate research surrounding Black education fails to account for the innate genius found in all children (Murrell, 2002; Perry et al., 2003; Wilson, 1992). AGHA continues to counter negative stereotypes about Black students through its demonstration of rigor, relevancy, and cultural affirmation, which are embedded in the Afrocentric learning environment. Findings demonstrate that students and teachers at Asa G. Hilliard find the learning environment to be engaging, relevant, and interdisciplinary. Additionally, the participants view their Afrocentric education as both culturally and socially important. Students and teachers at Asa G. Hilliard expressed increased self-awareness, greater ancestral knowledge, and a comprehensive grasp of world history from a nonhegemonic perspective. These are outcomes presumably beneficial for all people. When considering the lack of multiculturalism found in traditional public schools, Afrocentricity should be considered as an alternative model of education and inclusion. The implications for large-scale implementation may rest on the willingness of policymakers to explore best practice in education.

In closing, an excerpt from Plato's *Laws* provides an excellent summation of the final points of this study. Plato includes an interesting dialogue between two Greek citizens—a nameless Athenian and Clinias—in 348 BCE about Egypt's exceptional education system. This seemingly comical exchange between two unrelated Greeks surprisingly has direct educational relevance today.

> *Athenian:* One ought to declare, then, that the freeborn children should learn as much of these subjects as the innumerable crowd of children in Egypt learn along with their letters. First, as regards counting, lessons have been invented for the merest infants to learn, by way of play and fun—modes of dividing up apples and chaplets, so that the same totals are adjusted to larger and smaller groups, and modes of sorting out boxers and wrestlers, in byes and pairs, taking them alternately or consecutively, in their natural order. Moreover, by way of play, the teachers mix together bowls made of gold, bronze, silver and the like, and others distribute them, as I said, by groups of a single kind, adapting the rules of elementary arithmetic to play; and thus they are of service to the pupils for their future tasks of drilling, leading and marching armies, or of household management, and they render them both more helpful in every way to themselves and more alert. The next step of the teachers is to clear away, by lessons in weights and measures, a certain kind of ignorance, both absurd and disgraceful, which is naturally inherent in all men touching lines, surfaces and solids.
>
> *Clinias:* What ignorance do you mean, and of what kind is it?
>
> *Athenian:* My dear Clinias, when I was told quite lately of our condition in regard to this matter, I was utterly astounded myself: it seemed to me to be the condition of guzzling swine rather than of human beings, and I was ashamed, not only of myself, but of all the Greek world. (Plato, 348 BCE [1968], p. 819).

As displayed in the above conversation between an Athenian and Clinias, the Egyptians continuously baffled the ancient Greeks. The Hellenic world, as described by the Athenian, was too late in matters of educational reform, even before the first century. The Egyptians mastered effective ways to educate their students, and made sure to embed *rigor* and *relevancy* within the curriculum as early as infancy. Clinias, unknowing of the Greeks' ignorance, was baffled by the Athenian, who provided firsthand accounts of Egyptian education. In this brief exchange, the Athenian and Clinias share "shame" in Greece's outdated approaches for its students.

Just as the above dialogue captures Africa's immortal place in the human record, the power of the Egyptian ancestors continuously traverse time. Just as the Athenian and Clinias wish to disseminate the Egyptians' knowledge and teaching methods across their Grecian world, so too does this book aim to highlight the necessity of Afrocentric educational practices to promote healing and restoration.

Appendix A:
Teacher/Administrator Interview Protocol 1

Goal of the Study: I want to better understand the teachers and administrator experiences at Asa G. Hilliard Academy and identify how Afrocentric education can have utility for all students.

Type/Focus of Question	Question
Background	Tell me about yourself. How long have you been at [Asa G. Hilliard] Academy?
Descriptive	What do you do here at [Asa G. Hilliard] Academy? Tell me about your typical day.
Descriptive	What are the joys of teaching here? What are the challenges?
Descriptive	What is (or has been) your most rewarding experience since teaching here?
Introductory	What do you like about the learning environment at this school? What do you dislike about the learning environment at this school?
Reflective	Do you feel that the teaching environment at this school is helpful for students? Why or why not?
Reflective	How do you observe African values and traditions displayed at this school?
Reflective	What is your favorite moment in Black history? Do you have a favorite historical figure or role model?
Theoretical	What does the word "Afrocentricity" mean to you?
Reflective	What are your perceptions about Africa? What are some words that immediately come to mind?
Theoretical	How would you describe an African-centered education?
Curriculum	What are the benefits of African-centered curriculum models for students of color?
Prediction	How do you believe these curriculum designs could benefit all students?
Prediction	What improvements would you suggest for the curriculum at this school?

Appendix B:
Teacher/Administrator Interview Protocol 2

Goal of the Study: I want to better understand the teachers and administrator experiences at Asa G. Hilliard Academy and identify how Afrocentric education can have utility for all students.

Type/Focus of Question	Question
Reflective	How does teaching at [Asa G. Hilliard] Academy compare to other teaching positions or jobs you've had?
Reflective	Describe a moment when you expanded your knowledge about African or African American history.
Reflective	Describe a moment when you witnessed a student expand their knowledge about African or African American history.
Reflective	What is the role of Afrocentricity in teaching African American students?
Prediction	Do you believe any child could attend this school? Why or why not?
Reflective	In your opinion, what makes this school unique?
Prediction	How can environment and school practices at [Asa G. Hilliard] help other students in the community?
Prediction	What do you think are people's misconceptions about this school? Why do you think more families don't explore [Asa G. Hilliard] as a viable option for their children?
Prediction	What are ways African-centered education practices could be implemented in a public school?
Predictions	How can Afrocentricity be used as a tool of inclusion?
Reflective	Why is Afrocentricity/African-centered education helpful in shaping student identities?

Appendix C: Student Interview Protocol

Goal of the Study: I want to understand how middle school students at Asa G. Hilliard Academy identify the benefits of Afrocentric education and its utility for all students.

Type/Focus of Question	Question
Background	Tell me about yourself. How long have you been at [Asa G. Hilliard] Academy?
Descriptive	What do you do here at [Asa G. Hilliard] Academy? Tell me about your typical day.
Descriptive	What is the most enjoyable aspect about this school? What are the challenges that you face as a student here?
Descriptive	What is (or has been) the most rewarding aspect about being a student here?
Introductory	What do you like about this school? What do you dislike about this school?
Introductory	How do you view your teachers here at this school?
Curriculum	What are some things you've learned at this school that remind you of Africa?
Curriculum	Do you feel your education here at [Asa G. Hilliard] has helped you?
Reflective	What African traditions do you see at this school?
Reflective	How would you describe Africa?
Reflective	How have African traditions helped you view yourself?
Reflective	How has this school shaped your knowledge about Africa, African history, or African American events?
Reflective	What is your favorite moment in Black history? Do you have a favorite historical figure or role model? Who, and why are they your favorite?
Prediction	Do you believe anyone could attend this school? Why or why not?
Reflective	How is this school different from previous schools you've attended?
Reflective	How would you describe the friendships you've made with teachers and students at this school? Have they been helpful?
Prediction	What are ways that this school could help other students?
Prediction	What improvements would you suggest to make the school better?
Prediction	What would you like to see in a high school here?

Appendix D:
Student Written Essay Prompt

Goal of the Study: I want to understand how middle school students at Asa G. Hilliard Academy identify the benefits of Afrocentric education and its utility for all students.

Type/Focus of Question	Question
Reflective	What are your experiences since going to this school? Describe ways that an African-centered education (Asa G. Hilliard Academy) was either a positive or negative influence on your education? If you could tell someone about this school, what would you say?

Appendix E:
Afrocentric Learning Observation Rubric

Goal of the Study: I want to understand how Asa G. Hilliard Academy facilitates an Afrocentric learning environment, as outlined in the school's mission and objectives.

Asa G. Hilliard Academy has built its program around the concept currently known as "African-Centered" education. Our holistic approach is based on the premise that children will only excel academically and intellectually when the curriculum, teaching methodology, and environment reflects the builders of yesterday and the ideas of the future. Our belief in universal knowledge provides each student with the skills to meet the challenges of tomorrow. We use African Principles to teach and cultivate character and creativity with each student.

Name	Definition	Evidences	Observed Example
Umoja (Unity)	Unity stresses the importance of togetherness for the family and the community, which is reflected in the African saying, "I am We," or "I am because We are."	• Students work together in collaborative groups. • The familial environment of the school/classroom is evident. • Group collaboration is encouraged more than individualism.	November 21, 11:00 am Cafeteria observation: The cafeteria manager and head cook let a select group of middle school students help cook and serve the younger students for lunch. This was an embedded component of their Home Economics class. The younger students enjoyed seeing the "older kids." There was an evident sense of "community" between the younger students and older students. Many of the younger students clapped and cheered "YAY!!" when the older students served them their lunch.
Kujichagulia (Self-Determination)	Self-Determination requires that we define our common interests and make decisions that are in the best interest of our family and community.	• Students and teacher have unified learning goals. • Classroom decisions are made with family interests and the community in mind. • Students exhibit self-determination and perseverance when completing assignments.	November 20, 10:20 am Ms. Humphries led K–1st grade students in a discussion about the Wampanoag Indian Tribe. One of the students said that the English settlers helped the Native Americans—but before Ms. Humphries could say anything—children interrupted and said "NO! The Native Americans helped the settlers! They were there first!" Later in the lesson, Ms. Humphries asked, "What kinds of foods do you think the Native Americans ate who lived along the coast?" One of the students said corn. Another said fish. Ms. Humphries said, "very good . . . why do you think they ate fish?" she asked. After about three tries, one of the students said, "Because they were near water and rivers and that means they were fishermen!" Ms. Humphries then proceeded in a lesson on how the Native Americans were resourceful and kind.

| Ujima (Collective Work and Responsibility) | Collective Work and Responsibility reminds us of our obligation to the past, present, and future, and that we have a role to play in the community, society, and world. | • Students critically discuss how lesson connects to past, present, and future.
• Students discuss the significance of classroom assignments in relation to the larger society/community.
• Students identify their own sense of agency or "obligation" to collectively help society. | December 5, 10:00 am
Art teacher engages middle school students in a discussion about the Eric Garner case. He opens class with a loud announcement. "CLASS! WE HAVE A PROBLEM! A man was choked to death for illegally selling cigarettes!"
Students immediately offer their opinions about the case, either for or against the decision. Everyone engages in dialogue about the criminal justice system, hypocrisy, and how each of them are impacted.
Without prompting, they begin to centralize themselves within their own education. The teacher plays devil's advocate for a couple of the students' points, while the students reenact the scenario.
The class was outraged and immediately created social action signs for anti-police violence demonstrations. |
| Ujamaa (Cooperative Economics) | Cooperative Economics emphasizes our collective economic strength and encourages us to meet common needs through mutual support. | • Classrooms collaborate with one another.
• Students participate in civic engagement and help the surrounding community and/or the surrounding community's aid is evident in the classroom.
• The learning environment is welcoming toward visitors, administration, and anyone from the surrounding community. | October 24, 1:15 pm
Local artist from the community led middle school students in an art lesson. Students studied 20th-century panel art and took inspiration from Jacob Lawrence, a famous Black painter. |

Name	Definition	Evidences	Observed Example
Nia (Purpose)	Purpose encourages us to look within ourselves and to set personal goals that are beneficial to the community.	• Assignments connect to the larger surrounding community. • Classroom assignments serve a purpose and are not interpreted as "busywork." • Students are allowed to set personal goals for assignments.	December 5, 1:05 pm After the Eric Garner discussion, Mr. Lacey, the technology and drama teacher, took time to teach life skills to the middle school boys that day. He continuously stressed, if a police officer comes up behind you and you're driving a car– "KEEP YOUR HAND ON 10 and 2!!! DO NOT MOVE! Your life is too precious." In light of the news events, the lesson's purpose connected students to current events in the surrounding community.
Kuumba (Creativity)	Creativity makes use of our creative energies to build and maintain a strong and vibrant community.	• Classroom environment/ instruction is energetic and vibrant. • Instruction is engaging for various learning styles. • Instruction contains some "nontraditional" components to enhance effectiveness.	October 21st, 8:30 am Devotion observation: Ms. Saleem's class started singing and chanting about positive behavior and their ability to succeed. Students were given opportunities to dance and sing along with the chant, which was a fun- and spirit-filled away to start the day. It was extremely engaging and energetic.

Imani (Faith)	Faith focuses on honoring the best of our traditions, draws on the best in ourselves, and helps us strive for a higher level of life for humankind, by affirming our self-worth and confidence in our ability to succeed and triumph in righteous struggle.	• Students are verbally affirmed in a positive way. • Positive written affirmations are clearly displayed in classroom environment. • Teachers are affirmed in a positive way.	December 17th, 7:00 pm Kwanzaa Program observation: Students, teachers, staff, and parents engaged in a "liberation ceremony" where they lighted candles to remember ancestors who had transitioned on. It was a time for everyone to reflect on person's legacy and life. It was also a time to share about gratefulness and thankfulness.

Appendix F: Research Design Flow Chart

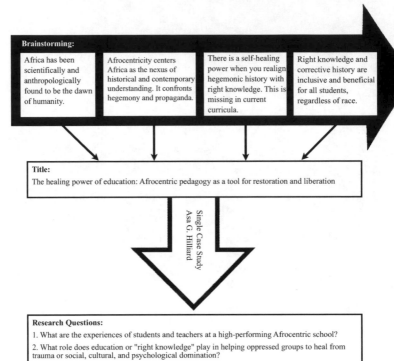

Brainstorming:

Africa has been scientifically and anthropologically found to be the dawn of humanity.

Afrocentricity centers Africa as the nexus of historical and contemporary understanding. It confronts hegemony and propaganda.

There is a self-healing power when you realign hegemonic history with right knowledge. This is missing in current curricula.

Right knowledge and corrective history are inclusive and beneficial for all students, regardless of race.

Title:
The healing power of education: Afrocentric pedagogy as a tool for restoration and liberation

Single Case Study
Asa G. Hilliard

Research Questions:
1. What are the experiences of students and teachers at a high-performing Afrocentric school?
2. What role does education or "right knowledge" play in helping oppressed groups to heal from trauma or social, cultural, and psychological domination?

Data Collection:
Interview students, teachers, and the administrator at Asa G. Hilliard Academy to examine participant experiences at an African-centered school and determine how Afrocentric education could be used as a healing mechanism for addressing social, cultural, and psychological domination.

Engage students in a writing prompt to receive open-ended responses regarding their perceptions of African-centered education.

Conduct classroom/school observations.

Appendix G: Daily Devotion ("The Seven Principles")

We the students of Asa G. Hilliard Academy believe that the seven principles will teach us the values of life:

UMOJA (oo-MO-jah)—Unity—to strive for and maintain unity in the
 family, community, nation and race.
KUJICHAGULIA (koo-jee-cha-goo-LEE-ah)—Self-determination—to
 define ourselves, name ourselves, create for ourselves, and speak for
 ourselves.
UJIMA (oo-JEE-mah)—Collective work and responsibility—to build and
 maintain our community together and make our sisters' and brothers'
 problems our own and solve them together.
UJAMAA (oo-jah-MAH)—Cooperative economics—to build and maintain
 our own stores, shops and other businesses and to profit from them
 together.
NIA (NEE-ah)—Purpose—to make our collective vocation to building of
 our community to restore our people to their traditional greatness.
KUUMBA (koo-OOM-bah)—Creativity—to do as much as we can to
 leave our community more beautiful and beneficial than we inherited it.
IMANI (ee-MAH-nee)—Faith—to believe with our heart in our people,
 our parents, our teachers, our leaders, and the righteousness and victory
 of our struggle.

Appendix H: Daily Devotion ("Nobility")

True worth is in being, not seeming—
In doing, each day that goes by,
Some little good—not in dreaming
Of great things to do by and by.
For whatever men say in their blindness,
And spite of the fancies of youth,
There's nothing so kingly as kindness,
And nothing so royal as truth.
We get back our mete as we measure—
We cannot do wrong and feel right,
Nor can we give pain and gain pleasure,
For justice avenges each slight.
The air for the wing of the sparrow,
The bush for the robin and wren,
But always the path that is narrow
And straight, for the children of men.
'Tis not in the pages of story
The heart of its ills to beguile,
Though he who makes courtship to glory
Gives all that he hath for her smile.
For when from her heights he has won her,
Alas! It is only to prove
That nothing's so sacred as honor,
And nothing so loyal as love!
We cannot make bargains for blisses,
Nor catch them like fishes in nets;
And sometimes the thing our life misses
Helps more than the thing which it gets.
For good lieth not in pursuing,
Nor gaining of great nor or small,
But just in the doing, and doing
As we would be done by, is all.
Through envy, through malice, through hating,
Against the world, early and late,
No jot of our courage abating—
Our part is to work and to wait.
And slight is the sting of his trouble
Whose winnings are less than his worth;
For he who is honest is noble,
Whatever his fortunes or birth.

Appendix I: Daily Devotion ("The Ultimate Student")

By Collins (Westside Prep), Fred Hampton, Franklin Philips

The world belongs to us . . . *So gaze* upon this triumphant *piercing* sight—
the builders of the pyramids and vital contributors to the magnificent,
glorious wonders of America's present and future.

We are the ultimate students . . . who attribute our extremely high self-
esteem and our tough as nails disposition to our philosophical belief
"that no one can make you feel inferior without your consent."

We are the epitome of the expression "Excellence breeds excellence."
We are tried, true and tested under fire in a tough, competitive
environment. We reach for the unreached. WE take care of business. We
are resilient, heroically bold, extremely candid, swift of mind, proud,
yet humble.

We are the ultimate students who renew our quest for excellence every day.
We seize the moment, we do not look back, we make big plans, we aim
high. We always play to win.

We are the ultimate students . . . to whom much is given, much is
expected.

We do not rest on our laurels, nor do we place any limits on our
intellectual or spiritual achievement. We never settle for "just getting by,
making excuses, taking short cuts, cutting corners, beating the system
or goofing-off."

We are not eager to follow others; we are not impressed with glitter or
glam, nor are we swayed by peer pressure.

We elect instead to soar like the eagle always striving to achieve the magic
and honor of leadership before we settle for the lesser, easier role of
following others.

We are the ultimate students . . . We measure our success not by what we
are, but by what we could be; not by what we have done, but by what
we can do.

We possess extreme confidence, character and self-abnegation.
We are not timid, intimidated or small minded.

Tomorrow belongs to us, and yesterday's accomplishments will pale in
comparison without academic achievements . . . We are adventurous,
creative, daring and willing to accomplish what others say *cannot be
done*.

We are the ultimate students . . . Who are *respected* for inquiring, tameless,
universal minds. We do not rest until our thoughts turn to actions.

We think beyond the traditional by reaching deeper into the unknown, by
asking "What If?", "What About?", and "What Else?"

We are the ultimate students . . . When we try, we do not cheat. When we
lose, we do not cry. And, when we compete, we take no prisoners—
none.

The world belongs to us . . . The future belongs to us . . . And today begins
with us . . . *The Ultimate Students*.

Appendix J: Daily Devotion ("I Have The Power")

I have the power to choose, and that makes me a powerful person.
I have the power to make the right choices.
I have the power to choose to be honest.
I have the power to choose to be kind.
I have the power to ask my parents, caregivers, or teachers when
I'm not sure what choice to make.
I have the power!

Appendix K: Daily Devotion ("Can't")

"Can't" is a favorite word of some children.
Here is the case against it.
Can't is the worst word that's written or spoken;
Doing more harm here than slander and lies;
On it is many a strong spirit broken,
And with it many a good purpose dies.
It springs from the lips of the thoughtless each morning
And robs us of courage we need through the day
It rings in our ears like a timely sent warning
And laughs when we falter and fall by the way.
Can't is the father of feeble endeavor,
The parent of terror and half-hearted work;
It weakens the efforts of artisans clever,
And makes of the toiler an indolent shirk.
It poisons the soul of the man with a vision,
It stifles in infancy many a plan;
It greets honest toiling with open derision
And mocks at the hopes and the dreams of a man.
Can't is a word none should speak without blushing;
To utter it should be a symbol of shame;
Ambition and courage it daily is crushing;
It blights a man's purpose and shortens his aim.
Despise it with all of your hatred of error;
Refuse it the lodgment it seeks in your brain;
Arm against it as a creature of terror,
And all that you dream of you someday shall gain.
Can't is a word that is foe to ambition,
An enemy ambushed to shatter your will;
Its prey is forever the man with a mission
And bows but to courage and patience and skill.
Hate it, with hatred that's deep and undying,
For once it is welcomed 'twill break any man;
Whatever the goal you are seeking, keep trying
And answer this demon by saying: "I can."

Appendix L: Daily Devotion ("Lift Every Voice and Sing")

By James Weldon Johnson

Lift every voice and sing
Till earth and heaven ring
Ring with the harmonies of Liberty;
Let our rejoicing rise,
High as the listening skies, let it resound loud as the rolling sea
Sing a song full of faith that the dark past has taught us,
Sing a song full of the hope that the present has brought us;
Facing the rising sun of our new day begun,
Let us march on till victory is won.

Stony the road we trod,
Bitter the chast'ning rod,
Felt in the day when hope unborn had died;
Yet with a steady beat,
Have not our weary feet,
Come to the place for which our fathers sighed?
We have come over a way that with tears has been watered,
We have come, treading our path through the blood of the slaughtered,
Out from the gloomy past, till now we stand at last
Where the white gleam of our star is cast.

God of our weary years,
God of our silent tears,
Thou who has brought us thus far on the way;
Thou who has by thy might,
Led us into the light,
Keep us forever in the path, we pray
Lest our feet stray from the places, our God, where we met thee,
Lest our hearts, drunk with the wine of the world, we forget thee,
Shadowed beneath the hand,
May we forever stand,
True to our God,
True to our native land.

Appendix M: Research Context

My mother said I must always be intolerant of ignorance but understanding of illiteracy. That some people, unable to go to school, were more educated and more intelligent than college professors.

—Maya Angelou, 1969

I have never encountered any children in any group who are not geniuses. There is no mystery on how to teach them. The first thing you do is treat them like human beings and the second thing you do is love them.

—Asa G. Hilliard III, 1994

This appendix outlines the research method used for this study, including the research outline, sample selection, data-gathering process, analysis of the data, limitations of the research method, and basic assumptions. This appendix provides a discussion on the research method and responds to two critical questions of the book: (1) What are the experiences of students and teachers at a high-performing Afrocentric school? (2) What role does education or "right knowledge" play in helping oppressed groups to heal from trauma or social, cultural, and psychological domination? In the book, the terms "Afrocentric" and "African-centered" are used interchangeably. Overall, the single case study research method used allowed for an in-depth examination of a specific school site (Creswell, 2013; Glense, 2011).

ROLE OF THE AUTHOR RESEARCHERS

The authors are both former middle school teachers in large metropolitan public school systems. During this time, they taught language arts and social studies, respectively. While teaching, one of them noticed a keen interest in African American history, specifically during the school's designated Black History Month, among students. The principal of the school at this time allowed for more curriculum flexibility during the month of February (Black History Month), and the then-teacher used this added freedom for historical examinations of African American history, as well as current events that impacted urban Black students. This point demonstrates a teaching and curriculum development background for middle school students. Through their experience, the authors frequently questioned the effectiveness of standardized curricula that were not engaging for students. The change resulting from this questioning helped shape both of the author researchers' quests to better understand alternative forms of curricula.

Through the aforementioned experiences as educators, the authors cannot deny the influence of these moments on this study. We advocate for alternative and culturally inclusive forms of curricula, based on seeing the effectiveness of such models in past experiences. One author admits while in graduate school having some hesitation regarding the term "Afrocentricity," as it was often negatively propagated and feared. Through a specific doctoral class, *Education as Self-Healing Power*, this author instead found benefits in Afrocentricity as a tool of mediation, healing, and inclusion. As the authors began to realign the true meaning of Afrocentric theory, former experiences as public school educators were inseparable from the unseen possibilities of Afrocentricity, especially for 21st-century students. These experiences are important to the book's positioning. We aim to neutralize the bias from past practitioner and researcher experiences in order to present the findings objectively.

As former middle school educators, the authors have an increased interest in effective curriculum designs for students. Since both researchers are familiar with middle school curricula, state standards, and curriculum development, there is a keen interest in developing more engaging curriculum models for students. Thus, the authors volunteered at the school site periodically throughout the 2013–2014 school year in order to observe a tangible example of Afrocentric practices in education. Both authors are familiar with some staff at the school, but were unfamiliar with the middle school student population. The author researchers carefully bracketed the data collected at the site in order to account for any biases that might occur from formerly knowing some of the staff and teachers. All data from the site location were analyzed with particular attention paid to any indication of former knowledge of participants.

Afrocentricity, as mentioned, is a continuous, reflexive, and introspective journey toward truth and understanding. Thus, this research was not aimed to critique and assess the effectiveness of Afrocentricity being used at the participating school site; rather, we aimed to identify ways in which the school served as a form of healing and restoration for African American students. The continuum and never-ending process involved with Afrocentricity is important to identify. Appendix F in the book provides a flow chart that outlines the thought processes for conceptualizing this research.

THEORETICAL FRAMEWORK

As noted in Chapter 1 of the book, Afrocentric theory is a theoretical framework that focuses keenly on African-centeredness. It is also a theory that undergirds various school designs, such as the one in this book. In short, Afrocentricity positions the African Diaspora and continental Africa at the center of discussion. It also reestablishes African people as *participants* versus *objects* (Asante, 1998). Out of respect for the nature of this work, Afrocentricity was the most ideal theory that aligned with exploring the importance of African-centered school designs. In essence, it includes both the *theoretical* and *educational* perspectives being studied.

Researcher and theorist Molefi Asante describes Afrocentricity's distinctive paradigm differences:

> Afrocentricity is essentially the idea that African persons are the subjects, that is, human agents, working out our own destinies within the context of our historical experiences as opposed to being objects in the margins of European experiences. It is a way of viewing reality that places us in the center of our culture and social environment. When a person believes that the society is only to be used, that people are only to be victimized, that neighborhoods are alien, he or she is capable of the worst kinds of actions. Afrocentricity creates a framework for dealing with this type of dislocation. (Asante, 1993, p. 124)

To appreciate the tenets of this theory, it must be understood how Afrocentricity can be both a study's topic (i.e., Afrocentric school model) and a theoretical framework that guides the book.

AFROCENTRICITY

As noted, Afrocentricity places Africa at the center (Asante, 1993, 1998; Lemert, 2010). This theoretical framework essentially removes Africa from the margins of Eurocentric analysis and posits that people of African descent are valuable contributors to their own history (Ani, 1994; Asante, 1998). Asante asserts that Africa should be at the center of historical and societal analysis, and for factual reasons. Wiggan (2010) describes Afrocentricity as "the indispensable perspective on the centrality of Africa and [B]lack studies" (p. 131). The critical need for Africa's "indispensable" perspective is relevant, not only regarding precolonial history, but also in contemporary discussions as well. Asante (1998) argues, "African Americans are a preeminently cultured people within American society, and our contributions to what is called 'popular American culture' are immense" (p. 9). Accepting Afrocentricity requires the dismissal of exclusive Eurocentric thought and the welcoming of other cultural perspectives (Ani, 1994; Asante, 1993, 1998).

Another aspect of Afrocentricity is the rejection of Eurocentric paradigms as the definitive measure of the Black experience. This is also important when selecting theoretical frameworks. Afrocentricity postulates its preeminent role in describing the African experience, and posits that it should be used without the validation or substantiation of other theories. Asante (1998) further questions, "How can the oppressed use the same theories as the oppressors? Is it possible that established European theory regards its view as the best way to understand?" (p. 181). Establishing a separate paradigm for "Africa" is the only theoretical framework that could accurately depict African perspectives alongside other multicultural, critical, and conflict frameworks.

Afrocentricity is also a theoretical framework that guides education. Traoré (2007) suggests that educators teach history, for example, based on "compiled [stories] of Africa told from their own perspective, filtered through the lens of long-standing colonial domination of the African nations" (p. 62). Thus, many African American students have little interest in a curriculum that is obviously nonreflective of their people. History and literature are often dedicated to Western ideals, and ignore the multiculturalism frequently represented in American classrooms (Karenga, 1995). Traoré (2007) further argues that telling a more Afrocentric story involves "making available the accomplishments of people of African descent, and learning more themselves about the continent and its people, not just its land masses and natural resources, but its human resources" (p. 70). In spite of its critics, the usefulness of the Afrocentric perspective is evident. Asante (1998) argues that "without the Afrocentric perspective, the imposition of the European line as universal hinders cultural understanding and demeans humanity" (p. 11). The Afrocentric analysis of the world deconstructs the pervasive and hegemonic way that Eurocentric education diminishes other cultures (Karenga, 2002; Murrell, 2002). For this current work, it is central that an Afrocentric perspective is used to frame a study on an African-centered school (Pellerin, 2012). Any other theory would not adequately capture the primary goals of this research.

CASE STUDY METHOD

The purpose of this study was to explore the experiences and perceptions of students and teachers at an Afrocentric school. In addition, this study aimed to determine Afrocentricity and *education as self-healing power*. To achieve this goal, it was important to capture the teacher, student, and administrator perspectives. All of the stakeholders' perspectives were important to this study's design. This study was intended to capture the experiences at one specific school; thus, a single case study method was the best qualitative method. In this study, the single school site for the case was Asa G. Hilliard Academy, or AGHA (pseudonym). Since the research aimed to explore an "unusual interest in and of itself," the case study intent was *intrinsic* in nature (Creswell, 2013, p. 98).

According to Yin (2003), "a case study is an empirical inquiry that: investigates a contemporary phenomenon within its real-life context, especially when the boundaries between phenomenon and context are not clearly evident" (p. 13). The real-life context for this study was the school environment at Asa G. Hilliard Academy. Classroom observations were conducted to document instructional and curriculum practices that differed from the mainstream, hegemonic pedagogy. Afrocentric classroom strategies include, but are not limited to: student-centered learning, positive affirmation, familial classroom environment, respect for community, higher-order thinking, and group activities (Dei, 2012; King et al., 2014; Ladson-Billings, 1994; Murrell, 2002). In addition to classroom observations, interviews were conducted with teachers, students, and the school's administrator regarding their thoughts and perceptions of AGHA. Last, student essay responses were collected to an open-ended prompt regarding the student's experiences at AGHA. This data helped to capture student perceptions of their Afrocentric schooling experiences.

Using a single case study was most beneficial for this study because of the singular school site. Data were collected from three primary sources in hopes of gathering rich depictions that exposed the unique learning experiences at AGHA. These data sources included interview transcripts, classroom observation notes, and student essay responses. For a single case study, it was imperative that the modes of data collection were in-depth and consisted of "many forms of qualitative data, ranging from interviews, to observations, to documents, to audiovisual materials" (Creswell, 2013, p. 98). Creswell suggests that relying on one form of data for single case studies is usually an ineffective way of capturing the entire case.

INSTRUMENTATION

This study aimed to understand the nature of an Afrocentric/African-centered school, specifically at one site. As mentioned earlier, Afrocentricity is an interpretive concept that falls on a continuum of truth and understanding. Thus, it was important to understand how this study's particular school defined the term "Afrocentricity" or "African-centeredness." The school's mission statement identified Afrocentricity's role in the Asa G. Hilliard learning environment:

> [AGHA] has built its program around the concept, currently known as "African-Centered" education. [AGHA's] holistic approach is based upon the premise that children will only excel academically and intellectually when the curriculum, teaching methodology, and environment reflect the builders of yesterday and the ideas of the future. [AGHA's] belief in universal knowledge provides each student with the skills to meet the challenges of tomorrow. [AGHA] uses African Principles to teach and cultivate character and creativity with each student. ("What We Do," 2013, para. 1)

The school site (Asa G. Hilliard) uses the seven principles of Nguzo Saba. As displayed in Table M.1, these seven principles are umoja (unity), kujichagulia (self-determination), ujima (collective work and responsibility), ujamaa (cooperative economics), nia (purpose), kuumba (creativity), and imani (faith).

Nguzo Saba's seven principles most famously align with the holiday Kwanzaa, which also promotes personal and group healing. The school had no former affiliation with Maulana Karenga or the Kwanzaa holiday specifically; instead, the school used the aforementioned principles as an applicable school mission statement and creed. The book's Appendix E demonstrates how these seven principles were used as a metric for observation. Nguzo Saba was not a formal assessment; rather, this research design used the seven principles as a guide when assessing Afrocentricity throughout the school and in the classroom. Instructors and school personnel were not bound to the metrics used in the observation rubric; instead the project

Table M.1. Nguzo Saba: The Seven Principles

Name	Definition
Umoja (Unity)	To strive for and maintain unity in the family, community, nation, and race
Kujichagulia (Self-Determination)	To define ourselves, name ourselves, create for ourselves, and speak for ourselves
Ujima (Collective Work and Responsibility)	To build and maintain our community together and make our brothers' and sisters' problems our problems and to solve them together
Ujamaa (Cooperative Economics)	To build and maintain our own stores, shops, and other businesses and to profit from them together
Nia (Purpose)	To make our collective vocation the building and developing of our community in order to restore our people to their traditional greatness
Kuumba (Creativity)	To do always as much as we can, in the way we can, in order to leave our community more beautiful and beneficial than we inherited it
Imani (Faith)	To believe with all our heart in our people, our parents, our teachers, our leaders, and the righteousness and victory of our struggle

Source: Karenga (1965).

aimed to observe how AGHA differentiated its instructional style from traditional schools.

THE SCHOOL SETTING

The setting for this single case study was a private school in a metropolitan, urban city in Georgia. Asa G. Hilliard Academy (pseudonym), or AGHA, is self-described as an African-centered school. As established earlier, African-centered is synonymous with Afrocentric in this research. At this site, Afrocentricity's *self-healing power* was examined by interviewing 15 5th- to 8th-grade students, four teachers, and one administrator. The research setting for this study was critical to the case study design. This allowed for observations of participants in their natural settings that did not disrupt their day-to-day routines (Creswell, 2013; Glense, 2011). For case studies, specifically, physical boundaries, as exemplified in the research setting, are critical for maintaining the "case" (Yin, 2003). AGHA served as the study's case. Some preliminary demographics of the school site are shown in Table M.2.

As we can calculate from the data in Table M.2, the average tuition is $7,860 per year for each student. This suggests that the student population came from middle- to upper-middle class families. The above information was obtained from the school's administrator and school website.

Teachers were observed in their classrooms as a part of the case study. Interviews and student essays were conducted in a separate space available within the focal school (Asa G. Hilliard Academy), such as an administrative office or counselor's room. In order to maintain confidentiality within the school locale, noninvasive times were chosen to conduct interviews. For example, teachers were interviewed during their individual planning periods or after school. Students were interviewed individually after school or

Table M.2. Asa G. Hilliard Academy Snapshot

Years in Existence	20+	
Grades Offered	Pre-K–8th	
Number of Students	100	
Number of Teachers	12	
Number of Administrators	1	
Racial Demographic (students and teacher)	100% African American	
Student Tuition (per year)	Pre-K	$7,140
	K–3rd	$8,000
	4th–6th	$8,100
	7th–8th	$8,200

during the lunch hour. Each interview was conducted individually on different days or times to ensure that participants maintained privacy.

SAMPLING

This study focused on one specific school site, AGHA. Because the site is small, including approximately 100 students and 12 teachers, purposive sampling was used. Purposive sampling was important to ensure that the study would not violate participant confidentiality. There were 20 participants total, including four teachers, one administrator, and 15 5th- to 8th-grade students. AGHA had approximately 20 to 25 enrolled 5th- to 8th-grade school students at the time of data collection, and it was important to capture as many participant experiences as possible for the case study. Twenty total participants provided insights on Afrocentric education, from varying perspectives. Although interviewing parents would have been helpful, doing so was beyond the scope of the study. Since Asa G. Hilliard is a private school and parents are required to pay tuition, it was assumed that families were educated and/or had a sort of "cultural awareness."

Purposive sampling was used for the student and teacher participants. An explanation of the specific sampling procedures is provided in detail in the sections below. Purposive sampling was particularly important in this case study in order to offer variety in the sample (Creswell, 2013). In this study, purposive sampling was important in selecting participants across different age ranges. Purposive sampling also allowed us to ensure that different demographics (male and female) were represented (Creswell, 2013; Glense, 2011). The following sections outline the different purposive sampling selection criteria used for both students and teachers.

STUDENT SELECTION

The student sample size contained 15 students ranging from 5th to 8th grade. This number was derived from the school's available middle school population (which ranges from 20 to 25 students). In order to obtain student consent, the school's monthly middle school parent meetings were attended prior to the commencement of the study. This meeting was prearranged with the administrator and conducted at the school site. This meeting was held to present the study's objectives to parents and students in order to recruit participants. Students were asked to complete one individual 30-minute interview, along with one written 30-minute essay. Preference was given to those students who had attended the school (AGHA) the longest (as indicated by their age and tenure at the school). As noted, purposive sampling was used to include the oldest students for the study—especially those in 7th and

8th grades. Purposive sampling also ensured that an even number of male and female participants was represented. In total, this study contained eight male participants and seven female participants.

TEACHER AND ADMINISTRATOR SELECTION

The teacher sample size included four participants, a number derived from the available teachers at the school site. Teacher and staff meetings were attended, as prearranged by the school administrator, and participants were presented the objectives of the study. The study's objectives were explained to the teachers, and the voluntary nature of participation was reiterated. Teachers and the administrator were asked to complete two 45-minute interviews, totaling 1.5 hours. Questions were openly answered and addressed concerns from the teachers regarding the study. Consent forms were presented to teachers to complete at the staff meetings. Each participant returned their forms voluntarily for the study.

There was only one administrator at the school site, who was asked to participate in the study. The administrator was made aware that participation in the study was completely voluntary. A meeting was held with the administrator to explain the objectives of the study and openly answer questions.

DATA COLLECTION, CODING, AND ANALYSIS, AND PHASES 1–3

Data Collection

Creswell (2013) mentions that collecting various forms of data is imperative for effective case studies. For single case studies, in particular, diverse groups of data are essential (Creswell, 2013; Glense, 2011). In this study, teachers, students, and the administrator were each vital aspects of the study, and contributed useful perspectives in *intrinsically* understanding the experience at AGHA (Creswell, 2013). Various data sources were gathered, including classroom observations, interviews, and students' written essays. The observations totaled to 20+ hours per month, and spanned across each of the participants' classrooms.

Additionally, the four teacher participants, along with the one administrator participant, individually engaged in two audiotaped interviews. These interviews lasted 45 minutes each, which totaled to 1.5 hours per teacher participant. The 15 student participants engaged in one 30-minute audiotaped interview, along with one written reflection essay lasting an additional 30 minutes, totaling 1 hour. Teacher and administrator interviews were arranged to accommodate their individual planning and work schedules (either during planning periods or before/after school). Student interviews and written essays were also arranged during nonacademic times (either lunch, extracurricular activity, or after school). The open-ended, semi-structured interviews were conducted using the approved interview protocol questions, as designated in the IRB protocol (see Appendixes A–C in the book). As indicated, students were asked different interview questions than the teachers and administrators. Interviews and field notes occurred congruently throughout the study, as designated later in phase 2 of the data collection timeline.

Data Analysis and Coding

As discussed, the data sources for this research study consisted of interviews, classroom observations, and discourse analysis of students' written essays. A holistic analysis of AGHA was used, and specifically highlighted various themes of inclusion within participant experiences (Creswell, 2013). The holistic analysis simply means that the entire case was analyzed in order to more accurately understand the phenomenon as a whole (Creswell, 2013). While it is clear that verbal interviews required coding and analysis, it is important to understand the other analysis processes for classroom observations and student essays. Field notes were collected during classroom observations. Open-ended notes were taken to document the Afrocentric evidences in the instructional style and curricular activities observed throughout the school (see the book's Appendix E). Student essays were written and completed individually by the students (see Appendix D). Audio recordings were used for interviews (see Appendixes A–C) and then transcribed.

Field notes and interview transcriptions were closely analyzed and coded (using open and axial coding), looking for themes, patterns, and variations within the written responses (Creswell, 2013). As mentioned, a holistic approach to analysis was used (Creswell, 2013). This started with open coding to identify common themes. Next, axial coding was used to categorize small segments of the field notes and interview transcripts according to identified words or phrases. During this phase, data were organized based on the two research questions and categorized into major themes. The themes represented reflect the experiences of teachers, students, and administrator attending an urban private Afrocentric school. Participants' data were analyzed using the same collective themes, each with their varying perspectives and experiences. Next, themes were identified that emerged from the open coding process, which later identified other themes and subthemes. For student essays, common themes were categorized and sorted according to students' written responses. Focused coding and line-by-line analysis were performed, which allowed for topical connections in the students' written reflection responses.

All data were collected and stored on a secure, password-protected laptop and stored in a locked cabinet at times when not in use. All participants' names were removed from the findings, and pseudonyms were used. Last, all participants were given the opportunity to review the transcriptions gathered throughout the research process.

Phase 1: Planning

The first phase of research planning occurred during the months of April 2014 through August 2014. During this phase, confirmation was received from the AGHA principal for site selection agreement. Next step: While working with the principal, meeting dates for the participants were arranged, including the staff meeting (for teachers) and parent meeting (for students) for the 2014–2015 school year. Additionally, in phase 1, the IRB was completed and submitted to the university for compliance on a human-subject study. During this phase, all of the necessary informed consents were secured from parents, teachers, and administrators.

Phase 2: Data Collection

Phase 2 of the study involved data collection. This phase was conducted August 2014 through December 2014 and involved two distinct steps. First, interviews were conducted with the participants. During this time, field notes were collected, as well as students' written narratives. None of these data-gathering processes were conducted in a particular order. Because this is a single case study, the participants' time and schedules were respected, and data were collected based on their availability. Ultimately, the goal was to capture the essence of the school culture without disrupting day-to-day activities. Next, participants were allowed to review their interview transcripts to ensure member checking and reinforce validity. Once finalized, the transcripts were analyzed and coded for relevant themes.

Phase 3: Follow-Up

Phase 3 occurred December 2014 through February 2015. This phase consisted of analyzing the data using open and axial coding. NVivo qualitative software was used to complete the coding and triangulation of data. During this phase, relevant themes were found that connected to the study. This information became imperatively important when determining the role of Afrocentricity and education as self-healing power.

Basic Assumptions

Several assumptions are associated with this research. First, traditional public school curricula are hegemonized and mainstream, and overwhelmingly teach European and middle-class ethos (Delpit, 2006a; King, 2005; Perry et al., 2003). Many parents find traditional schools lacking in multiculturalism and inclusion, which substantiates the importance of Afrocentric and African-centered schools as plausible school models.

Next, the theoretical framework that shaped this research is an interpretive word with many meanings. "Afrocentricity" is not only the guiding theory for the research but is also a type of school model that many districts have adopted and utilized. It is assumed that the guiding theory and school model are connected, and that the theory informs the school design. The discussion presented in Chapter 3 of the book demonstrates that many schools like AGHA exist across the United States, Canada, and throughout the world. It is an assumption that Afrocentric schools are similar in design, and have a distinction from traditional school designs. It is also an assumption that Afrocentric schools have additional curricular and pedagogical flexibility, in comparison to traditional school models.

SUMMARY

Using a single case study method, which is a qualitative research technique, we were able to investigate the benefits of Afrocentricity as an educational tool of inclusion. Classroom observations were conducted, as well as student and teacher interviews, and student essay responses were gathered. Gathering data from multiple sources enabled us to more accurately capture the school environment of AGHA. Teachers were recruited during staff meetings and voluntarily signed up to participate in the study. Students were recruited at the school's parent meeting. Because the student participants are minors (under 18), parent consent was obtained for participants. Middle school student participants (in 5th–8th grade) were recruited for the study. Again, 7th- and 8th-grade students were purposively selected due to their age and tenure at AGHA.

For classroom observations, teachers were observed through the lens of Nguzo Saba, which are seven principles of Afrocentric education (see Appendix E). The findings from this study are beneficial for educators, researchers, and curriculum developers because it connects Afrocentric education with curricular inclusion. In addition, the study recasts African-centered/Afrocentric education as a tool of healing, wholeness, and restoration. The findings found in Chapters 5 and 6 answer key questions regarding the role of Afrocentric education for students. These questions include: (1) What are the experiences of students and teachers at a high-performing

Afrocentric school? And (2) What role does education or right knowledge play in helping oppressed groups to heal from trauma or social, cultural, and psychological domination? Chapter 4 of the book presents a snapshot of the school site, as well as the study's participants. Whereas Chapters 5 and 6 present the findings of the study, Chapter 7 provides discussion and recommendations.

References

Accomando, C. (2003). Demanding a voice among the pettifoggers: Sojourner Truth as legal actor. *Multi-Ethnic Literatures and the Idea of Social Justice, 28*(1), 61–86.

Adams, V. N., & Stevenson, H. C. (2012). Media socialization, black media images and black adolescent identity. In D. T. Slaughter-Defoe (Ed.), *Racial stereotyping and child development* (pp. 28–46). Karger.

Adeleke, T. (2009). *The case against Afrocentrism.* University Press of Mississippi.

Adeleke, T. (1994). Martin R. Delany's philosophy of education: A neglected aspect of African American liberation thought. *Journal of Negro Education, 62*(2), 221–236.

Adler, K. S. (1992). "Always leading our men in service and sacrifice": Amy Jacques Garvey, feminist black nationalist. *Gender and Society, 6*(3), 346–375.

Adogamhe, P. G. (2008). Pan-Africanism revisited: Vision and reality of African unity and development. *African Review of Integration, 2*(2), 1–34.

Agyepong, R. (2010). Rethinking anti-racism and equity education: Issues of curriculum and development of teachers. *Our Schools Our Shelves, 19*(3), 75–85.

Akbar, N. (1998). *Know thy self.* Mind Productions and Associates.

Alford, K. W. (2000). The early intellectual growth and development of William Leo Hansberry and the birth of African studies. *Journal of Black Studies, 30*(3), 269–293.

Allen, A. M. (2009). Introduction: Africentric inclusive curriculum project by the Toronto District School Board. Toronto District School Board. pp. 8–9.

Allen, A. M. (2010). Beyond Kentes and Kwanzaa: Reconceptualizing the African school and curriculum using principles of anti-racism education. *Our Books Our Shelves, 19*(3), 327–340.

Anderson, D. S. (2016). Black Olmecs and White Egyptians: A parable for professional archaeological responses to pseudoarcheology. In J. J. Card & D. S. Anderson (Eds.), *Lost city, found pyramid: Understanding alternative archaeologies and pseudoscientific practices* (pp. 68–80). University of Alabama Press.

Angell, S. W. (1992). *Bishop Henry McNeal Turner and African-American religion in the south.* University of Tennessee Press.

Ani, M. (1998). *Let the circle be unbroken: The implications of African spirituality in the diaspora.* Red Sea Press.

Ani, M. (1994). *Yurugu: An Afrikan-centered critique of European cultural thought and behavior.* Nkonimfo Publications.

Anselmi, S. M., & Peters, D. B. (1995, August). School context effects in Black adolescents' perceptions of self and the future. Paper presented at the annual meeting of the American Psychological Association, New York, NY.

Anyon, J. (2005). *Radical possibilities: Public policy, urban education, and a new social movement.* Routledge.

Appiah, A. (1990). Alexander Crummell and the invention of African. *The Massachusetts Review*, 31(3), 385–406.

Archie, M. M. (1997). *The centered school: An Afrocentric developmental project for urban schools* (Doctoral Dissertation). Retrieved from ProQuest Dissertation and Theses Database.

Aristotle. (350 BCE [1966]). *Metaphysics, Vol 1.* (W. D. Ross, Trans.). Oxford Clarendon Press.

Asante, M. K. (1990). *Kemet, Afrocentricity, and knowledge.* Africa World Press.

Asante, M. K. (1991). The Afrocentric idea in education. *The Journal of Negro Education*, 60(2), 170–180.

Asante, M. K. (1993). *Malcolm X as cultural hero and other Afrocentric essays.* Africa World Press, Inc.

Asante, M. K. (1998*). The Afrocentric idea.* Temple University Press.

Asante, M. K. (2000). *The Egyptian philosophers: Ancient African voices from Imhotep to Akhenaten.* African World Images.

Asante, M. K. (2003). *Afrocentricity: The theory of social change.* African American Images.

Asante, M. K. (2009a). *The Asante principles for the Afrocentric curriculum.* http://www.asante.net/articles/6/the-asante-principles-for-the-afrocentric-curriculum

Asante, M. K. (2009b). *Afrocentricity: Toward a new understanding of African thought in the world.* http://www.asante.net/articles/5/afrocentricity-toward-a-new-understanding-of-african-thought-in-the-world

Asante, M. K. (2010). Afrocentricity and Africology: Theory and practice in the discipline. In J. R. Davidson (Ed.), *African American studies* (pp. 35–52). Edinburgh University Press.

Asante, M. K., & Karenga, M. (2006). *Handbook of black studies.* Sage.

Austin, A. (2006). *Achieving blackness: Race, black nationalism, and Afrocentrism in the twentieth century.* New York University Press.

Awad, I. (2011). Critical multiculturalism and deliberative democracy: Opening spaces for more inclusive communication. *Javnost—The Public*, 18(3), 39–54.

Ayeko-Kümmeth, J., & Sandner, P. (2018). *Queen Muhumuza: Fighting colonialism in East Africa.* Deutsche Welle: African Roots. https://www.dw.com/en/queen-muhumuza-fighting-colonialism-in-east-africa/a-42522227

Bachynski, K. (2018, June 4). *American medicine was built on the backs of slaves. And it still affects how doctors treat patients today.* The Washington Post. https://www.washingtonpost.com/news/made-by-history/wp/2018/06/04/american-medicine-was-built-on-the-backs-of-slaves-and-it-still-affects-how-doctors-treat-patients-today/?utm_term=.a967ba83d60c

Baker, B. D. (2018, July 17). *How money matters for schools: School finance series.* Learning Policy Institute. https://learningpolicyinstitute.org/product/how-money-matters-brief

Baker, T. (2020, February 13). *The power of teachers to transform. Useable knowledge: Relevant research for today's educators.* Harvard Graduate School of Education. https://www.gse.harvard.edu/news/uk/20/02/power-teachers-transform

Banks, V. K. (1998). *Florida social studies leaders' perceptions regarding an Afrocentric curriculum* (Doctoral Dissertation). Retrieved from ProQuest Dissertation and Theses Database.

Barton, P. A. (2001). *A history of the African-Olmecs: Black civilization of America from prehistoric times to the present era.* AuthorHouse.

Beese, J., & Liang, X. (2010). Do resources matter? PISA science achievement comparisons between students in the United States, Canada and Finland. *Improving Schools, 13*(3), 266–279.

Bell, J. A. (2001). High-performing, high-poverty schools. *Thrust for Educational Leadership, 31*(1), 8–11.

ben-Jochannan, Y. A. A. (2016). We, the sons and daughters of "Africa's" great sperms and ovum, let us this day of 6086 N.Y. / 1986 C.E. speak as one voice, academically. *Africology: The Journal of Pan African Studies, 8*(10), 19–47.

Binder, A. J. (2000). Why do some curricular challenges work while others do not? The case of three Afrocentric challenges. *Sociology of Education, 73*(2), 69–91.

Bireda, M. (2002). *Cultures in conflict: Eliminating racial profiling in school discipline.* Scarecrow Press, Inc.

Black, E. (2012). *War against the weak: Eugenics and America's campaign to create a master race.* Dialog Press.

Blackett, R. (1977). Martin R. Delany and Robert Campbell: Black Americans in search of an African colony. *Journal of Negro History, 62*(1), 1–25.

Blakeslee, S. (1975, June 4). School for blacks offers money-back guarantee. *New York Times*, p. 30.

Bloom, C. M., & Owens, E. W. (2013). Principals' perception of influence on factors affecting student achievement in low- and high-achieving urban high schools. *Education and Urban Society, 45*(2), 208–233. doi:10.1177/0013124511406916

Bortolot, A. I. (2003, October). *Women leaders in African history: Anza Nzinga, Queen of Ndongo.* The Metropolitan Museum of Art. https://www.metmuseum.org/toah/hd/pwmn_2/hd_pwmn_2.htm

Breasted, J. H. (1930). *The Edwin Smith papyrus surgical papers* (Vol. 1). University of Chicago Press.

Brown, P. (1996). Educational achievement in a multiethnic society: The case for an Afrocentric model. *The International Journal of Africana Studies, 4*(1–2), 99–119.

Bush, V. L. (2004). Access, school choice, and independent black institutions: A historical perspective. *Journal of Black Studies, 34*(3), 386–401.

Campbell, M. C. (1988). *The Maroons of Jamaica 1655–1796: A history of resistance, collaboration, and betrayal.* Bergin & Garvey Publishers.

Chace, A. B. (1927). *The Rhind mathematical papyrus* (Vol. 1). Mathematical Association of America.

Chase, A. (1977). *The legacy of Malthus: The social costs of the new scientific racism.* Random House.

Chavez, N. (2020, November 1). *Unrest after Walter Wallace Jr. shooting boiled over from the disconnect between a Philadelphia community and police.* CNN. https://www.cnn.com/2020/11/01/us/philadelphia-police-community-tensions-walter-wallace/index.html

Chenoweth, K. (2007). *It's being done.* Harvard Education Press.

Chenoweth, K. (2009). *How it's being done.* Harvard Education Press.

Children's Defense Fund. (2017). *State of America's Children Report.* Children's Defense Fund

Chiorazzi, A. (2015, October 6). *The spirituality of Africa.* The Harvard Gazette. https://news.harvard.edu/gazette/story/2015/10/the-spirituality-of-africa

Clarke, J. H. (1977). The University of Sankore at Timbuctoo: A neglected achievement in black intellectual history. *The Western Journal of Black Studies, 1*(2), 142–146.

Clarke, J. H. (1993). *Christopher Columbus and the Afrikan holocaust: Slavery and the rise of European capitalism.* Eworld Inc.

Costello, D., & Duvall, T. (2020, May 15). *Minute by minute: What happened the night police fatally shot Breonna Taylor.* USA Today. https://www.usatoday.com/story/news/nation/2020/05/15/minute-minute-account-breonna-taylor-fatal-shooting-louisville-police/5196867002

Crawford, M. (2003). African American intellectual history: Philosophy and ethos. In J. L. Conyers (Ed.), *Afrocentricity and the academy: Essays on theory and practice* (pp. 129–140). McFarland and Company.

Crenshaw, K. W. (1991). Mapping the margins: Intersectionality, identity politics, and violence against women of color. *Stanford Law Review, 43,* 1241–1299.

Creswell, J. W. (2013). *Qualitative inquiry and research design: Choosing among five traditions.* Sage.

Daley, S. (2002, January 30). *Exploited in life and death, South African to go home.* New York Times. https://www.nytimes.com/2002/01/30/world/exploited-in-life-and-death-south-african-to-go-home.html

Darling-Hammond, L. (2000). Teacher quality and student achievement. *Educational Policy and Analysis Archives, 8*(1), 1–44.

Darling-Hammond, L. (2010). *The flat world and education: How America's commitment to equity will determine our future.* Teachers College Press.

Darling-Hammond, L. (2017). *Empowered educators: How high-performing systems shape teaching quality around the world.* Jossey Bass.

de Montellano, B. O., Haslip-Viera, G., & Barbour, W. (2015). They were NOT here before Columbus: Afrocentric hyperdiffusionism in the 1990s. *Ethnohistory, 44*(2), 199–234.

DeGury, J. (2017). *Post-traumatic slave syndrome: America's legacy of enduring injury and healing.* Author.

Dei, G. J. (1994). Afrocentricity: A cornerstone of pedagogy. *Anthropology and Education Quarterly, 25*(1), 2–28.

Dei, G. J. (1996). The role of Afrocentricity in the inclusive curriculum in Canadian schools. *Canadian Journal of Education, 21*(2), 170–186.

Dei, G. J. (2003). Communication across the tracks: Challenges for anti-racist educators in Ontario today. *Orbit, 33*(3), 2–5.

Dei, G. J. (2012). *Teaching Africa: Towards a transgressive pedagogy.* Springer.

Dei, G. J. S., Asgharzadeh, A., Bahador, S. E., & Shahjahan, R. A. (2006). *Schooling and difference in Africa: Democratic challenges in a contemporary context.* University of Toronto Press.

Dei, G. J. S., James, I. M., Karumanchery, L. L., James-Wilson, S., & Zine, J. (2000). *Removing the margins: The challenges and possibilities of inclusive schooling.* Canadian Scholars' Press.

Deliso, M. (2020, June 2). *LGBTQ community calls for justice after Tony McDade, a black trans man, shot and killed by police.* ABC News. https://abcnews.go.com/US/lgbtq-community-calls-justice-black-trans-man-shot/story?id=71022981

Delpit, L. D. (2006a). *Other people's children: Cultural conflict in the classroom.* New Press.

Delpit, L. D. (2006b). Lessons from teachers. *Journal of Teacher Education*, 57(3), 220–231.

Dennis, R. M. (1995). Social Darwinism, scientific racism, and the metaphysics of race. *Journal of Negro Education*. 64(3), 243–252.

Dillard, C. B., & Neal, A. (2020). I am because we are: (Re)membering ubuntu in the pedagogy of black women teachers from Africa to America and back again. *Theory into Practice*. doi:10.1080/00405841.2020.1773183

Diop, C. A. (1974). *The African origin of civilization: Myth or reality*. Lawrence Hill Books.

Diop, C. A. (1981). *Civilization or barbarism: An authentic anthropology*. Lawrence Hill Books.

Diop, C. A. (1987). *Pre-colonial black Africa: A comparative study of the political and social systems of Europe and black Africa, from antiquity to the formation of modern states*. Lawrence Hill Books.

Donald, B. (2016, January 12). *Stanford study suggests academic benefits to ethnic studies courses*. Stanford News. https://news.stanford.edu/2016/01/12/ethnic -studies-benefits-011216

Dove, N. D. E. (1993). The emergence of black supplementary schools: Resistance to racism in the United Kingdom. *Urban Education*, 27(4), 430–447.

Dragnea, C., & Erling, S. (2008). *The effectiveness of Africentric (black-focused) schools in closing student success and achievement gaps: A review of literature*. Toronto District School Board.

Drake, S. C. (1959). Pan-Africanism: What is it? *Africa Today*, 6(1), 6–10.

Durden, T. R. (2007). African centered schooling: Facilitating holistic excellence for black children. *Negro Educational Review*, 58(1–2), 23–34.

Dynarski, M., & Kainz, K. (2015, November 20). *Why federal spending on disad- vantaged students (Title I) doesn't work*. Brookings. https://www.brookings.edu /research/why-federal-spending-on-disadvantaged-students-title-i-doesnt-work

Edwards, S. D., Makunga, N. V., Thwala, J. D., & Mbele, P. B. (2009). The role of the ancestors in healing. *Indilinga: African Journal of Indigenous Knowledge Systems*, 8(1), 1–11 .

Education Week. (2019). *How each state performed on school spending and equity (map and rankings)*. https://www.edweek.org/policy-politics/how-each-state -performed-on-school-spending-and-equity-map-and-rankings

Egalite, A. J., & Kisida, B. (2016, August 19). *The many ways teacher diversity may benefit students*. Brookings. https://www.brookings.edu/blog/brown-center -chalkboard/2016/08/19/the-many-ways-teacher-diversity-may-benefit-students

El-Gammal, S. Y. (1993). Pharmacy and medicine education in ancient Egypt. *Bulle- tin of the Indian Institute of History of Medicine*, 23(1), 37–48.

Emdin, C. (2016). *For white folks who teach in the hood . . . and the rest of y'all too: Reality pedagogy and urban education*. Beacon Press.

Engel, K. (2012, January 12). *Ana Nzinga Mbande, fearless African queen*. AWH. https ://amazingwomeninhistory.com/anna-nzinga-mbande-fearless-africa-queen

Evans, G. (2018, March 2). *The unwelcome revival of 'race science.'* The Guardian. https://www.theguardian.com/news/2018/mar/02/the-unwelcome-revival-of -race-science

Evans-Winters, V. E. (2011). *Teaching black girls: Resiliency in urban classrooms*. Peter Lang.

Frazier, E. F. (1974). *The Negro church in America*. Schocken Books.

FreeSVG.org. (2019). *Nanny of the Maroons*. "Simple nanny in brown-colored drawing." [Digital Image]. https://freesvg.org/nanny-illustration

Freire, P. (2000). *Pedagogy of the oppressed*. Continuum International Publishing Group.

Fu-Kiau, K. K. B. (1980 [2001]). *African cosmology of the bantu-kongo: Tying the spiritual knot, principles of life & living*. African Tree Press.

Gates, H. L. (1991). Beware of the new pharaohs. *Newsweek, 118*(13), 47.

Gay, G. (2000). *Culturally responsive teaching: Theory, research and practice*. Teachers College Press.

Gbaba, J. T. (2009). *The Chiandeh Afrocentric curriculum and textbook experience: Exploring children's responses to an Afrocentric curriculum* (Doctoral Dissertation). Retrieved from ProQuest Dissertation and Theses Database.

George, J., & Puente, M. (2015, March 14). *Baltimore leaders agree: City has a race problem*. The Baltimore Sun. http://www.baltimoresun.com/news/maryland /baltimore-city/bs-md-ci-baltimore-racism-20150314-story.html

Giddings, G. J. (2001). Infusion of Afrocentric content into the school curriculum: Towards an effective movement. *Journal of Black Studies, 21*(4), 462–482.

Giddings, J. R. (2015). *The exiles of Florida: The crimes committed by our government against the maroons, who fled from South Carolina and other slave states, seeking protection under Spanish laws*. CreateSpace Independent Publishing Platform.

Gill, W. (1991). Jewish day schools and Afrocentric paradigms as models for educating African American youth. *Journal of Negro Education, 60*(4), 566–580.

Gillham, N. W. (2001). Sir Francis Galton and the birth of eugenics. *Annual Review of Genetics, 35*, 83–101.

Ginwright, S. A. (2004). *Black in school: Afrocentric reform, urban youth, and the promise of hip-hop culture*. Teachers College Press.

Glense, C. (2011). *Becoming qualitative researchers: An introduction* (4th ed.). Pearson.

Gottlieb, K. (2000). *Mother of us all: A history of Queen Nanny, leader of the Windward Jamaica Maroons*. African World Press.

Gramsci, A. (1999). *Selections from the prison notebooks*. The Electric Book Company Ltd.

Greenberg, G. (1996). *The Moses mystery: The African origins of the Jewish people*. Carol Publication Group.

Gross, B. (1932). Freedom's journal and rights for all. *Journal of Negro History, 17*(3), 241-86.

Guthrie, R. V. (2004). *Even the rat was white: A historical view of psychology* (2nd ed.). Pearson Education.

Halsall, P. (1997). *Sojourner Truth: "Ain't I a Woman?," December 1851*. Modern History Sourcebook. https://sourcebooks.fordham.edu/mod/sojtruth-woman.asp

Hammer, D. (1994). *School choice: Why you need it—how you get it*. Cato Institute.

Harriet Tubman Historical Society. (2019). *Harriet Tubman, the Moses of her people*. http://www.harriet-tubman.org/moses-underground-railroad

Hartigan, J. (2010). *Race in the 21st century: Ethnographic approaches*. Oxford.

Haslip-Viera, G., de Montellano, B. O., & Barbour, W. (1997). Robbing native American cultures: Van Sertima's Afrocentricity and the Olmecs. *Current Anthropology, 38*(3), 419–441.

Hernen, T. A. (2016). The impact of No Child Left Behind Act and Common Core State Standards on curriculum and the diverse learner. *International Journal of Education and Human Development, 2*(3), 15–20.

Herodotus. (440 BCE [2014]). *The history of Herodotus, volume 1* (G. C. Macaulay, Trans.). CreateSpace Independent Publishing Platform.

Hilberth, M., & Slate, J. R. (2014). Middle school black and white student assignment to discipline consequences: A clear lack of equity. *Education and Urban Society, 46*(3), 312–328.

Hilliard, A. G. (1998). *SBA: The reawakening of the African mind.* Makare Publishing.

Hilliard, A. G., & Amankwatia, N. B. (1998). *African power: Affirming African indigenous socialization in the face of the culture wars.* Makare Publishing Company.

Hilliard, A. G., Sizemore, B. A., Daniels, E., Green, C., Johnson, J. A., Pasteur, A. B., . . . Strozier, Y. (1984). *Saving the African American child: A report of the National Alliance of Black School Educators, Inc.* National Alliance of Black School Educators.

Hilliard, A. G., Williams, L., & Damali, N. (1987). *The teachings of Ptahhotep: The oldest book in the world.* Blackwood Press.

Hilliard, C. B. (1998). *Intellectual traditions of pre-colonial Africa.* McGraw-Hill.

Holt, K. C. (1991). A rationale for creating African-American immersion schools. *Educational Leadership, 49*(4), 18.

Homer (~762 BCE [1990]). *The Iliad* (R. Fagles, Trans.). Viking.

hooks, b. (1994). *Teaching to transgress: Education as the practice of freedom.* Routledge.

Hoover, M. E. R. (1992). The Nairobi Day School: An African American independent school, 1966–1984. *Journal of Negro Education, 61*(2), 201–210.

Hopkins, R. (1997). *Educating black males: Critical lessons in schooling, community, and power.* SUNY Press.

Hopson, R. K. M., Hotep, U., Schneider, D. L., & Turenne, I. G. (2010). What's educational leadership without an African-centered perspective? Explorations and extrapolations. *Urban Education, 45*(6), 777–796.

Huerta, A. (2020, May 15). *The right to ethnic studies in higher education.* Inside Higher Ed. https://www.insidehighered.com/advice/2020/05/15/why-students -should-be-required-take-ethnic-studies-opinion

Human Rights Watch. (2020, May 12). *Covid-19 fueling anti-Asian racism and xenophobia worldwide.* Human Rights Watch. https://www.hrw.org/news/2020 /05/12/covid-19-fueling-anti-asian-racism-and-xenophobia-worldwide

Ighodaro, E., & Wiggan, G. (2011). *Curriculum violence: America's new civil rights issue.* Nova Science Publishers.

Irvine, J. J. (1990). *Black students and school failure: Policies, practices, and prescriptions.* Praeger.

Ito, T. A., & Urland, G. R. (2003). Race and gender on the brain: Electrocortical measures of attention to the race and gender of multiply categorizable individuals. *Journal of Personality and Social Psychology. 85,* 616–626.

Jackson, C. (1994). The feasibility of an Afrocentric curriculum. *Southern Social Studies Journal, 20*(1), 60–74.

Jackson, J. G. (1970). *Introduction to African civilizations.* Kensington Publishing Group.

James, G. G. M. (2010). *Stolen legacy: The Egyptian origins of western philosophy.* Feather Trail Press.

Jan, T. (2017, December 13). *News media offers consistently warped portrayals of black families, study finds.* The Washington Post. https://www.washingtonpost .com/news/wonk/wp/2017/12/13/news-media-offers-consistently-warped -portrayals-of-black-families-study-finds/?utm_term=.a5fbd6ae5d1f

Joyce, J. A. (2005). *Black studies as human studies: Critical essays and interviews.* SUNY Press.

Karenga, M. (1965). *Nguzo Saba: The seven principles.* http://officialkwanzaawebsite .org/NguzoSaba.shtml

Karenga, M. (1966). *The African American holiday of Kwanzaa.* University of Sankore Press.

Karenga, M. (1984). *Selections from the Husia: Sacred wisdom of ancient Egypt.* University of Sankore Press.

Karenga, M. (1995). Afrocentricity and multicultural education: Concept, challenge and contribution. In B. P. Bowser, T. Jones, & G. A. Young (Eds.), *Towards the multicultural university* (pp. 41–61). Praeger.

Karenga, M. (2002). *Introduction to black studies.* University of Sankore Press.

Kearney, W. S., Herrington, D. E., & Aguilar, D. V. (2012). Beating the odds: Exploring the 90/90/90 phenomenon. *Equity and Excellence in Education, 45*(2), 239–249.

Keller, M. (2006, August 6). *The scandal at the zoo.* New York Times. https://www .nytimes.com/2006/08/06/nyregion/thecity/06zoo.html

Kelly, R. D. G. (2016, March 7). *Black study, Black struggle.* Boston Review: A Political and Literary Forum. http://bostonreview.net/forum/robin-d-g-kelley-black -study-black-struggle

Kenyatta, K. (1998). *Guide to implementing Afrikan-centered education.* Afrikan Way Investments.

Kifano, S. (1996). Afrocentric education in supplementary schools: Paradigm and practice at the Mary McLeod Bethune institute. *Journal of Negro Education, 65*(2), 209–218.

Kim, C. Y., Losen, D. J., & Hewitt, D. T. (2010). *The school-to-prison pipeline.* New York University Press.

King, J. E. (2005). *Black education: A transformative research and action agenda for the new century.* Lawrence Erlbaum.

King, J. E., & Swartz, E. E. (2016). *The Afrocentric praxis of teaching for freedom: Connecting culture to learning.* Routledge.

King, J. E., & Swartz, E. E. (2018). *Heritage knowledge in the curriculum: Retrieving an African episteme.* Routledge.

King, J. E., Swartz, E. E., Campbell, L., Lemons-Smith, S., & López, E. (2014). *Re-membering history in student and teacher learning: An Afrocentric culturally informed praxis.* Routledge.

Kozol, J. (2005). *The shame of the nation: Apartheid schooling in America.* Random House.

Kunjufu, J. (2002). *Black students middle class teachers.* African American Images.

Ladson-Billings, G. (1994). *The dreamkeepers: Successful teachers of African American children.* Jossey-Bass.

Lang, C. (2020, September 29). *President Trump has attacked critical race theory. Here's what to know about the intellectual movement*. TIME Magazine. https://time.com/5891138/critical-race-theory-explained/

Larson, K. C. (2004). *Bound for the promised land: Harriet Tubman, portrait of an American hero*. Ballantine.

Law, R. (1989). Between the sea and the lagoons: The interaction of maritime and inland navigation on the precolonial slave coast. *Cahiers d'Études Africaines, 29*(114), 209–237.

Leake, D. O., & Leake, B. L. (1992a). Islands of hope: Milwaukee's African American immersion schools. *Journal of Negro Education, 61*(1), 24–29.

Leake, D. O., & Leake, B. L. (1992b). African-American immersion schools in Milwaukee: From the inside. *Phi Delta Kappa, 73*(10), 783–785.

Learning Policy Institute. (2018, July 17). *Research shows that when it comes to student achievement, money matters*. Learning Policy Institute. https://learningpolicyinstitute.org/press-release/research-shows-student-achievement-money-matters

Leatherby, L., Ray, A., Singhvi, A., Triebert, C., Watkins, D., & Willis, H. (2021, January 12). *How a presidential rally turned into a capitol rampage*. The New York Times. https://www.nytimes.com/interactive/2021/01/12/us/capitol-mob-timeline.html

Ledwith, S. (2014, April 3). *The Rwandan genocide: From imperialism to barbarism*. Counterfire. https://www.counterfire.org/articles/history/17141-the-rwandan-genocide-from-imperialism-to-barbarism

Lee, C. (1992). Profile of an independent black institution: African-centered education at work. *The Journal of Negro Education, 61*(2), 160–177.

Lee, C., Lomotey, K., & Shujaa, M. (1990). How shall we sing our sacred song in a strange land? The dilemma of double consciousness and the complexities of an African-centered pedagogy. *The Journal of Education, 172*, 45–61.

Lefkowitz, M. (1997). *Not out of Africa: How "Afrocentrism" became an excuse to teach myth as history*. Basic Books.

Lemert, C. (2010). *Social theory: The multicultural and classic readings* (4th ed.). Westview Press.

Library of Congress. (1811). *Love and beauty–Sartjee the Hottentot Venus* [Digital Print]. https://www.loc.gov/item/2007680266

Library of Congress. (1864). *Sojourner Truth: I sell the shadow to support the substance* [Photograph]. Library of Congress, Rare Book and Special Collections Division, Alfred Whital Stern Collection of Lincolniana https://www.loc.gov/item/scsm000880

Library of Congress. (1911). *Photograph of Harriet Tubman* [Photograph]. https://www.loc.gov/item/rbcmiller002657

Library of Congress. (1915/1916). *Ota Bengi* [Glass Negatives]. Library of Congress, Prints & Photographs Division, [reproduction number, e.g., LC-B2-1234]. https://www.loc.gov/resource/ggbain.22741

Little, B. (2016, April 21). *Harriet the spy: How Tubman helped the union army*. National Geographic. https://news.nationalgeographic.com/2016/04/160421-harriet-tubman-20-dollar-bill-union-spy-history

Loewen, J. W. (1995). *Lies my teacher told me: Everything your American history textbook got wrong*. The New Press.

Losen, D. J., & Gillespie, J. (2012). *Opportunities suspended: The disparate impact of disciplinary exclusion from school.* eScholarship, University of California.

Mamdani, M. (2001). *When victims become killers: Colonialism, nativism, and genocide in Rwanda.* Princeton University Press.

Manley, O. I. (1997). *The centered school: An Afrocentric developmental project for urban schools* (Doctoral Dissertation). Retrieved from ProQuest Dissertation and Theses Database.

Marcus Garvey School. (2019). *School background.* http://mgsla.org/school-background

Marryshaw, T. A. (1917). *Cycles of civilization.* B.W.I. Printed at the Office of The West Indies.

McCaskie, T. C. (2007). The life and afterlife of Yaa Asantewaa. *Journal of the International African Institute, 77*(2), 151–179.

McLaughlin, E. C. (2020, May 12). *What we know about Ahmaud Arbery's killing.* CNN. https://www.cnn.com/2020/05/11/us/ahmaud-arbery-mcmichael-what -we-know/index.html

McQueen, P. (2014). "Ain't I a woman?": Feminist theory and the politics of recognition. In P. McQueen (Ed.), *Subjectivity, gender and the struggle for recognition* (pp. 18–40). Palgrave.

The Met Museum. (2006). *Head of Ahmose I, ca. 1550–1525 B.C.* [Digital Image]. https://www.metmuseum.org/art/collection/search/547950

Mickelson, R. (2001). Subverting Swann: First and second generation segregation in the Charlotte-Mecklenburg Schools. *American Educational Research Journal, 38,* 215–252.

Milner, H. R., & Hoy, A. N. (2003). A case study of an African American teacher's self-efficacy, stereotype threat, and persistence. *Teaching and Teacher Education, 19,* 263–276.

Minister, M. (2012). Female, black, and able: Representations of Sojourner Truth and theories of embodiment. *Disability Studies Quarterly, 32*(1). doi: 10.18061 /dsq.v32i1.3030

Mitchell, K. (2003). *Standing in the gap: A critical case study of the MAAT Academy* (Doctoral Dissertation). Retrieved from ProQuest Dissertation and Theses Database.

Mohan, G., & Zack-Williams, A. B. (2002). Globalisation from below: Conceptualising the role of African diasporas in Africa's development. *Review of African Political Economy, 29*(92), 211–236.

Moss, A. A., Jr. (1981). *The American negro academy: Voice of the talented tenth.* Louisiana State University Press.

Moulthorp, D. (2015, February 19). *Cleveland's race problem: How longstanding injustice could cripple the city's rebirth.* Politico Magazine. http://www.politico .com/magazine/story/2015/02/cleveland-segregation-115320

Mumbere, D. (2018, August 29). *Germany returns Namibia genocide skulls.* Africa News. http://www.africanews.com/2018/08/29/photos-germany-returns -namibia-genocide-skull

Murphy, P. P. (2020, June 3). *New video appears to show three police officers kneeling on George Floyd.* CNN News. https://www.cnn.com/2020/05/29/us/george -floyd-new-video-officers-kneel-trnd/index.html

Murrell, P. C. (1993). Afrocentric immersion: Academic and personal development of African American males in public schools. In T. Perry & J. Fraser (Eds.),

Freedom's plow: Teaching in the multicultural classroom (pp. 231–259). Routledge.

Murrell, P. C. (1999). Chartering the village: The making of an African-centered charter school. *Urban Education, 33,* 565–583.

Murrell, P. C. (2002). *African-centered pedagogy: Developing schools of achievement for African American children.* SUNY Press.

National Assessment of Educational Progress. (2017a). *National achievement-level results.* Nation's Report Card. https://www.nationsreportcard.gov/reading_2017/nation/achievement?grade=4

National Assessment of Educational Progress. (2017b). *National achievement-level results.* Nation's Report Card. https://www.nationsreportcard.gov/math_2017/nation/achievement?grade=4

National Center for Education Statistics. (2017a). *Number and percentage distribution of teachers in public and private elementary and secondary schools, by selected teacher characteristics: Selected years, 1987-88 through 2015-16.* https://nces.ed.gov/programs/digest/d17/tables/dt17_209.10.asp?current=yes

National Center for Education Statistics. (2017b). *Number and percentage distribution of teachers in public elementary and secondary schools, by race/ethnicity and selected teacher and school characteristics: 2015–16.* https://nces.ed.gov/programs/digest/d17/tables/dt17_209.23.asp

National Center for Education Statistics. (2017c). *Enrollment and percentage distribution in public elementary and secondary schools, by race/ethnicity and level of education: Fall 1999 through fall 2027.* https://nces.ed.gov/programs/digest/d17/tables/dt17_203.60.asp

National Center for Education Statistics. (2020). *Public high school graduation rates.* https://nces.ed.gov/programs/coe/indicator_coi.asp

National Library of Medicine. (2002, September 16). *Greek medicine.* https://www.nlm.nih.gov/hmd/greek/greek_oath.html

Newkirk, P. (2015). *Spectacle: The astonishing life of Ota Benga.* Harper Collins.

Ngũgĩ, T. (1986). *Decolonising the mind: The politics of language in African literature.* J. Currey.

Nieto, S. (1992). *Affirming diversity: The sociopolitical context of multicultural education.* Longman.

Nieto, S., & Bode, P. (2008). *Affirming diversity, the sociopolitical context of multicultural education* (5th ed.). Allyn & Bacon.

Nobles, W. (1990). The infusion of African and African-American content: A question of content and intent. In A. Hilliard, L. Payton-Stewart, & L. Williams (Eds.), *Infusion of African and Black in the school curriculum* (pp. 5–25). Third World Press.

Obenga, T. (2004). *African philosophy: The Pharaonic period 2780–330 BC.* Per Ankh.

Okafor, V. O. (1998). The functional implications of Afrocentrism. In J. D. Hamlet (Ed.), *Afrocentric vision: Studies in culture and communication* (pp. 209–228). Sage.

Olson, J. E., & Bourne, E. G. (Eds.). (1906[2006]). *Original narratives of early American history: The northmen Columbus and Cabot 985-1503.* Project Gutenberg. https://www.gutenberg.org/files/18571/18571-h/18571-h.htm

Onyeweuenyi, I. C. (2005). *The African origin of Greek philosophy: An exercise on Afrocentrism*. University of Nigeria Press.

The Opportunity Agenda. (2011). *Media representations and the impact on the lives of black men and boys*. http://racialequitytools.org/resourcefiles/Media-Impact-onLives-of-Black-Men-and-Boys-OppAgenda.pdf

Osler, W. (1913 [2013]). *The evolution of modern medicine. A series of lectures delivered at Yale University*. Project Gutenberg. https://www.gutenberg.org/files/1566/1566-h/1566-h.htm

Painter, N. I. (2000). Truth, Sojourner (1799–26 November 1883). *American National Biography*. http://www.anb.org/view/10.1093/anb/9780198606697.001.0001/anb-9780198606697-e-1500706

Parkinson, J. (2016). *The significance of Sarah Baartman*. BBC News. https://www.bbc.com/news/magazine-35240987

Pellerin, M. (2012). Benefits of Afrocentricity in exploring social phenomena: Understanding Afrocentricity as a social science methodology. *The Journal of Pan African Studies*, *5*(4), 149–160.

Peltier, L. F. (1990). *Fractures: A history and iconography of their treatment*. Norman Publishing.

Perez, J., Jr. & Guadiano, N. (2020, September 17). *Trump blasts 1619 Project as DeVos praises alternative Black history curriculum*. Politico. https://www.politico.com/news/2020/09/17/devos-black-history-1776-unites-417186

Perry, T., Steele, C., & Hilliard, A. (2003). *Young, gifted and black*. Beacon Press.

Peterson, S. (2001). *Me against my brother: At war in Somalia, Sudan, and Rwanda*. Routledge.

Piert, J. H. (2006). *SBA (teaching, wisdom, and study): An exploration of the experiences of African American young people who attend an African centered school* (Doctoral Dissertation). Retrieved from ProQuest Dissertation and Theses Database.

Piert, J. H. (2013). Thirty years in the storm: Leadership at an African-centered school. *Urban Review*, *45*, 376–394.

Pinch, G. (2002). *Handbook of Egyptian mythology*. ABC-CLIO Publishers.

Plato. (348 BCE [1968]). *Laws*. (R.G. Bury, Trans.). Harvard University Press.

Plutarch. (75 CE [2012]). *Parallel lives vol. 1*. SMK Books.

Pollard, D., & Ajirotutu, C. (2000). *African-centered schooling in theory and practice*. Bergin & Garvey.

Portland Public Schools. (1987). *Portland Baseline Essays*. http://www.pps.k12.or.us/files/curriculum/prefc-af.pdf

Program for International Student Assessment [PISA]. (2015a). *Mathematics literacy: Average scores*. National Center for Education Statistics. https://nces.ed.gov/surveys/pisa/pisa2015/pisa2015highlights_5.asp

Program for International Student Assessment [PISA]. (2015b). *Science literacy: Average scores*. National Center for Education Statistics. https://nces.ed.gov/surveys/pisa/pisa2015/pisa2015highlights_3.asp

Program for International Student Assessment [PISA]. (2015c). *Reading literacy: Average scores*. National Center for Education Statistics. https://nces.ed.gov/surveys/pisa/pisa2015/pisa2015highlights_4.asp

Progress in International Reading Literacy Study [PIRLS]. (2016). *PIRLS and ePIRLS results*. National Center for Education Statistics. https://nces.ed.gov/surveys/pirls/pirls2016/tables/pirls2016_table01.asp

Pulsipher, D. (2019, February 8). *Yaa Asantewaa (mid 1800s-1921)*. BlackPast. https://www.blackpast.org/global-african-history/yaa-asantewaa-mid-1800s-1921

Rattan, A., & Ambady, N. (2013). Diversity ideologies and intergroup relations: An examination of colorblindness and multiculturalism. *European Journal of Social Psychology, 43,* 2–21.

Ratteray, J. D. (1990). African American achievement: A research agenda emphasizing independent schools. In. K. Lomotey (Ed.), *Going to school: The African American Experience* (pp. 197–208). State University of New York Press.

Ratteray, J. D. (1994). The search for access and context in the education of African Americans. In M. J. Shujaa (Ed.), *Too much schooling, too little education: The paradox of black life in white societies* (pp. 123–141). Africa World Press.

Ravitch, D. (1990). Multiculturalism: E pluribus plures. *The American Scholar, 59*(3), 337–354.

Rayford, D. D. (2012). *A phenomenological case study of seventh-grade African American male students at the Africentric School in Columbus, Ohio* (Doctoral Dissertation). Retrieved from ProQuest Dissertation and Theses Database.

Reese, B. (2001). *An Afrocentric education in an urban school: A case study* (Doctoral Dissertation). Retrieved from ProQuest Dissertation and Theses Database.

Rickford, R. J. (2016). *We are an African people: Independent education, black power, and the radical imagination.* Oxford University Press.

Roberts, M. A. (2010). Toward a theory of culturally relevant critical teacher care: African American teachers' definitions and perceptions of care for African American students. *Journal of Moral Education, 39*(4), 449–467.

Robinson, T. Y., & Jeremiah, M. (2011). The development of an African-centered urban high school by trial and error. *Schools: Studies in Education, 8*(2), 311–328.

Rodney, W. (2011). *How Europe underdeveloped Africa.* Black Classic Press.

Romero, A. F. (2010). At war with the state in order to save the lives of our children: The battle of ethnic studies in Arizona. *Black Scholar, 40*(4), 7–15.

Rury, J. L. (1983). The New York African free school, 1827–1836: Conflict over community control of black education. *Phylon, 44*(3), 187–197.

Sanders, E. T. W., & Reed, P. L. (1995). An investigation of the possible effects of an immersion as compared to a traditional program for African American males. *Urban Education, 30*(1), 93–112.

Schlesinger, A. M. (1998). *The disuniting of America: Reflections on a multicultural society.* W.W. Norton.

Serageldin, I. (2013). Ancient Alexandria and the dawn of medical science. *Global Cardiology Science and Practice, 2013*(4), 1–10.

Sharma, T. (2010). *Jane-Finch black youth perspectives of Africentric schooling in Toronto* (Doctoral Dissertation). Retrieved from ProQuest Dissertation and Theses Database.

Shockley, K. G. (2003). *When culture and education meet: An ethnographic investigation of an Africentric private school in Washington, DC* (Doctoral Dissertation). Retrieved from ProQuest Dissertation and Theses Database.

Shockley, K. G. (2011). Reaching African American students: Profile of an Afrocentric teacher. *Journal of Black studies, 42*(7), 1027–1046.

Shockley, K. G., & Frederick, R. M. (2010). Constructs and dimensions of Afrocentric Education. *Journal of Black Studies, 40*(6), 1212–1233.

Simon, M., & Sidner, S. (2021, January 11). *Decoding the extremist symbols and groups at the Capitol Hill insurrection.* CNN. https://www.cnn.com/2021/01/09/us/capitol-hill-insurrection-extremist-flags-soh/index.html

Singer, J. D., & Braun, H. I. (2018). Testing international assessments. *Science, 360*(6384), 38–40.

Sizemore, B. A. (1990). The politics of curriculum, race, and class. *Journal of Negro Education, 59*(1), 77–85.

Skiba, R. J., Michael, R. S., Nardo, A. B., & Peterson, R. L. (2002). The color of school discipline: Sources of racial and gender disproportionality in school punishment. *The Urban Review, 34*(4), 317–342.

Smith, S. (2014). *Black feminism and intersectionality.* International Socialist Review. https://isreview.org/issue/91/black-feminism-and-intersectionality

Span, C. M. (2002). Black Milwaukee's challenge to the cycle of urban miseducation: Milwaukee's African American immersion schools. *Urban Education, 37*(5), 610–630.

Spigner, C. (n.d.). *Henry McNeal Turner (1834–1915): Minister, Chaplin in the union army and advocate for emigration to Liberia.* Social Welfare History Project. http://socialwelfare.library.vcu.edu/religious/turner-henry-mcneal

Spring, J. (2005). *Conflict of interests: The politics of American education* (5th ed.). McGraw-Hill.

Squire, M. S. (2012). *The development of an African-centered school—the first 20 years* (Doctoral Dissertation). Retrieved from ProQuest Dissertation and Theses Database.

Stapleton, T. J. (2017). *A history of genocide in Africa.* Praeger.

Stein, S. J. (2004). *The culture of educational policy.* Teachers College Press.

Stiglitz, J. (2002). *Globalization and its discontents.* W.W. Norton.

Tauheed, L. F. (2008). Black political economy in the 21st century: Exploring the interface of economics and black studies addressing the challenge of Harold Cruse. *Journal of Black Studies, 38*(5), 692–730.

Taylor, U. Y. (2000). "Negro women are great thinkers as well as doers": Amy Jacques-Garvey and community feminism, 1924–1927. *Journal of Women's History, 12*(2), 104–126.

Toch, T. (1998, April 27). The new education bazaar. *U.S. News and World Report,* p. 34.

Toldson, I., & Lewis, C. (2012). *Challenging the status quo: Academic success among school-age African-American males.* Congressional Black Caucus Foundation, Inc.

Torney-Purta, J., & Amadeo, J. (2013). International large-scale assessments: Challenges reporting and potentials for secondary analysis. *Comparative and International Education, 8*(3), 248–258.

Townsend, B. (2000). The disproportionate discipline of African American learners: Reducing school suspensions and expulsions. *Exceptional Children, 66*(3), 381–391.

Townsend, H. L. (2005). *African American empowerment: A qualitative case study of an African-centered school in Pennsylvania* (Doctoral Dissertation). Retrieved from ProQuest Dissertation and Theses Database.

Traoré, R. (2002). *Implementing Afrocentricity: A case study of African and African American students in an urban high school in America* (Doctoral Dissertation). Retrieved from ProQuest Dissertation and Theses Database.

Traoré, R. (2007). Implementing Afrocentricity: Connecting students of African descent to their cultural heritage. *The Journal of Pan African Studies, 1*(10), 62–78.

Trends in International Mathematics and Science Study [TIMSS]. (2015a). *Mathematics for grades 4 and 8: Averages.* National Center for Education Statistics. https://nces.ed.gov/timss/timss2015/timss2015_table02.asp

Trends in International Mathematics and Science Study [TIMSS]. (2015b). *Science for grades 4 and 8: Averages.* National Center for Education Statistics. https://nces.ed.gov/timss/timss2015/timss2015_table23.asp

Truth, S. (1851). *Modern history sourcebook: Sojourner Truth: "Ain't I a woman?"* Fordham University. https://sourcebooks.fordham.edu/mod/sojtruth-woman.asp

Understanding, S. (2013). *When the world was black* (Vol. 1). Supreme Design.

U.S. Census Bureau. (2011). *The Black population: 2010.* https://www.census.gov/prod/cen2010/briefs/c2010br-06.pdf

U.S. Census Bureau. (2015). *Projections of the size and composition of the U.S. population: 2014 to 2060: Estimates and projections.* https://www.census.gov/content/dam/Census/library/publications/2015/demo/p25-1143.pdf

U.S. Census Bureau. (2018). *Regions and Divisions of the United States.* https://www2.census.gov/geo/pdfs/maps-data/maps/reference/us_regdiv.pdf

U.S. Department of Education. (2016). *Prevalence of teachers without full state certification and variation across schools and states* (p. 40). https://www2.ed.gov/rschstat/eval/teaching/teachers-without-certification/report.pdf

U.S. Department of Education, Office of Civil Rights. (2012). *Revealing the truths about our nation's schools.* United States Department of Education Office of Civil Rights.

Van Sertima, I. (1976 [2003]). *They came before Columbus: The African presence in ancient America.* Random House.

Washington, H. A. (2008). *Medical apartheid: The dark history of medical experimentation on black Americans from colonial times to the present.* Harlem Moon Broadway Books.

Webb, B. J. (1996). *The impact of an Afrocentric educational experience on school functioning of selected Black students* (Doctoral Dissertation). Retrieved from ProQuest Dissertation and Theses Database.

West, R. (2019). Yaa Asantewaa (Mid-1800s–1921). [Photograph]. *Blackast.org.* https://www.blackpast.org/global-african-history/yaa-asantewaa-mid-1800s-1921

What we do. (2013, September 14). http://[Asa G. Hilliard]academy.net/what-we-do

Whitewright, J. (2018). The ships and shipping of Indo-Roman trade: A view from the Egyptian red sea. *HEROM. Journal on Hellenistic and Roman Material Culture, 6*(2), 137–171

Wiggan, G. (2007). Race, school achievement and educational inequality: Towards a student-based inquiry perspective. *Review of Educational Research, 77*(3), 310–333.

Wiggan, G. (2010). Afrocentricity and the black intellectual tradition and education: Carter G. Woodson, W.E.B. Du Bois, and E. Franklin Frazier. *The Journal of Pan African Studies, 3*(9), 128–149.

Wiggan, G. (2018). Afterword: Black migrations and urban realities. *Black History Bulletin*, *81*(2), 30–33.

Wiggan, G., & Watson, M. J. (2016). Teaching the whole child: The importance of involvement, cultural responsiveness, and character development in nurturing high performing African American students. *The Urban Review*, *48*(5), 766–798.

Wiggan, G., & Watson-Vandiver, M. J. (2018). Urban school success: Lessons from a high achieving urban school, and students' reactions to Ferguson, Missouri. *Education and Urban Society*, *51*(8), 1074–1105.

Wiggan, G., Scott, L. M., Watson, M. J., & Reynolds, R. (2014). *Unshackled: Education for freedom, student achievement and personal emancipation*. Sense-Springer Publishers.

Wikimedia Commons. (2007). *Olmec head, Cabeza olmeca. Nationalmuseum für Anthropologie, Mexiko-Stadt* [Photograph]. https://commons.wikimedia.org/wiki/File:20041229-Olmec_Head_(Museo_Nacional_de_Antropolog%C3%ADa).jpg

Wikimedia Commons. (2010). *View of Great Pyramid at La Venta* [Photograph]. "La Venta Pirámide cara norte." https://commons.wikimedia.org/wiki/File:La_Venta_Pir%C3%A1mide_cara_norte.jpg

Wikimedia Commons. (2014). *Ann Zingha* [painting]. https://commons.wikimedia.org/wiki/File:Ann_Zingha.jpg

Wikimedia Commons. (2016). *Rhind papyrus problem 81* [Photograph]. https://commons.wikimedia.org/wiki/File:Rhind_Papyrus_Problem_81.png

Wikimedia Commons. (2017a). *Muhumusa ("Sultanin Mumusa" in the Original), ca. 1904* [Photograph]. https://commons.wikimedia.org/wiki/File:Muhumusa_(wei%C3%9F).jpg

Wikimedia Commons. (2017b). *Marcus Garvey with Amy Jacques Garvey, 1922* [Photograph]. https://commons.wikimedia.org/wiki/File:Marcus_Garvey_with_Amy_Jacques_Garvey,_1922.png

Wikimedia Commons. (2018). *The Rhind mathematical papyrus*. [Digital Image]. https://commons.wikimedia.org/wiki/File:Rhind_Mathematical_Papyrus.jpg

Wilder, C. S. (2014). *Ebony and ivy: Race, slavery and the troubled history of America's universities*. Bloomsburg.

Williams, C. (1961). *The rebirth of African civilization*. Third World Press.

Williams, C. (1987). *The destruction of black civilization: Great issues of a race from 4500 B.C. to 2000 A.D.* Third World Press.

Williams, W. (1999, July 20). *Liberty and the failures of government*. Independent Institute. https://www.independent.org/events/transcript.asp?id=39

Wilson, A. N. (1992). *Awakening the natural genius of black children*. Afrikan World InfoSystems.

Woodson, C. G. (1977). *The mis-education of the negro*. AMS Press. (Original work published 1933)

Yin, R. K. (2003). Introduction. In *Case study research: Design and methods* (3rd ed., pp. 1–18). Sage.

Zaslavsky, C. (1973). *Africa counts: Number and pattern in African cultures* (3rd ed.). Lawrence Hill Books.

Index

About the Authors

Marcia J. Watson-Vandiver is an assistant professor of elementary education at Towson University. She attended Mercer University in Macon, Georgia, where she received her B.S. in Middle Grades Education with specializations in language arts and social studies methods. She received her M.Ed. in Educational Policy and Leadership from Georgia State University and her Ph.D. in Curriculum and Instruction–Urban Education and Graduate Certificate in Africana Studies from the University of North Carolina at Charlotte. Marcia is the co-author of *Unshackled: Education for Freedom, Student Achievement and Personal Emancipation* and *Teacher Education to Enhance Diversity in STEM: Applying a Critical Postmodern Science Pedagogy*. She is also the co-editor of *Contemporary African American Families: Achievements, Challenges, and Empowerment Strategies in the 21st Century*. Marcia's research interests explore various intersections of Black education, including resistance pedagogy, historical and contemporary issues in urban education, critical multiculturalism, and transformative/emancipatory learning.

Greg Wiggan is a professor of urban education, adjunct professor of sociology, and affiliate faculty member of Africana Studies at the University of North Carolina at Charlotte. His research addresses world history [Caribbean Studies], history of education, urban education, and urban sociology in the context of school processes that promote high achievement among African American students and other underserved minority student populations. In doing so, his research also examines the broader connections among the history of urbanization, globalization processes, and the internationalization of education (comparative education) in urban schools. Some of his books include: *Global Issues in Education: Pedagogy, Policy, Practice, and the Minority Experience*; *Education in a Strange Land: Globalization, Urbanization, and Urban Schools—The Social and Educational Implications of the Geopolitical Economy*; *Curriculum Violence: America's New Civil Rights Issue*; *Education for the New Frontier: Race, Education and Triumph in Jim Crow America, 1867–1945*; *Following the Northern Star: Caribbean Identities and Education in North American Schools*; *Unshackled: Education for Freedom, Student Achievement, and Personal Emancipation*; *In Search of a Canon: European History and the Imperialist State*; *Last of the Black Titans: The Role of Historically Black Colleges and Universities in the 21st Century*; and *Dreaming of a Place Called Home: Local and International Perspectives on Teacher Education and School Diversity*, among others.